1

A Guide to Scottish Trusts 2006/07

Tom Traynor

Published by
Directory of Social Change
24 Stephenson Way
London NW1 2DP
Tel. 08450 77 77 07; Fax 020 7391 4804
E-mail: publications@dsc.org.uk
Website: www.dsc.org.uk
from whom further copies and a full books catalogue are available.

Directory of Social Change is a Registered Charity no. 800517

First published 2002
Second edition 2004
Third edition 2006

ISBN-10   1 903991 67 6
ISBN-13   987 1 903991 67 1

British Library Cataloguing in Publication Data

A catalogue record for this book is available from the British Library

Cover design by Keith Shaw
Typeset by CPI Tradespools, Chippenham
Printed and bound by Antony Rowe, Chippenham

All Directory of Social Change departments in London:
08450 77 77 07

Directory of Social Change Northern Office:
Federation House, Hope Street, Liverpool L1 9BW
Research 0151 708 0136

Contents

Introduction

Welcome to *A Guide to Scottish Trusts 2006/07*. The guide contains details of 346, mainly Scottish trusts, but also UK-wide trusts which give in Scotland, or ones that have a preference for a part of Scotland as well as elsewhere in the UK. In total, they gave grants of over £70 million, an increase of around £2 million on the last edition.

Gathering information

The ethos underpinning our directories is that trusts are public institutions, not private ones, and as such they benefit from being 'in the light of public scrutiny', to quote the Charity Commission for England & Wales. In essence, they should be publicly accountable and give information about what they do with their money.

Most of the trusts were extremely helpful and efficient in providing us with information. In carrying out our research, however, we occasionally came across trusts (or more specifically, the administrators of trusts such as solicitors or accountants) which refused to provide us with accounts or any other information. As of February 2006, these administrators are subject to the same obligations as charity administrators in England and Wales have been for many years, as the Charities and Trustee Investment (Scotland) Act 2005 comes into effect. Administrators will be obliged to send annual reports and accounts upon request.

In fulfilling requests for accounts, an administrator may charge 'such a fee as it thinks fit for complying with such a request; but such a fee must not exceed the cost of supplying the document requested'. Readers may note that occasionally a trust administrator requested a fee of £10 for a set of basic accounts, and in the case of one trust a £25 fee was requested. It is this editor's view that the purpose of these fees is to discourage requests for these documents rather than cover costs (compare, for example, the very reasonable and realistic £2 charge previously requested by the Shetland Charitable Trust for a full set of its annual report and accounts).

These prohibitive charges for accounts are one of the reasons why readers will find the occasional entry where there is no new or recent information, financial or otherwise, available on a particular trust. All trusts were sent a letter requesting information, followed as necessary by e-mails and telephone calls to the administrators. In some cases information was promised but never materialised; in others the 'administration fee' proved too costly. In the case of such entries all contact details were verified with those on file at the Office of the Scottish Charity Regulator and/or *www.workwithus.org*.

In the future, should a charity registered in Scotland refuse to send its accounts upon request, the advice from the Office of the Scottish Charity Regulator is to inform them in order for them to take action. Unfortunately, the Regulator has no immediate plans to make charity accounts available online through its website, or for the public to view at its offices, in the same way as the Charity Commission for England and Wales does.

Office of the Scottish Charity Regulator

As a result of the Charities and Trustee Investment (Scotland) Act 2005, the Office of the Scottish Charity Regulator (OSCR) changed from an executive agency to a statutory body with the power to determine charitable status, regulate fundraising, intervene in alleged mismanagement of charities and suspend trustees if necessary. The act also empowers the OSCR to maintain a publicly accessible statutory register of all charities that operate in Scotland.

For more information on the OSCR or to search the List of Scottish Charities, visit their website at *www.oscr.org.uk.*

Which trusts are in this guide?

Trusts are included in this guide which:

- have a preference for, or stated interest in, Scotland or part of Scotland

- make grants totalling £1,000 or more to organisations in Scotland

- give to organisations, not just to individuals.

Top 25 trusts in Scotland

The top 25 trusts in this guide (see the table on page 7) gave almost 78% of the money. The amount required to enter the top 25 rose slightly on the previous edition from £410,000 to £420,000. Several trusts are new to the top 25 in this edition: the Hunter Foundation and Laidlaw Youth Project (new additions to this guide) and the Cadogan Charity and the Dulverton Trust (featured in the top 25 in this edition now with an estimate of their grantmaking in Scotland). The four that have dropped out since last time are: the North British Hotel Trust (down from £735,000 to £390,000); the Mathew Trust (down from £410,000 to £137,000); the Alex Deas Charitable Trust (due to be wound up); and the Jordan Charitable Trust (the majority of whose money was given to its other preferential area of Herefordshire).

The Shetland Charitable Trust remains the largest trust within the top 25, giving more than the combined total of the next two nearest trusts – the Lloyds TSB Foundation for Scotland and the Robertson Trust. The geographical restrictions of this trust result alone in a staggering £696 per person being available in the Shetland Islands. To put this in perspective, in the rest of Scotland as a whole (excluding Shetland Charitable Trust/Highland & Islands), about £11 per person is available from the trusts in this guide. No other unitary authority area, or region in Scotland (or indeed England), comes

anywhere near the Shetland Islands in this respect, as the following table indicates.

GEOGRAPHICAL DISTRIBUTION OF GRANTS			
Chapter	Grant total	No. trusts	£ per person
Scotland – general	£45,688,000	201	£8.96
Regions			
Aberdeen & Perthshire	£1,578,000	37	£2.31
Central Scotland	£256,000	11	£0.47
Edinburgh, the Lothians & the Borders	£890,000	21	£1.00
Glasgow & the West of Scotland	£2,608,000	58	£1.68
Highlands & Islands*	£16,553,000	18	£720.00
*includes Shetlands, which alone has a grant capability of £696 per person.			

Throughout the whole of Scotland, including all regions and all trusts in this guide, £13.84 per head is available. Compare this to around £10 per head in London, £6.50 in the north of England, £4.50 in the Midlands, £5 in the south of England and £7.10 in Wales.

The Robertson Trust and the Lloyds TSB Foundation for Scotland again complete the top three, although they have changed places since the last edition. Both trusts continue to be very significant grantmakers, not least because applications can be made from anywhere in Scotland.

Of the top 25 trusts, only three have some geographical preference for areas within Scotland, namely for: Aberdeen & Perthshire (Aberdeen Endowments Trust); Edinburgh, the Lothians & the Borders (City of Edinburgh Charitable Trusts); and Highlands & Islands (Shetland Charitable Trust) – the majority of the top 25 trusts will award grants anywhere in Scotland.

'Scottish Universities' is the most specific cause to be supported by any of the top 25 trusts, with grants from the Carnegie Trust for the Universities of Scotland. Otherwise, a range of causes are supported, although a preference for welfare or medical research appears the most common.

The Top 25 Scottish Grant-making Trusts

£16,000,000	**Shetland Charitable Trust**	Social welfare, art and recreation, environment and amenity
£6,700,000	**The Robertson Trust**	General in Scotland
£5,300,000	**Lloyds TSB Foundation for Scotland**	Social and community needs, education and training, scientific, medical and social research
£3,880,000	**BBC Children in Need**	Welfare of disadvantaged children in the UK with a proportion of grants made in Scotland
£2,600,000	**P F Charitable Trust**	General, but particularly arts/heritage, health, welfare and education with a preference for Scotland
£2,500,000	**The Gannochy Trust**	General
£2,000,000	**Hugh Fraser Foundation**	General in the UK, especially western or deprived areas of Scotland
£1,500,000	**Carnegie Trust for the Universities of Scotland**	Scottish Universities
£1,500,000	**Northwood Charitable Trust**	Medical research, health, welfare, general
£1,500,000	**Scottish Community Foundation**	Community development, general
£1,400,000	**Hunter Foundation**	Education, young people, children
£1,000,000	**Dunard Fund**	Classical music, the visual arts
£1,000,000	**Balcraig Foundation**	Welfare, particularly children
£1,000,000	**Laidlaw Youth Project**	Children and young people
£790,000	**Souter Charitable Trust**	Christian evangelism and welfare, with a preference for Scotland
£775,000	**Cash for Kids - Radio Clyde**	Children
£743,000	**Voluntary Action Fund**	Voluntary projects engaging people as volunteers
£688,000	**Scottish Hospital Endowments Research Trust**	Medical research
£600,000	**Cadogan Charity**	General in the UK with a preference for Scotland
£600,000	**Chest Heart and Stroke Scotland**	Medical research, community services, representation
£574,000	**Aberdeen Endowments Trust**	Education and the arts
£500,000	**Dulverton Trust**	Youth and education, welfare, general in the UK and elsewhere with a proportion of grants made in Scotland
£500,000	**City of Edinburgh Charitable Trusts**	General
£450,000	**Tenovus Scotland**	Medical research
£420,000	**MacRobert Trust**	General

Please note: The above figures are for the amount given by the trusts in Scotland and not their overall grant total. Sometimes this is an estimation, as precise geographical breakdowns were not available.

Getting the most from this guide – a first stop in Scotland

The Directory of Social Change publishes a number of directories of grant-making trusts and the layout of entries, illustrated on page 11, is similar to the pattern established in these. As with all the guides, when quoting extensively from a trust's own correspondence or publicity we have used a different, sans-serif font to indicate this. Please also refer to page 10 for further information on how to use this guide.

We recommend this guide as the first-stop guide for every organisation carrying out fundraising in Scotland. Our experience shows that fundraisers will have more success if they tap into local money before competing for money which does not have the same geographical restrictions on it. Applicants are more likely to have success with local trusts, whose support can also give credibility to small organisations who are applying to national bodies.

How to apply to trusts

For guidance on making applications, please see 'How to make an application', on page 13. We would like to make just a few points here.

The competition for grants is high, and most trusts get many more applications than they can possibly fund. Research which leads to relevant and targeted applications is never wasted. In any case, it is bad practice to apply for grants if you do not fit the eligibility criteria. It only serves to annoy trustees, potentially causing problems for eligible applicants. It is also a waste of your time and resources.

Unsolicited applications

A number of trusts did not wish to be included in this guide, with several reasons being given for this. The most common were where a trust claimed to receive too many irrelevant applications and/or that they were a 'private' trust. No registered charity is private and, in our opinion, trustees and administrators of trusts should not resent applications for grants, but be committed to finding the most eligible cases for assistance.

Some trusts are established to support the same organisations each year, or target organisations they have found through their own research. Usually, they do not consider unsolicited applications. In such cases it is understandable that they do not wish to advertise their grant-making. However, we continue to include all trusts since our research also acts as a survey of all grant money available in Scotland.

Several trusts state that they will not consider unsolicited applications. It can be the case that this is stated simply as a deterrent to applicants. We therefore suggest that any applications to these trusts should be made with caution as there may be valid reasons for asking organisations not to apply. We advise you state in your letter that if your application cannot be considered the trust should not feel obliged to reply to your request – do not enclose an sae. If you do not receive a reply, do not chase them.

For best results, we encourage fundraisers to try to establish links between what the trust seems to be interested in and what their organisation is trying to do. Fundraisers are increasingly being advised to take a personal approach, with some trusts preferring to have a lot of contact with charities. Many trusts in this guide consider themselves too small to take such an interest in applicants. Undoubtedly there are restrictions on the voluntary time many trustees can give to their trust's work, but the Lintel Trust is one example of a trust in this guide that shows an openness to discussing with potential applicants how they may approach the trust.

Other sources of information

Of the total income of the voluntary sector in Scotland, 10% is received from grant-making trusts which in 2004 donated about £260 million. Nearly 27% of this money is accounted for by the trusts in this book, with other funds coming from more UK-wide and international trusts. This is the third highest source of income for Scottish voluntary organisations, after self-generated income (trading, rents, investments, etc.) and public sector grants. Details of many of these other trusts and sources of income are also available in Directory of Social Change guides, along with information about how to make successful applications.

A hard copy of our Books & Information catalogue may be obtained by e-mailing your request to books@dsc.org.uk Alternatively, an online version may be browsed at our website: *www.dsc.org.uk*. A PDF version can also be downloaded from the website.

Training

The Directory of Social Change runs training courses, aiming to equip the voluntary sector to effectively carry out their work, including fundraising training in Scotland. Courses include 'Foundation Course in Fundraising Practice', 'How to Raise Money from Trusts' and 'How to Win Major Gifts'. For further information on these and our courses in England, please ring our Customer Services team on 08450 77 77 07 (local rates apply) or visit *www.dsc.org.uk*.

Finally

The research for this guide has been done as fully and carefully as possible. We are grateful to the many trust officers, trustees and others who have helped us in this. Although draft entries were sent to all the charities concerned, and any comments noted, the text and any mistakes remain ours rather than theirs.

We are aware that some of the information in this guide is incomplete and will become out of date. We are equally sure that we have missed some relevant charities. We regret such imperfections and are always looking to improve our work. If you find mistakes or omissions in this guide, please let us know so they can be rectified in the future. A telephone call to the Research Department of the Directory of Social Change in Liverpool (0151 708 0136) – or an e-mail to north@dsc.org.uk – is all that is needed.

We intend to update this guide every two years as during this time trusts move, change their policy or cease to exist. You can get up-to-date information by subscribing to DSC's online database service *www.trustfunding.org.uk*. This gives you the most recent information and is updated regularly throughout the year. Changes to Scottish trust addresses can be checked at *www.oscr.org.uk* through the 'Index' link or *www.workwithus.org*.

To end on a positive note, there are more potential funders than you may think, some of which do not even receive enough applications. Several trusts had large, unspent surpluses. There are also a number of trusts whose expenditure has rocketed in recent years. We hope this gives you extra encouragement in fundraising and we wish you success.

How to use this guide

The contents

The guide contains 346 trusts, which are listed alphabetically in six sections as follows:

The first section is general. It includes trusts which can give throughout the country or in more than one regional area. The other sections are regional areas and include trusts which are restricted to these areas.

Finding the trusts you need

1. Within the regional section, look to see if there are any trusts for your particular town and that give to your type of work.

2. Also within the regional section see if there are any trusts which give across the region or wider parts of the region, for which you meet the criteria.

3. Turn to the Scotland – General section and check the criteria for those trusts to see whether you are eligible.

Sending off applications which show that the available information has not been read antagonises trusts and brings charities into disrepute within the trust world. Carefully targeted applications, on the other hand, are welcomed by most trusts and usually have a reasonably high rate of success.

A typical trust entry

The Fictitious Trust

£180,000 (2004/05)

Welfare

Beneficial area UK.

The Old Barn, Main Street, New Town ZC48 2QQ

Correspondent Ms A Grant, Appeals Secretary

Trustees *Lord Great; Lady Good; A T Home; T Rust; D Prest.*

Information available Full accounts were on file at the Charity Commission.

General The trust supports welfare charities in general, with emphasis on disability, homelessness and ethnic minorities. The trustees will support both capital and revenue projects. 'Specific projects are preferred to general running costs.'

In 2004/05 the trust had assets of £2.3 million and an income of £187,000. Over 200 grants were given totalling £180,000. Grants ranged from £100 to £20,000, with about half given in New Town. The largest grants were to: New Town Disability Group (£20,000), Homelessness UK (£18,000) and Asian Family Support (£15,000). There were 10 grants of £2,000 to £10,000, including those to the Charity Workers Benevolent Society, Children without Families, New Town CAB and Refugee Support Group.

Smaller grants were given to a variety of local charities, local branches of national charities and a few UK welfare charities.

Exclusions No grants to non-registered charities, individuals or religious organisations.

Applications In writing to the correspondent. Trustees meet in March and September each year. Applications should be received by the end of January and the end of July respectively.

Applications should include a brief description of the project and audited accounts. Unsuccessful applicants will not be informed unless an sae is provided.

Name of the charity

Grant total (not income) for the most recent year available

Summary of main activities
What the trust will do in practice rather than what its trust deed allows it to do

Geographical area of grant-giving including where the trust can legally give and where it gives in practice

Contact address; telephone and fax numbers; e-mail and website addresses if available

Contact person

Trustees

Sources of information we used and which are available to the applicant

Background/summary of activities
A quick indicator of the policy to show whether it is worth reading the rest of the entry

Financial information We try to note the assets, ordinary income and grant total, and comment on unusual figures

Typical grants range to indicate what a successful applicant can expect to receive

Large grants to indicate where the main money is going, often the clearest indication of trust priorities

Other examples of grants – listing typical beneficiaries, and where possible the purpose of the grant. We also indicate whether the trust gives one-off or recurrent grants

Exclusions – listing any area, subjects or types of grant the trust will not consider

Applications, including how to apply and when to submit an application

How to make an application

Applying to trusts

Here in Scotland, grants from charitable trusts and foundations play a significant role in the funding of the voluntary sector. Making applications can be tricky, but by following this plan of action, you should manage to avoid most of the common pitfalls.

Take your first step

The first step in a successful application is to clearly define the 'problem' which needs to be solved. This could be a new service which is urgently needed, a gap in your revenue which needs to be filled, the director's latest grand plan, a new building, or other capital need. I am going to use the term project, or problem, to describe the gap which you have identified. This is the first point at which your application can begin to fail. Some questions that you need to be able to answer, before you go much further, are:

- what, exactly, is the 'problem'?
- why has the problem occurred?
- is there any clear evidence to support this?
- how do you plan to solve the problem?
- who will benefit?
- where will it take place, and when?
- how much will it cost?
- who else is involved?
- how does this project fit in with your organisation's business or strategic plan?

It can be a lengthy process to try to gather all the information that you need but, unless you have a clear understanding of what the money is needed for, then it can be incredibly difficult to convince potential funders. This stage is often an opportunity for you to get out of the office and go see the need! Talk to service users who will benefit from the changes which your new funding will bring; talk to staff, volunteers, family members, or anyone who will be involved; build up a picture of what the project will look like. Try to get 'stories' from people that you can either build in to the application, or you can use in conversations with funders or assessors.

Research

Identify your potential funders. Use this book wisely. It contains most of the information that you need to know. Please don't use it as a source of names and addresses to 'blanket mail' trusts. Be selective, read through each trust's entry to make sure that your need fits the trust's grant-making priorities. It is also worth looking around your organisation to see whether any members of staff, directors, trustees, clients or volunteers are connected with, or know, anyone in a position to support your application. Did your chair of trustees go to school with the chair of a local trust? Does the director live next door to Lady Bountiful? A personal endorsement of your work is well worth having!

Think about why each particular funder might want to fund your cause. Trusts and foundations exist solely to give money away, but often have very clear criteria, usually set by the founder of the trust.

If the potential funder has an application form

This can make the process much easier, but there are pitfalls.

- Be careful that you meet the funder's objectives – although this information may not be built in to a specific question on the application form. If the funder's aim is 'to decrease social isolation within disadvantaged communities', you can almost guarantee that there won't be a specific question which asks how your project will 'decrease'. You have to ensure that this information is within the answers that you offer to their questions.

- Try to use language that the funder will understand.
- Remember that there are 'fads' in funding; for example, 'social inclusion' is a priority at the moment, while 'innovative' is out through complete over-use.
- Not wishing to overstate the obvious, but it does happen: don't forget to answer every question! Be clear and concise, but don't be frightened to use all of the space available if you need to.
- Make sure that you enclose your most recent annual report and accounts, but try not to add much more unless it adds real value to your application. For example, if you are applying for a new building, then an architect's drawing can help.
- Try to make sure that your application, and its enclosures, are 'photocopiable' because it is probably only a photocopy which will go to the committee!

If the funder does not have an application form

If there isn't a prescribed format for the application, one style which works successfully is a simple covering letter, a detailed paper on the project, with your latest annual report and accounts.

The usual rules apply:

- KISS – keep it simple, stupid
- AIDA – attract the reader's attention; create interest in your problem; make the reader desire to help; inspire action
- use a plain font of a reasonable size, usually 12 point
- lay out your information clearly and legibly
- try to use no more than two sides of A4 – ideally you should be able to put all the detail on one side!

The covering letter

The covering letter should contain:

- a paragraph of background on your organisation. In no more than 100 words, try

to establish the credibility of your organisation: What do you do? Why? Where? To whom? When were you established? Who else is involved? Are you international, national or local?

- a brief summary of the problem that has been identified and your proposed solution
- a concluding sentence offering to send further information, an invitation to visit, or whatever else you feel is appropriate
- your charity number
- accurate details of the person to be contacted for further information.

The application

The problem

- What is the problem?
- How has it arisen?
- Why and where is it occurring?
- Who is affected by it?
- How many people are involved?
- What evidence do you have? Have you conducted research, or has anyone else? Are there any statistics?

The solution

This is where you should show the objectives of the project and the specific, measurable outcomes you expect to achieve.

Measure

How will you know if the project is successful? What monitoring processes and procedures will you put in place?

Budget

- How much will it cost?
- When do you need the money?
- Who else is contributing, either in cash, or in kind?

Future funding

- Is this a pilot project, a one-off piece of work, or an ongoing activity?
- How will you continue to fund the project?

This is the standard information that most funders require. However, you should obey any specific instructions given by the funder.

Some additional dos and don'ts

Do:

- research, research, research
- **answer** all the questions on the application form concisely and accurately
- remember that funders want to **solve a problem**
- complete your application in plain English
- give your charity number
- ask for **exactly** what you need
- demonstrate that you have put specific measurement criteria in place
- show your organisation's commitment to equal opportunities
- include your most recent annual report and accounts.

Don't:

- ignore the funder's application criteria
- **assume** that the funder knows your work and will automatically fund you
- attach too much additional information
- use jargon
- use 'mail merge' without checking the details of each application are correct
- put 'refer to Annual Report', or 'see attached leaflet', in sections where funders are asking for specific information – answer the question fully.

Follow up

So, you have thought through your problem, come up with a fantastic solution, researched your potential funders, designed the most spectacular application that it is possible to submit, and sent it off. Now four things can happen:

- you don't hear anything at all, ever
- you receive a standard letter telling you that your application didn't meet the funder's criteria

- you get a request for further information, or a visit
- you receive a cheque.

Sadly, even though you have spent hours, days, weeks putting an application together that, as far as you can establish, exactly meets the funder's published criteria, you might still get a 'no'. It is worth trying to contact the funder to seek clarification on why the application was unsuccessful. This can help you to discover whether there is something fundamentally flawed in the application, or whether it failed for reasons completely beyond your control. Sometimes, particularly at the moment, funders seem to be inundated with good projects, but there just isn't enough money in the pot for them to give grants to everyone.

If you receive a request for further information, supply it promptly and accurately. If you get a telephone assessment, make sure that the person receiving the call is well briefed and has a clear understanding of the project, and your organisation. If you receive a visit, it is not like having royalty coming to visit, but ensure that staff know what is happening, and who is visiting.

When you receive a grant, make sure that you get a thank-you letter off to the funder immediately. Be careful of mail merge, and make sure that the letter has the correct funder's name and amount on it; believe me, people do get this wrong! Keep the funder up-to-date with developments during the life of the project. It is worth letting them know the good news, and about things that aren't working as you had predicted. To really be part of your 'team', funders want to build a relationship with you that is based on honesty and integrity.

Acknowledge the support of the funder in your annual report, if the funder wishes (some don't). Make sure that you invite them to any important functions, or events. Do not inundate them with information, but make them part of your network. Please treat your funders well. Then, when you next need some help, financial or otherwise, the first place to look is from within your existing network.

Susan Robinson FInstF
Institute of Fundraising Scotland

Scotland – General

The 1970 Trust

Disadvantaged minorities

£47,000 (2003/04)

Beneficial area UK.

c/o C W Pagan, Messrs Pagan Osborne, 12 St Catherine Street, Cupar, Fife KY15 4HN

Tel. 01334 653777 **Fax** 01334 655063

e-mail enquiries@pagan.co.uk

Correspondent David Rennie, Trustee

Trustees *David Rennie.*

Scottish Charity No. SC008788

Information available Information was provided by the trust.

General The trust states it supports small UK charities 'doing innovative, educational, or experimental work in the following fields:

- civil liberties (e.g. freedom of information; constitutional reform; humanising work; children's welfare)
- the public interest in the face of vested interest groups (such as the advertising, alcohol, road, war, pharmaceuticals and tobacco industries)
- disadvantaged minorities, multiracial work, prison reform
- new economics and intermediate technology
- public transport, pedestrians, bicycling, road crash prevention, traffic-calming, low-energy lifestyles
- preventative health.

Grants are usually of between £300 and £2,000 and for between one and three years, but they can sometimes cover longer periods.

In 2003/04 it had an income of £47,000, all of which was given in grants. Beneficiaries included Scarman Trust (£4,000), Roadpeace, Public Interest Research Centre and Earth Resources (£3,000 each) and Parents for Children, Parent to Parent, Slower Speeds Trust, Prisoners' Wives,

Pesticles, Blackcare and Shelter Winter Night (£2,000 each).

There were also 15 other grants of £1,000 each.

Exclusions No support for larger charities, those with religious connections, or individuals (except in rare cases – and then only through registered charities or educational bodies). No support to central or local government agencies.

Applications In writing to the correspondent. Proposals should be summarised on one page with one or two more pages of supporting information. The trust states that it regrettably only has time to reply to the very few applications it is able to fund and that it is fully committed for the next three years.

Aberbrothock Charitable Trust

General

£64,000 (2004)

Beneficial area East of Scotland, north of the Firth of Tay.

Thorntons Law LLP, Brothockbank House, Arbroath, Angus DD11 1NF

Tel. 01241 872683 **Fax** 01241 871541

Trustees G McNicol; J G Mathieson; Mrs A T L Grant; J D B Smart.

Scottish Charity No. SC003110

Information available Information was provided by the trust.

General The trust gives grants for the benefit of the community. It will consider the following causes: children/young people, disability, environment/conservation, hospitals/hospices and medical research.

In 2004 it had assets of £1.6 million and an income of £61,000. Grants were made totalling £64,000.

Previous beneficiaries include Red Cross, Colon Cancer Care, Princess Royal Trust, International League of Horses, Kids Out and Dundee Heritage Trust.

Exclusions The geographical restriction is strictly adhered to. Applications from outside the area, and/or from individuals, will not be considered.

Applications In writing to the correspondent. Trustees meet to consider grants in March, July and December.

The Adamson Trust

Children, under 16, who are physically or mentally disabled

About £55,000 (2003/04)

Beneficial area UK, but preference will be given to requests on behalf of Scottish children.

Barnshaw, Comrie Street, Crieff, Perthshire PH7 4BQ

Tel. 01764 656048

Correspondent K B Devine, Secretary

Trustees A R Muir, Chair; R C Farrell; J W H Allen; Dr H Kirkwood; Dr M MacDonald Simpson.

Scottish Charity No. SC016517

Information available Limited information was provided by the trust.

General Formerly known as Miss Agnes Gilchrist Adamson's Trust, grants are made to organisations providing holidays for children under 16 who are mentally or physically disabled. Donations are usually one-off.

In 2003/04 it had an income of around £60,000. Grants totalled about £55,000, most of which was given in grants to organisations, although some individuals were supported directly. No information was available on beneficiaries during the year.

Previous beneficiaries include Barnardo's Dundee Family Support Team, Children's Hospice Association Scotland, Lady Hoare Trust for Physically Disabled Children, Scottish Spina Bifida Association, React, Sense Scotland, Peak Holidays, Hopscotch Holidays, Over the Wall Gang Group, Scotland Yard Adventure Centre, Special Needs Adventure Play Ground, St

Nicholas' Special School – Edinburgh and Trefoil House.

Exclusions Unsolicited applications.

Applications On a form available from the correspondent. A copy of the latest audited accounts should be included together with details of the organisation, the number of children who would benefit and the proposed holiday. Applications are considered in January, May and September.

Age Concern Scotland Grants

Older people

About £50,000 (2004/05)

Beneficial area Scotland.

Causewayside House, 160 Causewayside, Edinburgh EH9 1PR

Tel. 0845 833 9315 **Fax** 0845 833 0759

e-mail enquiries@acscot.org.uk

website www.ageconcernscotland.org.uk

Correspondent Alan McMillan, Membership Resource Officer

Trustees Members of Age Concern Scotland's Assembly.

Scottish Charity No. SC010100

Information available Guidelines for applicants and a general leaflet are available.

General The organisation gives grants to voluntary and charitable groups working with older people in Scotland. Grants can be for up to £500 for equipment and materials for small local groups. A few larger grants, of up to £5,000, are given to members of Age Concern Scotland to start significant new projects.

From the organisation's website:
Age Concern Scotland Grants awards small grants to voluntary organisations working for the benefit of older people in Scotland.

Grants available for Age Concern Scotland Members

General Project Grants of up to £1,000 to support the development of new projects or services for older people, or to develop an existing project or service so that more people can benefit or so that the quality of service can be improved. You can apply for a range of costs associated with setting up or developing a service, such as volunteer expenses, equipment, materials, publicity, office equipment, or furnishings.

However, we cannot fund minibuses, holidays, outings, dinners and parties, everyday running costs, or major building works.

All applications are judged on their own merits, but we are keen to encourage applications for projects in which older people are involved in planning and delivery, which promote the active participation of older people, and which show a commitment to good practice principles.

Small Equipment Grants of up to £500 are available to help small local groups purchase equipment or materials in order to support activities for older people. Eligible items include kitchen utensils, crockery and cutlery, tables and chairs, arts and craft materials, musical instruments and games. Priority is given to small local organisations, normally with an annual income of less than £10,000.

Special Assistance Grants of up to £5,000 are available to start up a major new project or to significantly expand an existing project in order to improve the quality of life for older people in local communities. Evidence of a need for the service should come directly from older people, and older people should be involved in the planning and management of the service, with representation on the management committee. Only a few Special Assistance Grants are awarded each year, at the beginning of the calendar year.

Conference and Training Grants of up to £500 are available to enable member groups to develop and improve their work with older people through participation in relevant conferences and training events. You can apply for assistance with the cost of sending one or two representatives to attend a conference or training event, or for assistance with the cost of putting on a training event for a group of people.

Grant available for potential Age Concern Scotland Members

Small Equipment Grants of up to £500 are available to help small local groups purchase equipment or materials in order to support activities for older people. Eligible items include kitchen utensils, crockery and cutlery, tables and chairs, arts and craft materials, musical instruments and games. Priority is given to small local organisations, normally with an annual income of less than £10,000.

Unfortunately we cannot give grants to individuals, statutory authorities or commercial organisations.

All grants are assessed by Age Concern Scotland's Grants Committee, which meets every two months. Applications will be accepted at any time.

Exclusions No grants to statutory authorities, commercial organisations and individuals. No grants are awarded for minibuses, holidays/outings, dinners/parties, running costs, major building costs and general appeals.

Applications An application form and further details are available from the correspondent. Applications are considered every two months, except for the special assistance grants to Age Concern member organisations which are given in February.

The Sylvia Aitken Charitable Trust

Medical research and welfare, general

£163,000 (2003/04)

Beneficial area UK, with a preference for Scotland.

Fergusons Chartered Accountants, 24 Woodside, Houston, Renfrewshire PA6 7DD

Tel. 01505 610412 **Fax** 01505 614944

Correspondent Mrs N Ferguson, Administrator

Trustees *Mrs S M Aitken; Mrs M Harkis; J Ferguson.*

Scottish Charity No. SC010556

Information available Full accounts were provided by the trust.

General Whilst this trust has a preference for medical projects, it has general charitable purposes, making small grants to a wide range of small local organisations throughout the UK, particularly those in Scotland.

In 2003/04 the trust had assets of £3.2 million and an income of £135,000. Grants were made to organisations totalling £163,000. A payment of £28,000 was paid to a firm of chartered accountants, of which one of the trustees is a partner, for 'day to day management of the trust, accountancy and professional advice'. Even though wholly legal, these editors always regret such payments unless, to use the words of the Charity Commission, 'there is no realistic alternative'.

Almost half of the trust's charitable expenditure, as in the previous year, was given to Glasgow University for research connected with its Myeloma Cancer Project. Payments to the project during the year totalled £70,000.

With the exception of those to the above project, almost all of the trust's grants were for between £500 and £3,000. Larger grants included those to Hansel Foundation (£6,000) and British Heart Foundation/Glasgow University and Defeating Deafness (£5,000 each).

More typical grants included those to Rainbow Trust and Variety Club (£2,500 each), Friends of the Lake District, Scottish Motor Neurone Disease Association and Action on Elder Abuse (£2,000 each), Scottish Spina Bifida (£1,500) and Botton Village, St Mary's Hospice, Bobath Scotland and West of Scotland Deaf Children's Society (£1,000 each)

Grants of £500 each included those to Clover House Children's Complementary Therapy Centre, Scottish Adoption Association, Young Enterprise Scotland, Scottish Storytelling Forum, Shelter Scotland, Scottish International Relief and Capability Scotland.

Exclusions No grants to individuals: the trust can only support UK registered charities.

Applications In writing to the correspondent. Applicants should outline the charity's objectives and current projects for which funding may be required. The trustees meet at least twice a year, usually in March/April and September/October. Potential applicants should note, however, that the trust has previously stated that its funds are fully committed.

The AMW Charitable Trust

Religion, education, culture, poverty, sickness, disability, social welfare

£52,000 (2003/04)

Beneficial area Scotland only, with a priority for the West of Scotland.

c/o KPMG, 191 West George Street, Glasgow G2 2LJ

Tel. 0141 226 5511

Correspondent M J McColl

Trustees *Joy Travers; Campbell Denholm; Prof. R B Jack.*

Scottish Charity No. SC006959

Information available Information was provided by the trust.

General The trust supports charities in Scotland with a priority given to the west of Scotland. There is some preference for organisations concerned with benefiting young adults, disabled people and Christians.

In 2003/04 it had assets of £3.1 million and an income of £115,000. Grants were made to 25 organisations totalling £52,000. Donations were for amounts of either £10,000, £5,000, £2,500, or more typically, £500. Beneficiaries included The Dixon Community, Girl Guiding School, Kelvingrove Refurb Appeal, Lifeboats of the Cycle Appeal, Friends of Glasgow Humane Society, Maryhill Parish Church, Aberlour Child Care Trust, Dystonia Society, Glasgow School of Arts, Momentum, Hansel Foundation and Muscular Dystrophy Campaign.

Exclusions No grants for individuals, or to organisations outside Scotland.

Applications In writing to the correspondent. Appeals are not acknowledged and the trust only advises successful applicants.

James and Grace Anderson Trust

Cerebral palsy

£22,000 (2003/04)

Beneficial area UK.

32 Wardie Road, Edinburgh EH5 3LG

Tel. 0131 552 4062 **Fax** 0131 467 1333

e-mail tim.straton@virgin.net

Correspondent Tim D Straton, Trustee

Trustees *I K Ritchie; J Donald; J D M Urquhart; T D Straton.*

Scottish Charity No. SC004172

Information available Accounts were provided by the trust.

General The trust was established in 1974 and currently funds research into cerebral palsy. In 2003/04 it had assets amounting to £588,000 and an income of £27,000. Grants were made to two organisations totalling £22,000.

During the year the trust continued to support research in gait analysis with a view to alleviating the conditions arising from cerebral palsy.

The two grants were £19,000 to Lothian Primary Care NHS Trust towards gait analysis projects and £3,000 to Yorkhill NHS Trust. The sum of £500 was given to an individual.

Exclusions No grants are made: to individuals who do not have cerebral palsy; to projects not directly related to research into cure or alleviation of cerebral palsy; or as sponsorship of individuals.

Applications In writing to the correspondent. Trustees meet in May and October. Applications should be received by the previous month.

Mary Andrew Charitable Trust

General

£19,000 (2003/04)

Beneficial area UK, with a preference for Scotland.

Mitchells Roberton Solicitors, George House, 36 North Hanover Street, Glasgow G1 2AD

Tel. 0141 552 3422 **Fax** 0141 552 2935

e-mail darb@mitchells-roberton.co.uk

Correspondent David A R Ballantine, Trustee

Trustees E H Webster; D A R Ballantine; A J Campbell.

Scottish Charity No. SC021977

Information available Accounts were provided by the trust.

General The trust makes grants to a wide variety of causes. Areas of interest include churches; health and welfare; education and training; children and young people; and heritage. There is a preference for Scotland. In 2003/04 it had assets of £831,000, an income of £30,500 and made 36 grants totalling £19,000.

With the exception of three donations (£1,000 each to Marie Curie Cancer Care and Glasgow City Mission, and £250 to RSPB), all grants were for £500. Beneficiaries included Breast Cancer Care Scotland, Deafblind Scotland, Age Concern Scotland, Prince & Princess of Wales Hospice, Glasgow Old People's Welfare Association,

British Lung Foundation Scotland, East Lothian Special Needs Playschemes, Woodland Trust Scotland and Epilepsy Scotland.

Exclusions No grants to individuals or registered charities applying on behalf of individuals.

Applications In writing to the correspondent.

The Anne Duchess of Westminster's Charity

Youth, health and welfare, general

About £20,000 (2003/04)

Beneficial area UK, with preference for Cheshire, Scotland and Ireland.

Eaton Estate Office, Eaton Hall, Eaton Park, Eaton, Chester CH4 9ET

Correspondent Miss A Stubbs, Secretary

Trustees T J Marshall; D Ridley; Sir J James; Sir M Ridley; A Clowes.

Charity Commission no. 245177

Information available Accounts were on file at the Charity Commission.

General In 2003/04 the charity had an income of £21,000 and a total expenditure of £24,000. Grants were made totalling around £20,000. Further information for this year was not available.

Previous beneficiaries include Clywd Special Riding Centre, Riding for the Disabled Association, NSPCC, Distressed Gentlefolk's Aid Association, Eccleston and Pulford Parochial Church Council, Royal National Mission for Deep Sea Fishermen, Scottish Society for the Prevention of Cruelty to Animals, Injured Jockeys Fund, The People's Dispensary for Sick Animals – Scotland.

Exclusions No grants to individuals.

Applications In writing to the correspondent.

The John M Archer Charitable Trust

General

£35,000 (2004/05)

Beneficial area UK and overseas.

12 Broughton Place, Edinburgh EH1 3RX

Tel. 0131 556 4518

Correspondent Mrs Elizabeth Grant, Secretary

Trustees *Gilbert B Archer; Mrs I Morrison; Mrs A Morgan; Mrs W Grant; Mrs C Fraser; Mrs I C Smith.*

Scottish Charity No. SC010583

Information available Accounts were provided by the trust.

General The trust supports local, national and international organisations, in particular those concerned with:

- prevention or relief of individuals in need
- welfare of people who are sick, distressed or afflicted
- alleviation of need
- advancement of education
- advancement of religious or missionary work
- advancement of medical or scientific research and discovery
- preservation of Scottish heritage and the advancement of associated cultural activities.

In 2004/05 the trust had assets of £657,000 and an income of £49,000. Grants were made totalling £35,000. Nine organisations received grants of £1,000 or more. They were: Mercy Corps Scotland (£3,500), Royal Liverpool University Hospital – Macular Degeneration Research (£2,500), Merchants Trust – University Student Bursaries (£2,000), Castlebrae School Tutoring Programme (£1,500) and Romanian Hospital Supplies, Hospice of Hope Romania, Edinburgh Area Scout Council, George Watson's Family Foundation and Duke Street Church (£1,000 each).

Applications In writing to the correspondent.

The BAA Communities Trust

Local community

£565,000 (2003/04)

Beneficial area Local communities around the following BAA run airports: Heathrow, Gatwick, Stansted, Southampton, Edinburgh, Glasgow and Aberdeen. Limited help is available for projects in the area immediately surrounding BAA's HQ in Victoria, London.

BAA Communities Trust, 130 Wilton Road, London SW1V 1LQ

e-mail caroline_nicholls@baa.com

website www.baa.com

Correspondent Caroline Nicholls, Trustee

Trustees *M Agius; C Nicholls; M Toms.*

Charity Commission no. 1058617

Information available Information was provided by the trust.

General BAA plc established this trust, formerly the BAA 21st Century Communities Trust, in 1996/97 and is the main funder, donating 0.15% of pre-tax profits per annum. Support is concentrated in three areas: on projects which will be of local community benefit in the areas of education, environment and economic regeneration and employee volunteering; on projects put forward by BAA staff; on international projects aligned to aviation/travel and linked to volunteering work in communities.

The trust supports a wide variety of projects but only if they satisfy the criteria above. Proximity to the airports and proven community benefit are essential.

In 2003/04 the trust had assets of £667,000 and an income of £864,000. There were 115 grants made totalling £565,000.

The largest beneficiaries were Youth Games (£120,000 in five grants), Young Engineers (£52,000 in two grants), Hayes Skills Centre (£50,000), LEA Events UK (£34,000 in two grants) and Broxbourne Borough Council (£19,000).

Other grants include £15,000 each to Sussex Wildlife Trust and to support young people entering The Young Environmentalist of the Year Award, £12,000 towards the annual Fun Day for 500 local senior citizens to visit Folkestone, £10,000 to Stanwell Community Hall, Heathrow, £3,500 to Kilbarchan Guide Centre near Glasgow Airport, £2,000 each towards supporting the development of a school in Gambia and towards production costs of the first youth theatre production of Les Miserables in Sussex and £500 to a volunteer research assistant on a marine expedition to Madagascar.

The trust also provided the following, more recent examples of projects in Scotland that have received support:

During 2005 the trust [supported] the Voluntary Services Overseas Global Xchange programme with a donation of £156,000, half of which will be used to support a programme linking Glasgow and India.

The trust is sponsoring two Global Xchange schemes, one linked to local community projects around Heathrow and the other at Glasgow. For each scheme 18 volunteers aged between 18 and 25, half from the UK and half from Sri Lanka and India, will spend three months in the community around each airport and three months in the exchange country.

It has also donated £18,000 to the charity Create which delivered an innovative creative writing/ photography project for 30 students from Linwood High School in Glasgow.

Exclusions Anything which falls outside the criteria will not be considered. In particular, applications which benefit individuals only, whether or not they meet the other criteria, will fail. No support for religious or political projects. Grants will not be made to nationally based organisations unless the direct benefit will be felt locally and the other criteria are satisfied.

Applications In writing to the correspondent.

Dr James and Dr Bozena Bain Memorial Trust Fund

Religion, education
About £2,500 (2003/04)

Beneficial area UK, with a strong preference for Scotland.

Eshwood Hall, New Brancepeth, Durham DH7 7HG

Tel. 0191 373 4221 **Fax** 0191 373 0843

Correspondent T B Patterson, Trustee

Trustees *T B Patterson; M N Patterson.*

Charity Commission no. 328356

Information available Accounts were on file at the Charity Commission.

General This trust supports:

- a place for a student at Edinburgh University Faculty of Medicine who is Polish, or suitable in other ways
- the advancement of religion and religious education for training priests at Ampleforth College in York.

In 2003/04 it had an income of £24,500 and a total expenditure of £3,000. Grants were made totalling about £2,500. The trust seems to make larger grants every few years.

Previous beneficiaries have included Ardrossan Academy, Boys' Brigade, St Andrew's Church Youth Centre, West Kilbride Primary School and West Kilbride War Memorial Trust.

Applications In writing to the correspondent.

The Baird Trust

Maintenance and repair of churches and halls of the Church of Scotland
£247,000 (2004)

Beneficial area Scotland.

182 Bath Street, Glasgow G2 4HG

Tel. 0141 332 0476 **Fax** 0141 331 0874

Correspondent Ronald D Oakes, Secretary

Trustees *Miss Marianne Baird; Lieut Cmdr Edward F B Spragge; Col. Hon. W D Arbuthnott; Hon. Mrs Coltman; Maj. J Henry Callander; Maj. J M K Erskine; Revd J R McKay; Alan C Borthwick; D Elliot; A J Elliot.*

Scottish Charity No. SC016549

Information available Information was provided by the trust.

General 'The principal object of the trust, founded in 1873, is the provision of grants for the maintenance and repair of church buildings although it may also provide grant aid to other activities of the church, especially in the field of education. Under its Act of Parliament, the trust can assist only the Church of Scotland, of which church the nine trustees must be members.'

In 2004 it had assets of £6.8 million which generated an income of £292,000. Grants totalled around £247,000 of which £79,000 was given in sundry grants and £168,000 was given in 'voted' grants. Grants ranged from £300 to £10,000.

Beneficiaries of sundry grants included Church of Scotland Fund for Widows of Ministers (£10,000), Lodging House Mission (£9,000), Scottish Churches House (£8,000), Licentiates Book Tokens (£2,000) and Church of Scotland Board Ministry (£300).

Beneficiaries of 'voted' grants included St Andrew's Erskine Parish Church, Canisbay Church of Scotland, Dalserf Parish Church – Hamilton, London Road Church – Edinburgh, Kinross Parish Church, Newmachar Parish Church and St Michael's Parish Church – Edinburgh (£10,000 each). Smaller grants of £1,000 each were made to Airth Parish Church, South Parish Church – East Kilbride, Coltness Memorial Church – Newmains, Kinnaird Church – Dundee and Bellshill West Parish Church.

Applications In writing to the correspondent at any time.

The Balcraig Foundation

Welfare, particularly children

Between £1 million and £2 million a year

Beneficial area Scotland and Africa.

Balcraig House, Scone, Perth PH2 7PG

Tel. 01738 552303 **Fax** 01738 552101

Correspondent David McCleary, Secretary

Trustees *Ann Gloag; Pamela Gloag; David McCleary.*

Scottish Charity No. SC020037

Information available No recent information was available on this trust.

General Little is known about the workings of this trust in recent years. The trust declined our request for information in October 2005 and did not wish to appear in this guide. A previous

request for information was met with a compliment slip declining our request for a grant.

The following information remains from the previous edition of this guide.

In 2003 the trust stated that support for Mercy Ships would be continuing until at least Autumn 2004. Therefore, funds are usually fully committed, with the trust estimating that around £4 million was given towards Mercy Ships in 1999. The trust also stated that it was fundraising in order to make further grants to the cause. The current income levels for the trust are thought to be in the £1 million to £2 million bracket.

Applications As the trust only supports longtime beneficiaries, unsolicited applications are unlikely to be considered, although the trust did mention that applications are considered every two months. It appears from the earlier response we received that correspondence may not even be read by the trust.

Barfil Charitable Trust

General

£7,500 (2003/04)

Beneficial area Scotland, with preference for Dumfries.

Barfil, Crocketford, Dumfries DG2 8RW

Tel. 01556 690682 **Fax** 01556 690231

Correspondent The Trustees

Trustees *Bob Lee; Maggie Gordon; John Whittaker; Bill Lee; Bill Gordon.*

Scottish Charity No. SC018293

Information available Accounts were provided by the trust.

General The trust supports causes recommended by the trustees and local appeals in the Dumfries area. It may support any charitable purpose, but it is anticipated that this will primarily involve donations to other registered charities.

In 2003/04 it had assets of £158,000 and an income of £6,000. Grants were made to 15 organisations totalling £7,500

The largest grants were £1,000 each to Prison Me No-Way, Headway and Action Aid. Other beneficiaries included Association for Children with Heart Disorders and Renfrewshire Dance Project (£750 each), Wildfowl and Wetlands

Trust, Royal Highland Education Trust and Help the Aged (£500 each), National Kidney Research Fund (£400), BTCV Scotland (£300), Asperger's Syndrome Foundation and Send a Cow (£250 each), Helensburgh Tree Conservation Trust (£200), British Percheron Horse Society (£150) and Biodynamic Agricultural Association (£100).

Applications In writing to the correspondent.

The Kenneth Barge Memorial Trust

Local charities, disaster funds, developing countries, environment, military, religion

About £15,000

Beneficial area Worldwide, UK, Scotland.

c/o Messrs Raeburn Hope Solicitors, 77 Sinclair Street, Helensburgh G84 8TG

Tel. 01436 671221 **Fax** 01436 675888

e-mail ajdh@raeburnhope.co.uk

Scottish Charity No. SC006063

Information available No recent information was available.

General The trust supports local charitable organisations, charities in developing countries, military organisations and charities concerned with the environment and religion. Unfortunately up-to-date financial information was not available.

Grants have previously been made totalling around £15,000. Previous beneficiaries in Scotland include Action for ME in Scotland, Friends of Clydeview, Leprosy Mission, Scripture Union Scotland, Eredine Christian Trust, Marie Curie (Dumbarton), Thistle Foundation and Tullochan Trust.

It gives many annual grants and only a few new beneficiaries are supported each year. The trust states that it receives many more applications than it is able to support.

Applications In writing to the correspondent, but please note the above.

The Bartholomew Christian Trust

Christian organisations, poverty, education

£5,000 (2005)

Beneficial area Worldwide, but mainly UK.

Beathaich, Calgary, Isle of Mull, Argyll PA75 6QT

Tel. 01688 400240 **Fax** 01688 400240

Correspondent J E G Bartholomew, Trustee

Trustees *Commander I M Bartholomew; Mrs A Bartholomew; D G Bartholomew; A J Bartholomew; J E G Bartholomew.*

Scottish Charity No. SC012390

Information available Accounts were provided by the trust.

General The trust awards grants to Christian charitable organisations which promote the Christian faith, provide Christian education and work for the relief of poverty.

In 2005 grants, ranging from £100 to £500, totalled £5,000. Recent beneficiaries included Arab World Ministries, Youth for Christ, Christian National, Evangelical Alliance, Officers Christian Union, World Wildlife Fund, Grocers Trust Company, Release International, Signpost International and Israel and Christians Today.

Exclusions Grants are only awarded to registered charitable organisations. Grants are not awarded to pay for building work.

Applications In writing to the correspondent at the above address. Unsuccessful applications are not acknowledged.

BBC Children in Need

Welfare of disadvantaged children

£30.5 million (2003/04)

Beneficial area UK.

PO Box 76, London W3 6FS

Tel. 020 8576 7788 **Fax** 020 8008 3177

e-mail pudsey@bbc.co.uk

website bbc.co.uk/pudsey

Correspondent Sally Deighan, Chief Executive

Charity Commission no. 802052

Information available   Full information is available from the charity's website.

General   The charity makes around 2,000 grants a year in total, allocated in two rounds. Amounts range from a few hundred pounds to a normal maximum of about £100,000.

They are made for specific projects which directly help disadvantaged children and young people (aged 18 and under). About half of all applications result in a grant (though no doubt the success rate is higher for smaller applications and the amount given even in successful cases may often be less than the full amount requested).

Although most grants are for £5,000 or less, more than half the money goes in larger awards of over £35,000. Around half of its funds are given in one-off grants, the rest payable over two or three years.

The charity, registered in 1989, distributes the proceeds of the BBC's annual Children in Need appeal (first televised in 1980). In 2003 the appeal raised over £30 million. (The appeal in 2004 raised £17 million on the night, with the final total likely to be several million pounds more.)

Guidelines for applicants

General
The appeal gives grants to organisations working with disadvantaged children and young people who must be aged 18 years and under, living in the United Kingdom.

Their disadvantages will include:

- illness, distress, abuse or neglect
- any kind of disability
- behavioural or psychological problems
- living in poverty or situations of deprivation

The application should demonstrate how your project will change the lives of children for the better. It should be entirely focused on children. Where possible and appropriate it should take into account children's views and involve them in decision-making.

Advice to applicants
Organisations apply to us for a wide range of grants. The purpose and amount can vary enormously. From our experience we think that the following information might help an organisation to make a more effective application for a grant.

During the assessment of your application we will want to know more about:

- the background to your organisation and some knowledge of how it is governed
- how you work with other organisations and services in your area
- how your project was planned and what it hopes to achieve for children
- how you monitor/evaluate your work
- the child protection measures that are in operation
- job description(s), person specification(s) and expected salary level(s)
- the basis for costing equipment, services or activities
- the timing of other decisions with regard to multi-funding or complex projects.

The application form is designed to help us make an informed decision about your organisation and although some questions are probably easier to answer than others, you must complete the whole form otherwise we will not have enough information to make a decision.

We are committed to making sure our grants bring about changes for the better in children's lives and we want to support work that can do this.

The most important step in making a good application takes place before you even start to fill in the application form, and that is to plan your project well.

Good planning means:

- identifying in advance what difference you want to make for children
- realistically defining how the project will achieve this difference
- knowing how you will recognise whether the project has made the difference you want to make.

If you are applying for staff salaries:

- please state whether a salary is for a new post or an existing one
- make sure your costs include all the extras involved in employing staff e.g. recruitment, NI contributions, pension costs, inflation etc.
- enclose a job description, person specification, first year work plan and a completed Grant Breakdown form
- new posts funded by BBC Children in Need (except short term or sessional staff) must be publicly advertised
- during the assessment we will enquire about the organisation's skills to manage staff effectively.

(The application form itself has useful further guidance on completing individual questions.)

Grantmaking practice

Applications are assessed by a team of freelance assessors. Most of them are then considered, and grant decisions recommended, by advisory committees and staff at country or regional level. The assessment reports cover five main areas:

- The eligibility of the application
  Are the children disadvantaged?
  Is the organisation charitable?
- The acceptability of the project
  Is it well organised?
  Does it take child protection into account?
  Does it involve children, where relevant?
- The organisation's ability to carry out the project
  What is the organisation's capacity?
  What is its track record?
  What are its linkages with others, especially the local authority?
- The organisation's finances
  Is the organisation adequately managed financially?
  Are the project finances sensible?
- The mission
  What differences will be achieved for the children?
  How will this be monitored/evaluated?

Grants in 2003/04

The charity provides information about its grants as the decisions are made, twice each year, and without waiting for the end of the financial year concerned. However some of the analysis has to wait for the year end, so some information, particularly statistical information on the number and value of grants, was unavailable at the time of writing.

The charity received 3,808 applications (representing requests for a total of £143.5 million), with 1,782 applications being successful (47%), though many grants will have been for less than the full amount requested. The total amount awarded during the year was £30.5 million.

The 2003/04 grants were categorised as follows:

- to provide family support, welfare and care for children living in poverty and deprivation (£8,191,000)
- to involve children, many with physical and mental disabilities, in activities such as sport, drama, music and play (£7,426,000)
- to provide family support, welfare and care for children suffering through illness, distress, abuse or neglect (£4,159,000)
- to provide support and therapeutic services for children with disabilities, and advice or counselling services for children with special needs (£3,626,000)
- to help young people in trouble because of homelessness, drugs or solvent abuse, alcohol problems or eating disorders (£3,319,000)
- to playgroups, nurseries and other services for disadvantaged children under five (£1,935,000)
- to provide safe outdoor play facilities and holidays in the UK for children who need them (£1,135,000)
- to schools, hospitals and social services for activities and equipment for children which are in addition to those provided by the state (£743,000).

The charity notes that grants are targeted on areas of greatest need and the money is allocated geographically to ensure that grants are distributed in a balanced manner throughout the UK.

Examples of beneficiaries and projects supported include the following:

- Frank Buttle Trust: £789,000 for one year for small grants for disadvantaged children throughout the UK
- New School at West Heath: £244,000 for two years for the salary of a full-time Director of Centre, part-time assistant, video production, course materials and equipment
- Domestic Violence Intervention Project – London: £132,000 for three years for the salary of a specialist children's worker and funding for linked sessional work with children aged 5–18
- Newham Autism Centre: £107,000 for three years for the full-time salary of a family services worker for a project offering advice, support and information to families, plus IT equipment
- Renfield St Stephen's Church Centre – Glasgow: £98,500 for the provision of small individual grants for children in need
- Mental Health Advocacy in Pembrokeshire: £91,500 for three years for the salary of a full-time Mental Health Advocate for children and young people
- Haven House Project – Sheffield: £86,000 for three years for the salary of a full-time children's worker
- Christ Church Youth & Community Centre – Bootle: £81,500 for three years for the salaries of four part-time project workers, resources, volunteer expenses and transport for an after–school activities project
- Playback Trust – Midlothian: £81,000 for three years for the salary of a full-time trust

development manager working with children with physical disabilities and other complex needs
- Women's Aid Ynys Mon – Anglesey: £20,000 towards the salary of a part-time children's project worker
- Swansea and Brecon Diocesan Council for Social Responsibility: £14,500 towards the salaries of a full-time play co-ordinator and a part-time play worker
- Takeover Radio Children's Media Trust: £5,000 towards the costs of a radio training course for young carers
- Brent Educational Tuition Service: £2,000 for the cost of providing a sensory tunnel, raised flower beds and constructing pathways
- Coventry Youth Bowling Club: £500 for four lightweight bowling balls, training and transport to events.

Exclusions   The appeal does not consider applications from private individuals or the friends or families of individual children. In addition, grants will not be given for:

- trips and projects abroad
- medical treatment or medical research
- unspecified expenditure
- deficit funding or repayment of loans
- retrospective funding
- projects which are unable to start within 12 months
- distribution to another/other organisation(s)
- general appeals and endowment funds
- the relief of statutory responsibilities.

Applications   Straightforward and excellent application forms and guidelines are available from the website or from the following national offices:

England (and general helpline):
PO Box 76
London
W3 6FS
Tel: 020 8576 7788
Northern Ireland:
Broadcasting House
Ormeau Avenue
Belfast
BT2 8HQ
Tel: 02890 338221
Scotland:
BBC Edinburgh
Holyrood Road
Edinburgh
EH8 8JF
Tel: 0131 248 4225

Wales:
Broadcasting House
Llandaff
Cardiff
CF5 2YQ
Tel: 029 2032 2383

There are two closing dates for applications – 30 November and 30 March. Organisations may submit only one application and may apply on only one of these dates.
Applicants should allow up to five months after each closing date for notification of a decision. (For summer projects applications must be submitted by the November closing date or will be rejected because they cannot be processed in time.)

Bell's Nautical Trust

Maritime education

£17,000 (2003/04)

Beneficial area Scotland, with a preference for Leith.

11 Corrennie Gardens, Edinburgh EH10 6DG

Tel. 0131 447 9859

Correspondent   W H G Mathison

Trustees   *R S Salvesen; S J Boyd; G C Brown; J MacNeill; J W Sellars; N C Souter; Capt. A H F Wilks; Capt. J W O Simpson; Capt. R M Logan; J A G Lowe; G J Hughes; W Parker; J Taylor.*

Scottish Charity No. SC017199

Information available   Information was provided by the trust.

General   The trust supports maritime education. An average grant is £1,500, the largest can be £7,500. Grants are often given for equipment or towards travel/accommodation costs. Several grants are recurrent and about half the grants are given to Sea Cadets groups.

The removal of the Advance Corporation Tax Credit, which is being phased out by the government over a number of years, has unfortunately led to a reduction in the trust's income. In 2003/04 grants totalled £17,000. Recent beneficiaries have included sailing clubs, Sea Cadets groups, Sea Scouts, the Tall Ships, Jewel and Esk Valley College.

Applications An application form and guidelines are available from the correspondent. Trustees meet once a year to consider grants. Applications should be received by the end of November, grants are distributed in February.

The Bethesda Charitable Trust Fund

Christian, churches, welfare, general

See below

Beneficial area Preference for Scotland.

c/o 18 Ballieswell Drive, Bieldside, Aberdeen AB15 9AX

Tel. 01224 864460

e-mail jimw@truedeal.co.uk

Correspondent Jim Wilson, Trustee

Trustees *J Wilson; B Wilson; Mrs A R P Wilson.*

Scottish Charity No. SC007968

Information available Limited information was available.

General The trust supports Christian charities and churches for education and outreach. It will also give grants for general charitable purposes. Grants are usually one-off for capital projects, and can be for buildings. They rarely exceed £1,000.

It has recently resumed its grantmaking. In previous years grants totalled about £25,000. No further information was available.

Exclusions Grants are not given for expeditions, scholarships, individuals, housing or animal charities.

Applications In writing to the correspondent, including an sae. A trustee usually visits a charity considered for support.

The Birnie Trust

Minority sports

£7,500 a year

Beneficial area Scotland.

Johnston Carmichael, 10 Melville Crescent, Edinburgh EH3 7NS

Tel. 0131 220 2203 **Fax** 0131 220 1080

e-mail andrew.shepherd@jcca.co.uk

Correspondent Andrew W Shepherd

Trustees *Lt Col. E F Gordon; D A Connell; Mrs E A G Gordon; Dr L J King; N C Gordon; Mrs R E Simpson.*

Scottish Charity No. SC005509

Information available Information was provided by the trust.

General The assets of the trust are about £150,000 producing an income of about £7,500 a year, all of which is given in grants. Grants are to be applied for the benefit of young sportsmen and sportswomen who are pursuing a career in 'minority' sports. It is envisaged that the sportsmen and sportswomen will be aged between 16 and 21 years. However, the trustees have a discretion as to age.

Applications In writing to the correspondent, preferably including an sae.

Kenneth Blackwood Charitable Trust

General

Around £3,000 (2004/05)

Beneficial area Scotland.

Wylie & Bisset, 168 Bath Street, Glasgow G2 4TP

Tel. 0141 566 7000 **Fax** 0141 566 7001

Scottish Charity No. SC006726

Information available Limited information was available on this trust.

General This trust has general charitable purposes in Scotland. It is a small private trust and the funds are pre-selected each year. It has an annual income of around £3,000, the majority of which is made in grants.

Applications In writing to the correspondent. All funds are pre-selected and new applicants are very unlikely to be supported.

The Blair Foundation

Wildlife, access to countryside, general

£58,000 (2003/04)

Beneficial area UK, particularly southern England and Scotland; overseas.

Smith & Williamson, 1 Bishops Wharf, Walnut Tree Close, Guildford, Surrey GU1 4RA

Tel. 01483 407100 **Fax** 01483 407194

Correspondent Graham Healy, Trustee

Trustees *Robert Thornton; Jennifer Thornton; Graham Healy; Alan Thornton; Philippa Thornton.*

Charity Commission no. 801755

Information available Full accounts were provided by the trust, with a detailed narrative report.

General This foundation was originally established to create environmental conditions in which wildlife can prosper, as well as improving disability access to such areas. This work is focused on Scotland and southern England.

In 2003/04 the trust had assets of £1.9 million and an income of £653,000. Grants totalled £58,000 with beneficiaries including Ayrshire Wildlife Services (£14,000), Ayrshire Fiddle Orchestra (£5,000), Queen Elizabeth Foundation for the Disabled (£6,000) SENSE (£4,000), National Trust for Scotland – Culzean Castle (£1,500) and Blairquhan Castle, British Youth Opera, Royal Scottish National Opera and Scottish Academy for Autism (£1,000 each).

Exclusions Charities that have objectives the trustees consider harmful to the environment are not supported.

Applications In writing to the correspondent, for consideration at trustees' meetings held at least once a year. A receipt for donations is requested from all donees.

James Boyle's Trust

Relief of human suffering

About £10,000

Beneficial area Scotland.

34 Albyn Place, Aberdeen AB10 1FW

Tel. 01224 845845 **Fax** 01224 845800

Correspondent G W Stevenson, Trustee

Trustees *G Cunningham; J E F Thomson; G W Stevenson.*

Scottish Charity No. SC021125

Information available Information was provided by the trust.

General This trust was set up with funds of £116,000 on the death of James Boyle. Organisations are funded at the discretion of the trustees and grants are awarded 'for general or specific purposes of the charities named by the settlor'. No further or more up-to-date information was available.

Applications The trust states that there is no application procedure. Contact the correspondent at the above address for details.

Colonel T R Broughton's Charitable Trust

Older people, people who are infirm, ex-servicemen

£7,200 (2003/04)

Beneficial area Preference for Scotland.

Brodies LLP Solicitors, 15 Atholl Crescent, Edinburgh EH3 8HA

Tel. 0131 228 3777 **Fax** 0131 228 3878

e-mail andrew.dalgleish@brodies.co.uk

Correspondent Andrew M C Dalgleish

Trustees *C S R Stroyan; E J Cuthbertson; Brodies & Co (Trustees) Ltd.*

Scottish Charity No. SC003782

Information available Accounts were provided by the trust.

General The trust supports people who are elderly or infirm, with special reference to ex-servicemen.

In 2003/04 it had assets of £233,000 and an income of £9,000. After administration expenses of £2,500, grants totalling £7,200 were made to 6 organisations.

As in the previous year, the beneficiaries, receiving £1,200 each, were Edinburgh and Leith Age Concern, Ex–Services' Mental Welfare

Society, Lord Robert's Workshop, Marie Curie Cancer Care, National Benevolent Fund and Scottish Veterans' Residences.

Exclusions   No grants to individuals.

Applications   In writing to the correspondent. The trust has previously stated that its funds are usually fully committed.

Miss Marion Broughton's Charitable Trust

Older people, medical, disability, churches

£28,500 (2003/04)

Beneficial area Scotland, with a preference for the Lothians.

Brodies LLP Solicitors, 15 Atholl Crescent, Edinburgh EH3 8HA

Tel. 0131 228 3777 **Fax** 0131 228 3878

e-mail andrew.dalgleish@brodies.co.uk

Correspondent   Andrew M C Dalgleish, Trustee

Trustees   *Evan J Cuthbertson; Andrew M C Dalgleish.*

Scottish Charity No. SC009781

Information available   Accounts were provided by the trust.

General   This trust supports Scottish organisations working with children, older people and people who are disabled. It has a preference for the Lothians. Special emphasis is given to infirm and older people and also for exceptional work on the fabric of churches.

In 2003/04 it had assets of £823,000 and an income of £33,000. Grants were to 29 organisations totalling £28,500.

All grants were for either £500, £1,000 or £1,500. Beneficiaries included Cancer Research UK, Scottish Motor Neurone Disease Association, Multiple Sclerosis Society, Alzheimer's Scotland and Edinburgh & Leith Age Concern (£1,500 each), Anthony Nolan Trust, Capability Scotland, Salvation Army and Colon Cancer Concern (£1,000 each) and Health in Mind, British Red Cross Scotland, Scottish Spina Bifida Association,

Harlawhill Day Care Centre and Listening Books (£500 each).

Exclusions   No grants to individuals.

Applications   In writing to the correspondent but please note the trust states it is 'overburdened with applications' and not looking for more.

The Cadogan Charity

General

£1.2 million (2003/04)

Beneficial area UK, especially Kensington and Chelsea in London and Scotland.

18 Cadogan Gardens, London SW3 2RP

Tel. 020 7730 4567

Correspondent   P M Loutit, Secretary

Trustees   *Earl Cadogan; Countess Cadogan; Viscount Chelsea; Lady Anna Thomson.*

Charity Commission no. 247773

Information available   Accounts were on file at the Charity Commission.

General   There were four grants made of £100,000 or more in 2003/04, although most grants are for between £1,000 and £3,000 and go to a wide range of national organisations and some local ones in the Kensington and Chelsea area. About half the recipients have been supported in the previous year and the charity notes that 'contributions are given to a regular list of charities'.

The trust had an income of £1.2 million in 2003/04, derived mostly from its shares in the Cadogan Group Ltd.

The trust notes that it has been inundated with requests and has to turn down very many. 'We have our regular list of charities to whom we provide support and we entertain as many others as we can but, generally speaking, these charities must be either Scottish or London based and in the latter case a request from a Kensington and Chelsea based organisation would stand more chance of success.'

Grants in 2003/04

Grants were categorised as follows:

Category	No.	Total
Social welfare	76	£739,000
Medical research	21	£271,000
Military	5	£87,000
Education	5	£17,000
Animal welfare	3	£7,000
Conservation/environment	2	£55,000

Of the grants made, 12 were for £10,000 or more. They were made to Royal Hospital Chelsea Infirmary Building Appeal (£250,000), Leukemia Research Fund (£200,000), Great Ormond Street Hospital (£150,000), Royal Horticultural Society (£100,000), Pensioner's Mobility Fund (£75,000), Migratory Salmon Foundation (£50,000), Royal Marsden Cancer Campaign (£25,000) and Geoffrey de Havilland Flying Foundation, PRCDTR Didcot English Martyrs, SJ Noble Trust, St Paul's & Mary's Church – Glenrothes and Oatridge Agricultural College (£10,000).

Most of the smaller grants were for between £1,000 and £3,000. Beneficiaries included St John Ambulance (£7,500), Guild of Air Pilots and Navigators (£7,000), Diabetes UK (£6,000), Animals in War Memorial Fund, British Racing School Accommodation Appeal, Evelina Children's Hospital, Neuromuscular Centre, Trinity Hospice, Cancer Research UK and World Wildlife Fund (£5,000 each), Rainbow Trust Children's Charity, Alzheimer's Society, YMCA National Council and Royal Star & Garter Home (£3,000 each), Action in Addiction, British Tinnitus Association, National Missing Persons Helpline, Victim Support and British Lung Foundation (£2,000 each), Action for Blind People, Back to Work, Children with Aids Charity, Family Welfare Association, Queen Elizabeth's Foundation and Epilepsy Research Foundation (£1,000 each) and British Brain & Spine Foundation and Moorcroft Racehorse Welfare Centre (£500 each).

Exclusions No grants to individuals.

Applications In writing to the correspondent, who states: 'Please note that contributions are given to a regular list of charities.'

The Callander Charitable Trust

General
Not known

Beneficial area Falkirk, other parts of central Scotland and Galloway.

Messrs A J & A Graham, 105 West George Street, Glasgow G2 1QA

Tel. 0141 204 4225 **Fax** 0141 204 4511

Correspondent J A Aitkenhead

Scottish Charity No. SC016609

Information available Limited information was available on this trust.

General Donations are awarded to various charitable organisations for general charitable purposes. Principal donations are given for work in Falkirk, other parts of central Scotland and Galloway.

Unfortunately we were unable to obtain further information about the trust.

Exclusions No grants to individuals and non-registered charities.

Applications In writing to the correspondent.

The W A Cargill Charitable Trust

General
About £90,000

Beneficial area Scotland.

Miller Beckett & Jackson Solicitors, 190 St Vincent Street, Glasgow G2 5SP

Tel. 0141 204 2833 **Fax** 0141 248 7185

e-mail mail@millerbj.co.uk

Correspondent Norman A Fyfe, Trustee

Trustees *A C Fyfe; W G Peacock; N A Fyfe; Mirren Elizabeth Graham.*

Scottish Charity No. SC012076

Information available Limited information was provided by the trust.

General The trust supports a wide variety of organisations, as follows: welfare, local projects, hospices and medical research, recreational organisations for young people, schools, people with visual impairments, animals and wildlife and lifeboat services. It has the same address and trustees as two other trusts, DWT Cargill Fund and WA Cargill Fund, although they all operate independently.

Grants are made totalling about £90,000 each year. Despite providing accounts in the past, the administrators now make a charge for this information. No further information was available.

Previous beneficiaries include Church of Scotland, Crossroads (Scotland) Care Attendant Scheme, City of Glasgow Social Services, Glasgow Braendam Link, Trefoil House, Cornerstone Community Centre, Scottish Conservation Projects, National Asthma Campaign, Leonard Cheshire Foundation, Sighthill Youth Centre, Possil & Milton Forum on Disability, Stobhill Kidney Patients' Association, Cue & Review Recording Services, Dalmarnock Centre, St George & St Peter's Community Association, Towersey Foundation, Reality at Work – Scotland and National Children's Society.

Exclusions   No grants are given to individuals or organisations which have been 'nationalised or taken over by state/local authorities'.

Applications   In writing to the correspondent.

Caring for Kids (Radio Tay Charity Auction Trust)

Children and young people

£145,000 to individuals and organisations (2004/05)

Beneficial area Tayside, Angus and north east Fife.

Radio Tay Ltd, 6 North Isla Street, Dundee DD3 7JQ

Tel. 01382 200800 **Fax** 01382 423252

e-mail cfk@radiotay.co.uk

Correspondent   Alastair Brookes, Coordinator

Trustees   *Paul Smith, Chair; Arthur Ballingall; Boris Klapiscak; Lorraine Stevenson; Lady Fiona Fraser; Mrs M Young; Alison Wiseman; Norma Gamble.*

Scottish Charity No. SC008440

Information available   Information was provided by the trust.

General   The trust operates a year-round fundraising appeal, with the main fundraising event being the station's annual charity auction, for which gifts are donated by local businesses and individuals. All the money raised is distributed within the community covered by the radio service.

The trust's objects are to support children who are disabled, disadvantaged, deprived or otherwise in need, in Tayside, Angus and north east Fife. It aims to support those children who need assistance most. Around 10,000 children benefited from grants from the trust so far.

In 2004/05 it had an income of around £150,000, mostly from donations received. Grants to organisations and individuals totalled £145,000. Grants usually range from £30 to £2,500. No information was available on beneficiaries during the year.

Organisations previously receiving support include Ninewells Hospital, Strathmore Comfort Fund, Brechin Youth Project, Special Needs at Play, Youth Care and Oasis Youth Project.

Exclusions   No grants for staff wages or rent.

Applications   Application forms are available from the correspondent from early December. They must be returned by the end of January for consideration for the distribution in March. Applications from individuals must be recommended from a third party such as a social worker, doctor, head teacher, or charitable organisation and so on.

The Carnegie Trust for the Universities of Scotland

Scottish universities

£1.7 million (2004/05)

Beneficial area Scotland.

Cameron House, Abbey Park Place, Dunfermline, Fife KY12 7PZ

Tel. 01383 622148 **Fax** 01383 622149

e-mail jgray@carnegie-trust.org

website www.carnegie-trust.org

Correspondent Prof. Andrew Miller, Secretary and Treasurer

Trustees *Prof. Sir David Edward, Chair; Lady Balfour of Burleigh; Rt Hon. Lord Cameron of Lochbroom; Sir Tom B Hunter; Ms Eileen A Mackay; Calum A MacLeod; Sir Lewis Robertson; Rt Hon. Lord Wilson of Tillyorn; Richard Burns; Lord Kerr of Kinlochard; Janet Lowe; Revd Charles Robertson; David B B Smith; Ian Sword.*

Scottish Charity No. SC015600

Information available Detailed guidance notes and application forms for both personal research grants and for assistance with fees are available from the trust.

General This trust was established by Andrew Carnegie to improve and expand Scottish universities, to help pay tuition fees for students of Scottish 'birth or extraction', and to provide research and similar grants.

The original endowment was of US$10 million (a then unprecedented sum: at the time, total government assistance to all four Scottish universities was about £50,000 a year). The demands on the trust have changed greatly and there are now 13 Scottish universities in place of the original 4 that existed in 1901. The trust assists the universities by making capital grants (but see below), grants for research, scholarships and help with tuition.

By its royal charter, one half of the net income of the trust is to be applied to the improvement and expansion of the universities of Scotland and one half to the payment of fees of students of Scottish 'birth or extraction' in respect of courses leading to a degree from a Scottish university.

In 2003/04 the trust had assets of £50 million and an income of £1.9 million. A total of £1.7 million was given in grants. Capital grants to universities amounted to £395,000. Awards for advanced research and study totalled £1.3 million. Grants to students totalled £236,000.

The research grants have a maximum value of £2,000. They are intended to support low-cost research, for example to help with the costs of accessing archives, art galleries, libraries and museums and for travel and subsistence costs when field trips are conducted. During the year 251 research grants were given out of 281 applications, two-thirds of which were given to existing or retired members of staff and the remainder to postgraduates studying for a PhD at a Scottish university.

A category of larger grants has been introduced to assist projects which involve and are of benefit to Scottish universities as a whole. Grants awarded range from £8,000 to £30,000. These grants are not for individuals. Out of 12 applications received in 2003/04, 6 were successful.

The Carnegie Scholarships are made for the support of full-time research extending over three years at a university in the UK. During the year 12 new awards were made from 126 applications. Applicants must be nominated by a professor, reader or lecturer in a Scottish university.

To mark the centenary of the founder's benefaction, the trust has created the centenary fund. The initial purpose of this fund is to support the presence each year in Scottish universities of one or two outstanding scholars. The selection of these centenary professors is made from nominations by the universities. Two professorships were held in 2004.

The number of awards given for fee assistance for undergraduates in the year was 154 (from 187 applications). The trust also awards Vacation Scholarships designed to 'enable undergraduates of high academic merit to undertake a piece of research, usually in the summer vacation between their second and third years'. These are competitive awards, and names are submitted by deans of faculties by 1 April. There were 87 such awards made in the year from 133 applications.

Exclusions Research grants can be made only to staff and graduates of Scottish universities; costs of equipment, consumables, bench fees, radiocarbon dating and secretarial, technical and other assistance are specifically excluded. The trust does not give grants to individuals for attendance at conferences, travel (other than for research) or fees. Assistance is not given for the fees for second degree or postgraduate courses at Scottish universities. Only those born in Scotland, with a parent born in Scotland or with at least two years' secondary education in Scotland, are eligible to apply to the trust and awards made by other bodies will not be supplemented. Carnegie Scholarships are open only to those holding a degree with first-class honours from a Scottish university and nominated by a member of staff, although final year students who are expected to get first-class honours may also apply.

Applications Regulations and application forms can be obtained from the secretary and from the website. Preliminary telephone enquiries are welcome. Trustees meet in February, June, and November to consider research grants. Fee assistance is considered from April to 1 October for the coming session. Scholarships close on 15 March. Research grant closing dates are 15 January, 15 May and 15 October.

The Carnegie United Kingdom Trust

Social change

£1.1 million (2004)

Beneficial area UK, Ireland and internationally.

Comely Park House, Dunfermline, Fife KY12 7EJ

Tel. 01383 721445 **Fax** 01383 620682

e-mail charliecukt@dunf.fsnet.co.uk

website www.carnegieuktrust.org.uk

Correspondent Charlie McConnell, Chief Executive

Trustees *Millie Banerjee, Chair; Anthony Pender; David J Stobie; C Roy Woodrow; William Thompson; Dr David Fraser; Jeremy Holmes; Dr David Smith; Bill Livingstone; Robin Watson; James Doorley; Angus Hogg; Bhupendra Mistry; Douglas Scott; Jane Steele; Melanie Leech.*

Scottish Charity No. SC012799

Information available Information was provided by the trust.

General The following quote was taken from a press release issued by the trust in June 2005:

The trust has made a significant mark on the life of the people of Britain and Ireland, supporting libraries, education, the arts and social development for over ninety years.

Following the appointment of our new Chief Executive, Charlie McConnell, we have seen a radical change in the trust's focus.

The trust has ended its grantmaking programmes to focus upon strategic initiatives. Over the next few years, it will run strategic programmes on rural development, youth participation in civic life, strengthening democracy and civil society and promoting innovative philanthropy.

The UK trust is one of 25 Carnegie foundations and institutes worldwide. Carnegie left an estimated £15 billion (at today's value) for philanthropy in the early 20th century and is recognised internationally as an icon of 20th century philanthropy.

The trust believes that their capacity and profile as a foundation will be put to greater effect by concentrating in the coming years upon strategic social change initiatives, intended to benefit a far wider number of people than is possible through local grants programmes.

In 2004, the trust's final year as a grantmaker, it distributed £1.1 million in grants to organisations.

Exclusions The trust does not support any activities relating to armaments or war.

Applications 'The trust has closed its grants programme to focus exclusively on proactive commissions of inquiry and action research related to progressive social change.'

Cash for Kids – Radio Clyde

Children

£775,000 (2003/04)

Beneficial area Radio Clyde transmission area, i.e. west central Scotland.

CSV Clyde Action, 236 Clyde Street, Glasgow G1 4JH

Tel. 0141 204 1025 **Fax** 0141 248 2148

e-mail clydeaction@csv.org.uk

Correspondent Yvonne Wyper, Finance Manager

Trustees *Sir John Orr, Chair; Paul Cooney; Robert Caldwell; Kirsty Archer; Sheena Borthwick; Ewan Hunter.*

Scottish Charity No. SCO03334

Information available Accounts were provided by the charity.

General This is a Christmas appeal established by the radio station and CSV, a charity supporting media involvement in volunteering and in community support generally. The trust funds, via organisations such as playgroups, special schools or disability charities, small cash gifts for the benefit of individual children in need. Typically about 75,000 children benefit to the extent of £5 to £25 a head, or thereabouts. The trust seeks to 'reach those children who might otherwise face a bleaker Christmas'.

In 2003/04 the charity had an income of £954,000 (the charity will receive an additional £100,000 each year from the Hunter Foundation for 10 years, commencing 2004/05). Grants totalled £775,000. Only organisations receiving over 2% of the charity's gross income during the year are listed in the accounts – during the year just one organisation was listed, Make a Wish Foundation, which received £25,000. This leaves £750,000 unexplained in the accounts.

Exclusions   The trust does not fund trips in the summer or at Easter, equipment or salaries. Children benefiting must be aged 16 or under.

Applications   On a form available from the correspondent. 'To ensure proper stewardship of the funds raised, all nominations from those who believe the funds should be destined to a particular family or group have to be accompanied by a recommendation from an accredited body such as social work departments, Children 1st, head teachers, members of the clergy and community workers.'

The Cattanach Charitable Trust

'Community deprivation'
About £200,000

Beneficial area Scotland.

Royal Bank of Scotland plc, Trust & Estate Services, 2 Festival Square, Edinburgh EH3 9SU

Tel. 0131 523 2648 **Fax** 0131 228 9889

Trustees   *Royal Bank of Scotland plc; Colette Douglas Home; Lord MacLay; F W Fletcher; Adam Thomson; William Syson.*

Scottish Charity No. SC020902

Information available   Accounts are available from the trust for the prohibitive cost of almost £30.

General   For the five years from December 2002 to 2007 the trustees wish to concentrate on one individual theme, 'community deprivation', helping deprived communities to help themselves. This covers the full spectrum of community life, including health and employment issues, childcare, drug misuse, homelessness and disability.

The trustees welcome appeals from charities working in Scottish communities, including rural communities and small towns. They prefer to make a significant contribution to the funding of a distinct project that they feel will have a beneficial impact on the relevant community, rather than make a small contribution to a large project.

In addition, the trust will consider any appeals from charities named in the trust deed and any appeals they consider particularly compelling.

In recent years grants have been made totalling around £200,000. Unfortunately we were unable to view the latest accounts for this trust as the administrators required a £30 'administration fee'.

Previous beneficiaries include Raleigh International, Ruchill Furniture Project, Airborne Initiative, Samaritans, Tulloch Trust, Waverley Care, Larkhall and Childline Scotland.

Exclusions   Only registered charities can receive support. Grants will not be given to fund salaries of staff already in post.

Applications   A standard application form is available from the correspondent.

The trustees meet at the end of June and December and applications together with the charity's latest report and annual accounts must be received not less than three months before each meeting. Applications received after this deadline will only be considered if they are extraordinary, in which case they should be received not less than seven days prior to the meeting at which they are to be considered.

The trust may contact the applicant for further information prior to the trustees' meeting. All applicants are informed of the trustees' decision and, if successful, any conditions attached to it.

Celtic Charity Fund

Children, drug-related projects, promotion of ethnic and racial harmony
About £100,000

Beneficial area Preference for Scotland and Northern Ireland.

Celtic Football Club, Celtic Park, Glasgow G40 3RE

Tel. 08456 711888 **Fax** 0141 551 8106

e-mail ijamieson@celticfc.co.uk

website www.celticfc.co.uk

Correspondent Ian Jamieson, Public Relations Department

Trustees *Eric Riley; Kevin Sweeney; John Maguire.*

Scottish Charity No. SC024648

Information available No recent financial information was available.

General The fund raises its income through donations from Celtic supporters, staff and directors, the players, corporate clients, the general public and club funds. In addition to cash grants, hundreds of signed footballs, other items and complimentary tickets are also given away for charitable purposes.

The policy was originally to raise money to provide food for the poor of the East End of Glasgow and to encourage positive social integration between the Scottish and Irish people living in Glasgow. Today's policy reflects these original aims; the three main areas of support are as follows:

- children
- drug-related projects
- promoting religious and ethnic harmony.

It also supports three subsidiary areas which are:

- homelessness
- unemployment
- alleviation of suffering caused by illness and famine and to aid innocent families within areas of war.

No financial information has been available for the fund since 2000. Grants during that year were made totalling £100,000.

Applications An application form should be requested in writing from the trust. Trustees meet to consider grants in July each year.

Chest, Heart and Stroke Scotland

Medical research, community services, representation

£600,000 (2004/05)

Beneficial area Scotland.

65 North Castle Street, Edinburgh EH2 3LT

Tel. 0131 225 6963 **Fax** 0131 220 6313

e-mail admin@chss.org.uk

website www.chss.org.uk

Correspondent David H Clark, Chief Executive

Trustees *Prof. Charles Forbes, Chair; Dr Gavin Boyd; Colin McLean; Prof. Martin Dennis; Ms Hazel Fraser; Prof. James Friend; Dr David Franklin; Prof. Peter Langhorne; Prof. David Lidgate; Miss Valerie Lobban; Alasdair Macdonald; Mrs Alice Mackenzie; Dr Hazel McHaffie; John Moorhouse; Dr David Player; Dr Henry Prempeh; Prof. Lewis D Ritchie; Dr Roger G Smith; Dr Robert Stewart; Dr Douglas Stuart; Dr Brian Williams; Mrs Sandra Walker.*

Scottish Charity No. SC018761

Information available Full accounts were provided by the trust.

General Grants are given for support of research leading to the advancement of knowledge concerning the aetiology, diagnosis, prevention, treatment and/or social aspects of chest, heart and stoke disease.

In 2004/05 the trust had assets of £3.9 million and an income of £5.3 million, of which £2.5 million came from legacies. Grants were made during the year totalling £600,000.

Project grants and fellowships awarded during the year included those to:

- Western Infirmary – Glasgow, for trials on methods of overcoming corticosteroid resistance in asthma and COPD (£90,000)
- Ninewells Hospital – Dundee, to investigate the link between cardiovascular function and the intake of soft fruits (£90,000)
- Royal Infirmary – Glasgow, to study risk factors for venous thrombotic events in the elderly at risk (£86,000)
- Royal Infirmary – Aberdeen, to investigate the use of ECG in risk prediction following coronary artery bypass grafts (£82,000)
- University of Edinburgh, to investigate platelet and monocyte function in a South Asian population (£57,000)
- Highland NHS Board, to evaluate a pilot project of speech and language therapy in remote rural areas (£35,000).

A range of small research grants (up to £5,000 each) were also awarded.

'Applications directly relating to improvements in patient care, quality of life and health promotion are particularly welcomed.'

Exclusions Research involving animals is not funded. Research grants are restricted to those living and working in Scotland.

Applications For research grants contact David Clark at the address given.

Christian Education Association Scotland

Christian education

Around £5,000 (2004)

Beneficial area Scotland.

The Manse, Kinloch Rannoch, by Pitlochry PH16 5QA

Tel. 01882 632381

e-mail davidhamilton@onetel.net.uk

website www.ceas.org.uk

Correspondent Revd David G Hamilton, Executive Secretary

Scottish Charity No. SC011263

Information available Information was provided by the trust.

General This trust's objective is to fund research and development in the field of Christian education among children and young people. Recent projects include a major research initiative in the use of information technology in Christian education and the hosting of a day seminar, on children and spirituality, by CURBS.

Exclusions No grants for equipment.

Applications In writing to the correspondent.

John Christie Trust

Religion, missions, welfare of orphans

£80,000 (2004)

Beneficial area Scotland.

Tods Murray LLP, Edinburgh Quay, 133 Fountainbridge, Edinburgh EH3 9AG

Tel. 0131 656 2000 **Fax** 0131 656 2020

Correspondent The Trustees

Trustees J D Lennie; D W McLetchie; Mrs Ina Rankin; M J R Simpson; R York; H McMichael; Mrs E A Forrest.

Scottish Charity No. SC005291

Information available Information was provided by the trust.

General This trust supports the same organisations each year, most of which are concerned with religion, missionary work or the welfare of orphans. They are listed in the trust deed and receive the income in fixed, but not equal, proportions. If any of the charities change their activities substantially, the trustees can remove them from the list and decide how the resulting funds are distributed. Aside from these unexpected and unforeseeable circumstances, the trustees do not have the freedom to influence how the funds are spent.

In 2004 the trust had an income of £80,000, all of which was given in grants.

Applications Due to the nature of this trust unsolicited applications cannot be considered.

The Claremont Trust

Christian work, social welfare

£4,200 (2005)

Beneficial area Scotland and overseas.

15 The Row, Letham, Cupar, Fife KY15 7RS

Tel. 01337 810276

e-mail judithfairley@hotmail.com

Correspondent Mrs Judith Fairley, Secretary

Trustees Mrs C Davis; Mrs J Fairley; M Johnstone; J MacEwan; Mrs H Mein; K Pattison; A Sanderson; Mrs M A Ure.

Scottish Charity No. SC002721

Information available Information was provided by the trust.

General The trust was set up in 1948 to support groups which give practical expression to their faith in the life of society in Scotland and overseas. Founded on strong convictions of Christian social responsibility, it is ecumenical and states that it welcomes applications from inter-church and secular groups.

In 2005 grants were made totalling £4,200. Grants usually range between £250 and £600.

The trustees are keen to extend the scope of the trust through a larger number of longer-term grants, but so far comparatively few applications for such grants have been received. In an attempt to raise the trust's profile among potential grant recipients and potential donors, an article about the trust was prepared for distribution to a range of periodicals.

Beneficiaries during the year included Hope 4 Kids, Ecumenical Forum of Romania, Christian Women, Eighteen and Under, CasaAbba Project, Possibilities for East End Kids, Working Together for Change, Scottish Marriage Care, Shannon Trust and Kolali-Glasgow Partnership.

Exclusions Large building appeals, general appeals from well-established charities and applications from individuals for study or travel, whether in Scotland or abroad, are not considered.

Applications On a form available from the correspondent.

The Roger & Sarah Bancroft Clark Charitable Trust

Quaker, general

£85,000 (2003/04)

Beneficial area UK and overseas, with preference for Somerset and Scotland.

c/o KPMG LLP, 100 Temple Street, Bristol BS1 6AG

Trustees *Eleanor C Robertson; Mary P Lovell; S Caroline Gould; Roger S Goldby; Alice Clark; Robert B Robertson; Martin Lovell.*

Charity Commission no. 211513

Information available Full accounts were on file at the Charity Commission.

General The objects of the trust are general charitable purposes with particular reference to:

• Religious Society of Friends and associated bodies
• charities connected with Somerset
• education (for individuals).

For historical reasons the accounts for this trust were split into two separate funds, although it is administered as one. This entry will break the trust down into the two funds, even though they are essentially the same.

ECR Fund

In 2003/04 this fund had assets of £1.1 million which generated an income of £36,000. Grants totalled £10,000.

Grant beneficiaries included Religious Society of Friends (£2,000), National Galleries of Scotland, Oxfam, Prisoners of Conscience, Refugee Council and Scottish Women's Aid (£1,000 each), Amnesty International Charitable Trust (£600) and Hamlin Churchill Childbirth Injuries Fund, Shelter and Medical Foundation (£500 each).

SBC Fund

In 2003/04 it had assets of £5 million, which generated an income of £149,000. Grants were made to 134 institutions totalling £75,000 and 168 individuals totalling £41,000.

Beneficiaries included Britain Yearly Meeting (£10,000), Hickman Retirement Home (£6,000), Alfred Gilett Trust and OXFAM (£5,000 each), Retreat York Ltd and Society for the Protection of Ancient Buildings (£2,500 each) and Lydia Rous & Lucy Harrison Trust, Ulster Quaker Service Committee, Wilmington Friends and Wordsworth Trust (£2,000 each).

Applications In writing to the correspondent. There is no application form and telephone calls are not accepted. Trustees meet about three times a year. Applications will be acknowledged if an sae is enclosed or email address given.

The Clipper Foundation

General

£9,500 (2002/03)

Beneficial area UK, with some preference for Scotland.

21 Buckingham Gate, London SW1E 6LS [36 Queen Anne St W1G 9HY]

Tel. 020 7802 2700

Correspondent William L G Swan, Trustee

Trustees *Mrs Julie E U Macpherson; Nicholas W Smith; William L G Swan; Mrs Anne M Macpherson.*

Charity Commission no. 1062249

Information available Accounts were on file at the Charity Commission.

General Established in May 1997, in 2002/03 the foundation had an income of £76,000 and made grants totalling £9,500. The trust has previously informed us that it is using the extra income to build up its assets.

Four grants were made during the year to Raddery School Appeal (£4,000), Maggie's Centre (£3,000), Lochcarron Golf Club (£1,500) and British Blind Sport (£1,000).

Exclusions   No grants to individuals.

Applications   In writing to the correspondent.

Clyde Marine plc Charitable Trust

General, social welfare, medical/health

£23,000 (2004/05)

Beneficial area UK, with a preference for Scotland.

Cumbrae House, 15 Carlton Court, Glasgow G5 9JP

Tel. 0141 429 2181 **Fax** 0141 429 4348

e-mail ach@clyde-marine.com

website www.clyde-marine.com

Correspondent   Angela Hemphill, Trust Secretary

Scottish Charity No. SC001402

Information available   Information was provided by the trust.

General   The trust gives grants to a wide range of causes, especially organisations concerned with social welfare and medical and health causes. In 2004/05 the trust gave grants totalling £23,000. Most grants are recurrent, with beneficiaries each year including Prince & Princess of Wales Hospice, RNLI, Salvation Army, Macmillan Cancer Relief, Scottish Association for Mental Health, Glasgow City Mission and Princess Louise Scottish Hospital (Erskine Hospital).

Previous one–off grants have included those to Glasgow Seamen's Friends Society, Glasgow Veteran Seafarers' Association, TAK Tent, Trefoil Holiday and Adventure Centre for the Disabled.

Exclusions   Grants are not given to political or religious appeals.

Applications   In writing to the correspondent. The trustees meet in November to consider

grants. Applications should have been received by October.

Columba Charitable Trust

Health, children, general

£4,000 (2004/05)

Beneficial area Scotland and overseas.

Bird Semple, 21 Blythswood Square, Glasgow G2 4BL

Tel. 0141 304 3434

Correspondent   Thomas Monteith

Scottish Charity No. SC021517

Information available   Limited information was provided by the trust.

General   The trust makes donations to organisations, often dealing with health issues or with children.

In 2002/03 the trust made grants totalling £4,000. No further information was available.

Previous beneficiaries include Children 1st, Children's Hospice Association Scotland, Erskine Hospital, High Blood Pressure Foundation, Kelvingrove Refurbishment Appeal, Royal Blind Asylum & School and Water Aid.

Exclusions   No grants to individuals.

Applications   In writing to the correspondent. Applications are considered throughout the year.

Columba Trust

Catholic buildings, education, homelessness

£18,000 (2004/05)

Beneficial area Scotland.

Grant Thornton, 95 Bothwell Street, Glasgow G2 7SZ

Tel. 0141 223 0000 **Fax** 0141 223 0001

Correspondent   The Trustees

Scottish Charity No. SC008586

Information available   Information was provided by the trust.

General The trust's main aims are to support the following:

- students studying theology or related subjects
- charities working with people who are homeless
- projects associated with significant Catholic properties.

In the past the trust gave grants for Catholic educational purposes. It has since broadened its area of work to include the above categories. It has also decided to support a smaller number of charities each year and offer longer term funding of three to five years.

In 2004/05 it gave grants totalling £18,000. Grants normally range between £500 and £8,000. Beneficiaries have included St Mary's Cathedral, Lifeline (Pregnancy Counselling and Care), St Mary's Church – Greenock and Family House of Prayer.

Applications In writing to the correspondent. Trustees meet twice a year to consider grants in May and November.

The Martin Connell Charitable Trust

General

£147,000 (2004/05)

Beneficial area Scotland.

Messrs Maclay Murray & Spens, 151 St Vincent Street, Glasgow G2 5NJ

Tel. 0141 248 5011

Correspondent The Trustees

Scottish Charity No. SC009842

Information available Information was provided by the trust.

General The trust supports general charitable purposes in Scotland. In 2004/05 it had assets of £4.2 million, an income of £160,000 and gave £147,000 in grants.

Beneficiaries, receiving grants between £1,000 and £5,000, included Grampian Society for the Blind, Salvation Army, Talking Books and Yorkhill Sick Children.

Exclusions No grants to individuals.

Applications In writing to the correspondent. The trustees meet in June and December.

Gordon Cook Foundation

Education and training

About £200,000

Beneficial area UK.

3 Chattan Place, Aberdeen AB10 6RB

Tel. 01224 571010 **Fax** 01224 571010

e-mail i.b.brown@gordoncook.org.uk

website www.gordoncook.org.uk

Correspondent Mrs Irene B Brown, Foundation Secretary

Trustees G Ross, Chair; D A Adams; Prof. B J McGettrick; Dr P Clarke; Dr W Gatherer; J Marshall; C P Skene.

Scottish Charity No. SC017455

Information available Information was taken from the foundation's website.

General This foundation was set up in 1974 and is dedicated to the advancement and promotion of all aspects of education and training which are likely to promote 'character development' and 'citizenship'. The following information is taken from the foundation's own leaflet.

In recent years, the foundation has adopted the term 'Values Education' to denote the wide range of activity it seeks to support. This includes:

- the promotion of good citizenship in its widest terms, including aspects of moral, ethical and aesthetic education, youth work, cooperation between home and school, and coordinating work in school with leisure time pursuits
- the promotion of health education as it relates to values education
- supporting relevant aspects of moral and religious education
- helping parents, teachers and others to enhance the personal development of pupils and young people
- supporting developments in the school curriculum subjects which relate to values education
- helping pupils and young people to develop commitment to the value of work, industry and enterprise generally
- disseminating the significant results of relevant research and development.

No recent financial information was available, although previous research indicates that grants are made totalling around £200,000 each year.

The foundation has previously stated that it supports projects, including 'consultations' organised by Institute of Global Ethics, Professional Ethics, Business Ethics, Enterprise Ethics and Values Education in the Four Home Nations. Grants usually range from around £1,000 to £30,000. Previous beneficiaries include Norham Foundation, Health Education Board for Scotland, Citizen Foundation, North Lanarkshire Council and Northern College.

Exclusions   Individuals are unlikely to be funded.

Applications   The trustees are proactive in looking for projects to support; however, unsolicited applications may be considered if they fall within the foundation's criteria and are in accordance with current programmes. Forms may be obtained from the correspondent.

The Ernest Cook Trust

Education in environment, rural conservation, arts and crafts, often with youth focus; research

£1 million (2004/05)

Beneficial area UK.

Fairford Park, Fairford, Gloucestershire GL7 4JH

Tel. 01285 713273 **Fax** 01285 713417

e-mail grants@ernestcooktrust.org.uk

website www.ernestcooktrust.org.uk

Correspondent   Mrs Antonia Eliot, Grants administrator

Trustees   S A J P Bosanquet, Chair; M C Tuely; A W M Christie-Miller; P S W K Maclure; T R E Cook; H M Henderson.

Charity Commission no. 313497

Information available   Comprehensive information on grants and guidelines was provided by the trust.

General   The trust was founded in 1952 by the late Ernest Cook, a grandson of Thomas Cook, founder of the travel agency. The sale of the family travel business in 1928 generated enough wealth for him to direct his energies into the purchase and conservation of great houses and estates and the art works they contained. The trust's estates lie at Hatherop, Fairford, Slimbridge and Barnsley in Gloucestershire; Hartwell and Boarstall in Buckinghamshire; Little Dalby in Leicestershire; Trent in Dorset; and Filkins in Oxfordshire.

Any project supported by the trust must be clearly educational. The trustees are particularly interested in applications which provide opportunities for young people: these may either encourage the latter to gain qualifications to further their employment prospects, or they may assist training in crafts which are in danger of dying out.

The trustees are also keen to support applications which educate people about the rural environment and the countryside. Grants are also awarded for projects which educate young people in the arts, particularly if such work is linked to schools and the National Curriculum. In addition, a few research grants are awarded if the work covers areas of interest to the trustees.

Grants range from £100 to £3,000 in the small grants category, of which modest amounts for educational resources for small groups form a large part. At the two main meetings grants are mostly in the range of £3,000 and £10,000, with only a few larger awards for projects closely connected with the trust's land holdings and educational interests. For the first time in 2004/05, two exceptional awards of £50,000 each were made to Arkwright Scholarships to encourage young people to take up careers in engineering or technology and Forum for the Future to support the work programme of the organisation's Rural Economy Programme.

In 2004/05 the trust had an income of £2.8 million. A total of 264 grants were awarded, amounting to £1 million. Grants made were categorised as follows:

Arts and crafts

96 grants totalling £301,000 were made, ranging between £300 and £20,000. Grants were awarded to Gordon Highlanders Museum towards the cost of new educational materials for visiting schools (£6,800) and Dunedin Consort Trust to assist with the cost of a children's choral project which toured the area providing workshops which culminated in public performance and Grid Iron Theatre Company based in Edinburgh to run schools' workshops to accompany a play by the Scottish playwright Douglas Maxwell (£1,000 each).

Environment

82 grants totalling £387,000 were made, ranging between £300 and £20,000. Beneficiaries included Wild Things in Scotland to assist with the

2004/05 Forest Schools programme (£9,500) and Waterways Trust Scotland to help produce a resource pack to accompany the Wild over Waterways project aimed at enthusing primary school pupils about inland waterways (£6,000).

Research

3 grants totalling £15,000 were made, ranging between £3,000 and £7,000. A grant of £7,000 was made to National Institute of Agricultural Botany (NIAB) to make a two year award to an ECT studentship.

Exclusions Applicants must represent either registered charities or not-for-profit organisations. Grants are normally awarded on an annual basis and will not be awarded retrospectively. The following restrictions apply, as grants will not be made to:

* individuals
* agricultural colleges
* education work which is part of social support, therapy or medical treatment
* building and restoration work
* sports and recreational activities
* work overseas.

Support for wildlife trusts and for farming and wildlife advisory groups is largely restricted to those based in counties in which ECT owns land (Gloucestershire, Buckinghamshire, Leicestershire, Dorset and Oxfordshire).

Applications Trustees meet in April and November to consider grants in excess of £3,000; applications for these meetings should be submitted by 31st January and 31st August respectively. Meetings to consider grants of up to £3,000 are normally held in February, May, July, September and December. There is no application form and applicants are asked to focus their request on a specific educational need and to present clear and concise proposals on a maximum of two sheets of A4 paper. A simple budget for the project and a copy of the latest annual report and accounts should also be enclosed. Applicants are encouraged to contact the grants office if they require further details.

The Craignish Trust

Arts, education, environment, general

Around £109,000 (2003/04)

Beneficial area UK, with a preference for Scotland.

Messrs Geoghegan & Co, 6 St Colme Street, Edinburgh EH3 6AD

Tel. 0131 225 4681 **Fax** 0131 220 1132

e-mail lachlan.fernie@geoghegans.co.uk

Correspondent Lachlan K Fernie, Treasurer

Trustees *Clifford Hastings; Ms Caroline Younger; Ms Margaret Matheson.*

Scottish Charity No. SC016882

Information available Accounts were provided by the trust.

General This trust was established in 1961 by the late Sir William McEwan Younger; its funding criteria is summarised as follows:

* no grants to large national charities
* there is a Scottish bias, but not exclusively
* arts, particularly where innovative and/or involved in the community
* education
* environment
* organisations/projects of particular interest to a trustee.

In 2003/04 the trust had assets of £3.6 million, which generated an income of £138,000. Grants were given to 42 organisations totalling £109,000. Grants ranged from £500 to £11,500, although most were for £2,500 or less.

The largest grants during the year were made to Harmeny Education Trust (£11,500), Soil Association Scotland (£6,000) and Burma Educational Scholarship Trust, Henley Symphony Orchestra, Human Rights Watch Charitable Trust, Kilmartin House Museum, Stills and Grassmarket Project (£5,000 each).

Other beneficiaries included Craigiecau Ecology Centre, Donaldsons College, Edinburgh Youth Orchestra, Lomond & Clyde Pipe Band, Reforesting Scotland, Scottish Environment Trust, Shelter Scotland, Liberating Scots Trust, Woodland Trust Scotland and Youth Scotland.

Exclusions Running costs are not normally supported.

Applications There is no formal application form; applicants should write to the correspondent. Details of the project should be included together with a copy of the most recent audited accounts.

The Cray Trust

General

£51,000 (2004/05)

Beneficial area Mainly the east of Scotland.

c/o Springfords Accountants, Dundas House, Westfield Park, Eskbank, Midlothian EH22 3FB

Correspondent The Trustees

Trustees *P R Gammell; J E B Gammell.*

Scottish Charity No. SC005592

Information available Accounts were provided by the trust.

General In 2004/05 the trust had assets of £647,000 and an income of £54,000. A total of 150 grants were made amounting to £51,000. Grants ranged from £100 to £7,000, with the average payment being £340.

The trust's accounts list 12 payments of £1,000 or more. They were made to Mercy Corps Scotland (£7,000), Equine Grass Sickness Fund and National Galleries of Scotland (£5,000 each), Berwickshire RDA (£3,000) and Priory Church, Compass School, Mercy Ships, Centre for Human Ecology, Strathcarron Hospice, Nancy Ovens Trust, Oundle School and Landmark Trust (£1,000 each).

Grants of less than £1,000 each totalled £23,000.

Exclusions No support for political appeals and large UK or international charities. No grants to individuals.

Applications In writing to the correspondent. The trust stated: 'applications should be short and to the point. Grants are aimed to make a difference and so will seldom be made to large national charities unless for specific projects in east Scotland.'

Hamish and Doris Crichton's Charitable Trust

Animal welfare, conservation

About £10,000

Beneficial area Scotland, with a preference for Berwickshire/East Lothian.

Turcan Connell WS, Princes Exchange, 1 Earl Grey Street, Edinburgh EH3 9EE

Tel. 0131 228 8111 **Fax** 0131 228 8118

Correspondent Hubert Ross, Trustee

Trustees *G M Menzies; H J Ross.*

Scottish Charity No. SC000347

Information available Limited information was provided by the trust.

General This trust was established in 1999 and is the amalgamation of two trusts: The Hamish Crichton Charitable Trust and The Doris Crichton Charitable Trust. In previous years grants have been made totalling around £10,000. No further information was available.

Applications The trust does not solicit applications and is proactive in finding its beneficiaries.

The Cromarty Trust

Preservation of buildings, conservation, education

£21,000 (2003)

Beneficial area UK, with a preference for the Parish of Cromarty, Ross and Cromarty.

25 West Square, London SE11 4SP

Correspondent J Nightingale, Trustee

Trustees *Miss E V de B Murray; J B W Nightingale; A P Mc Nightingale; Mrs R Homfray.*

Charity Commission no. 272843

Information available Limited information was provided by the trust.

General It supports organisations mainly in the parish of Cromarty concerned with: preservation of buildings of historical or architectural interest; conservation of landscape; and education of the public in the history, character and wildlife of the parish.

In 2003 the trust had an income of £24,000 and gave grants totalling £21,000. No information was available on beneficiaries.

Applications Applications are not invited as the trustees take a proactive approach to grantmaking and the development of projects which they wish to support. Unsolicited appeals other than those from the parishes of Cromarty and Nigg will not receive a response.

The Cross Trust

Young people, music, drama, education

About £35,000 to organisations

Beneficial area Scotland.

McCash & Hunter Solicitors, 25 South Methven Street, Perth PH1 5ES

Tel. 01738 620451 **Fax** 01738 631155

Correspondent Mrs Dorothy Shaw, Assistant Secretary

Trustees *Revd Hon R D Buchanan-Smith; Dr R H MacDougall; Dr A R MacGregor; Mrs Clair Orr; Dougal Philip; Mark Webster.*

Scottish Charity No. SC008620

Information available No recent information was available.

General About 80% of the grants are given to individuals for educational purposes (including travel for their courses). Applicants must be of Scottish birth or parentage. Grants to organisations are normally made for music, drama or outdoor activities to benefit young people.

In previous years grants to individuals and organisations have totalled about £160,000 to £170,000. No further information was available.

Exclusions No retrospective applications will be considered.

Applications Application forms and guidance notes are available from the correspondent.

Cruden Foundation Ltd

General

£210,000 (2003/04)

Beneficial area Mainly Scotland.

Baberton House, Juniper Green, Edinburgh EH14 3HN

Correspondent M R A Matthews, Secretary

Trustees *N Lessels, Chair; M R A Matthews; J G Mitchell; A Johnston; M J Rowley; D D Walker.*

Scottish Charity No. SC004987

Information available Full accounts were available from the trust.

General The object of the foundation is to support and contribute to institutions for the benefit of the community. The policy of the company is to make donations to a wide range of mainly local charities.

In 2003/04 the trust had assets of £1.6 million and an income of £259,000. Grants totalled £210,000.

Grants ranged from £100 to £10,000 and were given to 263 charitable institutions. 8 were £5,000 or over and 52 were between £1,000 and £5,000. The largest grant of £10,000 was given each to Edinburgh International Festival, Neuro-otology Research Fund – Endowment Fund, Pitlochry Festival Theatre and Friends of Carberry.

Grants ranging from £1,000 to £5,000 include Edinburgh Academy Foundation (£2,500), Queen's Hall Edinburgh (£2,000) and Marie Curie Cancer Care Scotland (£1,500). 38 institutions received a grant of £1,000 including Dyslexia Institute, National Trust for Scotland and Thistle Foundation.

Smaller grants ranged from £100 to £750 and include Royal Scottish National Orchestra, Artlink, Edinburgh and Lothian Council on Alcohol and Scottish Wildlife Trust.

Exclusions No grants to individuals.

Applications In writing to the correspondent.

The Cunningham Trust

Medical research projects

£163,000 (2003/04)

Beneficial area Scotland.

Thorntons

~~Murray Donald & Caithness,~~ Solicitors, Kinburn Castle, St Andrews, Fife KY16 9DR

Angela Beth

Tel. 01334 477107 **Fax** 01334 476862

Correspondent The Trustees

Trustees *Prof. C Blake; A C Caithness; Dr D McD Greenhough.*

Scottish Charity No. SC013499

Information available Accounts were provided by the trust.

General This trust's main purpose is the encouragement of medical research and the relief of suffering. Since it was set up, in 1984, the income has been committed to medical research, mainly at Scottish university medical departments. It supports specific projects rather than giving general funding to research bodies.

In 2003/04 its assets totalled £6.1 million, generating an income of £259,000. Grants were made to five institutions totalling £163,000. The two largest grants were made to Aberdeen University – Department of Ophthalmology (£82,000) and St Andrew's University – School of Biomedical Sciences (£66,000).

A further three grants were made to Edinburgh University's Centre of Tropical Veterinary Medicine and Department of Biomedical Sciences (£5,000 each) and Aberdeen University – Department of Zoology (£4,500).

Exclusions Grants are unlikely to be made available to non-regular beneficiaries.

Applications Current information about dates and procedures for submitting applications is supplied to the deans of faculties of medicine of the Scottish universities. Applications need to be received by May and trustees meet in June and November. All applications must be submitted on the standard form, and early submission is advisable.

Robert O Curle Charitable Trust

Medical, health, medical research, environment, conservation and animal welfare

£7,000 (2004)

Beneficial area Scotland.

Shepherd & Wedderburn, Saltire Court, 20 Castle Terrace, Edinburgh EH1 2ET

Tel. 0131 473 5273 **Fax** 0131 228 1222

e-mail brian.robertson@shepwedd.co.uk

Correspondent W Brian Robertson, Administrator

Trustees *Hester Curle; W Brian Robertson.*

Scottish Charity No. SC018939

Information available Information was provided by the trust.

General The trust supports causes relating to animals, wildlife, the environment, conservation, medical research and the alleviation of suffering amongst older people and people who are ill.

In 2004 it gave £7,000 in grants. Beneficiaries included Seagull Trust, John Muir Trust, Scottish Native Woods, Asthma UK Scotland and Alzheimer's Scotland Action on Dementia.

Exclusions No grants to individuals. The trust will not fund organisations involved in the following areas: the arts, children/young people, education/training, overseas projects, religious appeals, sports/recreation and social welfare.

Applications In writing to the correspondent. Applications should be sent in October for consideration in December.

Reverend James Currie Memorial Trust

Poverty relief, education, medical, Christian religion

See below

Beneficial area Scotland.

Waddell & Mackintosh, 36 West Portland Street, Troon, Ayrshire KA10 6AB

Tel. 01292 312222

Correspondent   Mr Bailey

Trustees   *John M Mason, Chair;*
Miss Anne Clarke; Charles C McLeod Currie;
Robert D Kernohan; Mrs Mary G Sandeman;
Mrs Jessie M Bell; Gerald P Crean;
Mrs Margaret F Currie; James A Mackay;
Robert H Shepherd.

Scottish Charity No. SC021769

Information available   Information was provided by the trust.

General   The objects of the trust are the relief of poverty, to advance education, medical knowledge and Christian religion.

Over recent years the trustees have been trying to accumulate around £100,000 in assets from which the interest could be dispersed in grants. The 2004/05 accounts show that this amount has almost been reached. It is possible that grantmaking will begin sometime in 2006, although the amounts available for distribution will be modest. Contact the trust directly for up-to-date information.

Applications   In writing to the correspondent.

The Demigryphon Trust

Medical, education, children, general

£53,000 to organisations (2004/05)

Beneficial area UK, with a preference for Scotland.

Pollen House, 10–12 Cork Street, London W1S 3LW

Tel. 020 7439 9061

Correspondent   Alan Winborn, Secretary

Trustees   *The Cowdray Trust Ltd.*

Charity Commission no. 275821

Information available   Accounts were provided by the trust.

General   The trust supports a wide range of organisations and appears to have a preference for education, medical, children and Scottish organisations.

In 2004/05 the trust had assets of £2.3 million and an income of £76,000. Grants were made to

organisations totalling £53,000, ranging from £50 to £50,000.

There was one major beneficiary during the year, the Third Viscount Cowdray's Charity Trust, which received £50,000.

A further 13 small grants were made to organisation including the Aqualung Trust, Echt, Skene & Midmar Agricultural Association, First Merton Park Scout Group, Royal Northern Countryside Initiative, Selham Parochial Church Council and Willow Foundation.

In addition, payments totalling £29,000 were made to 31 older people.

Exclusions   No grants to individuals; only registered charities are supported.

Applications   In writing to the correspondent, including an sae. No application forms or guidelines are issued and there is no deadline. Only successful applications are acknowledged.

John Ferguson Denholm Charitable Trust

General

About £6,000 (2004/05)

Beneficial area Scotland.

Newton of Belltrees, Lochwinnoch, Renfrewshire PA12 4JL

Tel. 01505 842406 **Fax** 08700 517310

e-mail ian.denholm@btinternet.com

Correspondent   Sir Ian Denholm

Scottish Charity No. SC002503

Information available   Limited information was provided by the trust.

General   The trust supports selected recognised charities only. Grants were made in 2004/05 totalling about £6,000. No further information was available.

Previous beneficiaries include Treasurer Paisley Abbey, Children's Music Foundation, Erskine Hospital, Save the Children and Scotland & Newcastle Lymphoma Group.

Applications   In writing to the correspondent. But please note that the trust has stated that its income is fully committed.

The Drummond Trust

Evangelical Christian publications

£10,500 (2005)

Beneficial area UK and worldwide, with a preference for Scotland.

Messrs Hill & Robb, 3 Pitt Terrace, Stirling FK8 2EY

Tel. 01786 450985 **Fax** 01786 451360

e-mail douglaswhyte@hillandrobb.co.uk

Correspondent Douglas S Whyte

Trustees *J F Sinclair; Revd A Sheila Blount; D B Cannon; Miss M J S Henderson; Revd A A S Reid; Revd K G Russel; J K Sinclair, A J Skilling; Dr D A Smith.*

Scottish Charity No. SC011077

Information available Information was provided by the trust.

General The trust supports Christian publications which should be 'of sound Christian doctrine and outreach'. In 2004 the trust's assets amounted to £420,000, generating an income of £18,000. Grants in 2005 totalled £10,500 and ranged between £200 and £1,500. Beneficiaries included Wild Goose Publications and Christians in Sport. The trust also runs a series of lectures in partnership with University of Stirling.

Exclusions Scholarships are not awarded.

Applications Application forms are available from the correspondent at the above address. Trustees meet twice a year in March and September. Completed forms must be returned by 31 January or 31 July of each year.

The Dulverton Trust

Youth and education, welfare, general

£2.7 million (2004/05)

Beneficial area Unrestricted. Mainly UK in practice. An interest in the Cotswolds. Limited support to parts of Africa. Few grants for work in London or Northern Ireland.

5 St James's Place, London SW1A 1NP

Tel. 020 7629 9121 **Fax** 020 7495 6201

e-mail trust@dulverton.org

website www.dulverton.org

Correspondent Col. Christopher Bates, Director

Trustees *Col. David Fanshawe, Chair; Christopher Wills; Sir John Kemp-Welch; Lord Carrington; Tara Douglas-Home; Lord Dulverton; Earl of Gowrie; Dr Catherine Wills; Richard Fitzalan Howard; Sir Malcolm Rifkind; Dame Mary Richardson.*

Charity Commission no. 206426

Information available Good reports and accounts with analysed grants schedule; leaflet outlining 'Policy and Practice'.

General Grants were made during the year in the following categories, listed according to the value of grants with the greatest first:

- youth and education
- welfare
- Africa
- minor appeals
- conservation
- religion
- miscellaneous
- preservation
- peace and security
- local appeals.

The trust states that a number of grants fall within more than one category, making calculations approximate. Awards are seldom for more than £50,000 except to organisations that have established funding connections with the trust.

During 2004/05 the trust received 1,434 appeals for funding, 263 of which received a grant, making the success rate one in six. Though there are wide areas of 'exclusion' these can be funded if an application is recommended by a trustee. The grant total for the year was £2.7 million.

This is one of the trusts deriving from the tobacco-generated fortune of the Wills family. It has an endowment worth £73.5 million and a body of trustees which combines family members with others who have achieved distinction in public life.

The Dulverton Trust is unusual in saying that an application, outside its guidelines, may be accepted if it is supported by an individual trustee – most trusts say that their trustees decide their grantmaking intentions and policies first, and then stick to them.

Three of the trustees are from the Wills family, and the chairman David Fanshawe has an indirect family connection. There is a clear, reported family connection with the Cotswold area (though no longer apparently with Bristol, where many of the Wills factories were located). Sir John Kemp-Welch is a former Chairman of the London Stock Exchange; Lord Carrington, as a former foreign secretary, brings expertise to the trust's minor area of interest in peace and security; Sir Malcolm Rifkind, is also a former foreign secretary; and Lord Gowrie is best known for his interests in the arts.

Apart from a few special programmes described below, the trust makes one-off grants and will not normally consider further applications until a period of at least two years has passed. About one in six applications results in a grant, though not necessarily for the amount requested (but note that the trust, unusually, has been known to give more rather than less than the requested amount, when it has investigated the project concerned).

The following guidelines from the trust are in general terms and there is clearly flexibility in their interpretation in practice:

The main work of the trust is aimed at two major categories which are considered to be of particular relevance. These are youth and education and general welfare. Other areas of interest are conservation, religion (in which the main emphasis is the promotion and development of religious education in schools, principally through the Farmington Trust), followed by preservation and peace and security. Other causes considered by the trustees to have special merit are supported under the miscellaneous category. The trust supports charities throughout the United Kingdom, though is rarely able to support those operating in Greater London and Northern Ireland. Limited grants continue to be made to historic contacts and associations in east Africa, and occasional grants are made in response to appeals from South Africa.

Perennial grants represent a significant portion of the trust's work. These grants are limited to specific charities which lie in the mainstream of the trust's guidelines; the trustees review the size of each grant annually, and undertake to give a year's notice of cessation.

To focus the work of the trust and to allow grants to be made on a worthwhile scale, some exclusions to the general remit have been applied. Therefore, grants are never made to individuals and are not normally made in the following areas unless the project is recommended personally by a trustee, and is considered to be of special merit:

- the broad fields of medicine and health, including drug addiction and work with the mentally and physically handicapped, although exceptions are made from time to time for the development of physically disabled young people;
- projects concerning museums, galleries, libraries and exhibition centres;
- individual churches, cathedrals and other historic buildings (except for limited support under the preservation category), or heritage projects;
- the whole field of the arts, including theatre, music and drama;
- appeals concerned with sport, including sports centres and individual playing field projects;
- appeals from individual schools, colleges, universities or other educational establishments;
- expeditions and research projects.

Requests for grants are considered following an application to the director, who will examine each case in detail. He will discuss it with the applicant and usually, when time allows, one of the trust's staff will visit applicants for major grants anywhere in the United Kingdom. This policy allows a firsthand impression to be gained of the charity's work, and also allows discussions which foster connections with other charities operating in a similar field, or organisations providing useful services to the sector. Each application is treated on its merits and grants are made according to the worthiness of the cause, as presented. The final status of an application lies with the trustees who must confirm any recommendation by the director to reject an appeal.

Grants in 2004/05

The grants for 2004/05 were categorised as follows:

	No.	Total
Youth and education	40	£856,000
General welfare	32	£560,000
Africa	15	£266,000
Minor appeals	121	£225,000
Conservation	12	£219,000
Religion	5	£180,000
Miscellaneous	18	£174,000
Preservation	5	£93,000
Peace and security	5	£86,000
Local appeals (Cotswolds)	10	£25,000

The following is an outline of the trust's priorities and examples of grants in 2004/05:

Youth and education
'This is the trust's largest area of activity and is concerned in the main with help for disadvantaged youth. The trustees are also keen to

assist deserving youngsters who would otherwise be unable to achieve their true potential. In view of the enormous number of appeals within this category, priority will always be given to those which are open to all members of the community and are not aimed at any particular sector of society. The trustees are also concerned with promoting an understanding of the importance of industry and good industrial relations, and any such appeals will normally be considered in this category.'

This category represented nearly 32% of the trust's grant total. The largest number of perennial grants fall within this category. Beneficiaries included Oxford University Dulverton Scholarships (a continuing programme: £125,000), Atlantic College, for scholarships and bursaries (£56,500), Tall Ships Youth Trust (£34,000), Michael Palin Centre for Stammering Children (£29,000), National Library for the Blind (£25,000), ChildLine and Learning Through Action Trust (£20,000 each), Outward Bound Trust (£13,000), Glencoe Trust (£10,000), Endeavour (£7,000) and Queen Victoria School Dunblane (£3,000).

General welfare

'Particular emphasis is placed upon those appeals which deal with the very young and the problems suffered by the increasing proportion of elderly people within the UK. Support for those caring for others, especially young carers, is an area of particular interest as is the importance of marriage and the problems encountered within the family in the 21st Century.'

Just over 20% of the grant total went on general welfare grants during the year. The largest grant of £30,000 was made to Queen Elizabeth's Foundation. Other beneficiaries included Scottish Adoption Association (£26,000), Aberlour Child Care Trust and Scottish Churches Housing Action (£20,000 each), After Adoption (£15,000), Scottish Council for Voluntary Organisations (£12,000), Help the Aged (£10,000), Age Concern Scotland (£5,000) and Army Benevolent Trust (£1,000).

Africa

'Unless there are exceptional circumstances, assistance is given only to a very small number of organisations operating in east Africa, or occasionally South Africa, which have a long association with the trust.'

This category received a larger-than-normal allocation during 2004/05, with almost 10% of the grant total. The largest grant was made to the new Starehe Girls Centre in Kenya, which received £40,000. Other grants included those to Book Aid International (£30,000), Computer Aid International (£25,000), Rhodes University Trust (£15,000), Zimbabwe Agricultural Welfare Trust (£10,000), Kariandusi School Trust (£7,500) and Advantage Africa (£3,000).

Minor appeals

'The sum of £225,000 has been set aside by the trustees. These grants are aimed specifically at charitable organisations, usually operating at local or county level, where a small grant, currently to a maximum of £2,500, would make a significant difference to their ability to operate. Competition for these awards is intense and priority will usually be given to charities working in areas of severe deprivation. Appeals can fall within any of the other categories but, at this level, they are more usually within the areas of youth and education, general welfare and conservation.'

A total of 121 grants were awarded to organisations such as Scout groups, youth clubs and community associations, with an average value of £1,861.

Conservation

'General conservation issues within the UK are of prime importance with the emphasis being on the protection of wildlife habitats. Single species appeals are rarely considered.'

The largest grant of £30,000 was made to the Woodland Trust's Trafalgar Woods project. Other beneficiaries included BioRegional Development Fund (£20,000), Global Canopy Foundation and Scottish Wildlife Trust (£15,000 each) and Royal Society for Nature Conservation (£6,000).

Religion

'This category of appeal is concerned predominantly with the teaching of religious education in schools, especially at secondary level.'

The largest grant, as in the previous year, was made to Farmington Trust, which received £130,000. The four other beneficiaries in this category were Society for Promoting Christian Knowledge (£17,500), Mission to Seafarers (£17,000), Atlantic College – Launcelot Fleming Fellowship (£15,000) and Bibles for Children (£1,000).

Miscellaneous

'This category embraces appeals considered to be of particular merit in areas normally excluded by the trust, if they are recommended personally by a trustee. It also includes a limited number of appeals from charities which provide services for the benefit of the charitable sector as a whole.'

Beneficiaries included Cantraybridge Trust and Erskine Hospital (£25,000 each), REACH (£20,000), Broughton House and Harris Manchester College Oxford (£5,000 each), County Air Ambulance Trust (£3,000) and Devon Air Ambulance Trust (£500).

Preservation

'This is concerned with the preservation of heirlooms of outstanding historic and national importance. Whilst it occasionally includes support for churches and cathedrals, individual appeals can rarely be addressed due to the very large numbers of applications received. In order to provide some assistance in this area of activity, the trust makes annual awards to the Historic Churches Preservation Trust [£20,000 in 2004/05] and the Scottish Churches Architectural Heritage Trust [£8,000].'

The other three beneficiaries in this category were St Giles' Cathedral – Edinburgh (£25,000), Friends of War Memorials and Painswick Rococo Garden Trust (£20,000 each).

Peace and security

'The trust provides very limited support in this category, mainly through the awarding of annual grants to organisations which have a high degree of expertise in this area of activity.'

Grants were made to Encompass – Daniel Braden Reconciliation Trust (£30,000), Royal United Services Institute (£26,000), International Institute for Strategic Studies (£15,000), Royal Institute of International Affairs (£10,000) and Council on Christian Approaches to Defence & Disarmament (£5,000).

Local appeals

Ten grants were made to organisations in the Cotswolds ranging from £1,000 to £3,500.

Exclusions The trust does not operate within the broad fields of medicine and health, including drug and alcohol addiction and work with people who are mentally and physically disabled, although exceptions are made from time to time for the development of young people who are physically disabled. Also generally excluded are museums, galleries, libraries and exhibition centres, and individual churches, cathedrals and other historic buildings (except for limited support under the preservation category) or heritage projects. The whole field of the arts, including theatre, music and drama is excluded together with appeals from individual schools, colleges and universities. Appeals concerned with sport including sports centres and individual playing field projects are not considered.

No grants to overseas charities, except for limited support in Africa. Grants are not made to individuals or for expeditions.

The trust very seldom operates within the Greater London area, or in Northern Ireland except for specific, nominated charities.

Unless there are exceptional circumstances, the trust will not usually provide funding for salaries, major building projects, including the purchase of property or land, endowment appeals or appeals which seek to replace statutory funding.

Applications Applications should be made in writing to the director. Trustees meetings are held four times a year – in January, May, July and October (though decisions on small grants can be made more rapidly – if essential, very rapidly).

Initial enquiries by telephone, for example to establish eligibility, are welcomed.

Applications should, if possible, be restricted to a letter and maximum of two sheets of paper, and should include the applicant's registered charity number, a brief description of the background, aims and objectives of the charity, details of the specific appeal for which funding is sought together with the funding target, and the balance of funding outstanding at the time of application. Initial applications should always include a copy of the previous year's annual report and accounts.

All applications will receive a reply as soon as possible, although research and consultation may delay a response. All rejected applications will receive notification and an explanation for an appeal's rejection will be given.

The selection procedure can take between three to six months, so applicants are advised to apply in plenty of time if funding is required by a certain date.

Dunard Fund

Classical music, the visual arts

£1.4 million (2003/04)

Beneficial area UK, but with a strong interest in Scotland.

4 Royal Terrace, Edinburgh EH7 5AB

Tel. 0131 556 4043 **Fax** 0131 556 3969

Correspondent Mrs Carol Colburn Høgel, Trustee

Trustees *Carol Colburn Høgel; Elisabeth Norman; Catherine Høgel; Erik Høgel; Colin Liddell.*

Charity Commission no. 295790

Information available Accounts were on file at the Charity Commission.

General The charity, established in 1986, is funded annually by Marlow Holdings Limited, the food company responsible for the Quorn brand, of which the correspondent is both a director and a shareholder. It describes its grantmaking as follows:

'The funds are committed principally to the training for and performance of classical music at the highest standard and to education and display of the visual arts, also at international standard. A small percentage of the fund is dedicated to environmental projects.'

In 2003/04 the fund had assets totalling £2.4 million, an income of £868,000 (including a donation of £796,000 from its benefactor), and made 51 grants totalling £1.4 million. About half the trust's beneficiaries were Scottish organisations.

Culture and the Arts – £604,000 in total (24 grants)

Grants in Scotland included those to Edinburgh Festival Society, the largest beneficiary during the year, which received £305,000 in five grants. Other beneficiaries included Scottish National Gallery of Modern Art (£85,000), Maggie's Centres (£30,000 in two grants), Scottish National Photography Centre (£25,000) and Perth Festival of the Arts and Royal Scottish Academy (£10,000 each).

Music – £368,000 in total (22 grants)

Beneficiaries included Scottish Chamber Orchestra (£94,000 in two grants), Royal Scottish National Orchestra (£50,000), Lamp of Lothian Collegiate Trust (£20,000), Dunedin Consort (£18,000 in two grants), Scottish Ensemble (£10,000) and Newtown Concert Society – Edinburgh (£5,000).

Humanitarian and environmental – £52,000 in total (5 grants)

The largest beneficiary was Royal Edinburgh Gardens Edinburgh (£31,000 in two grants).

A further 27 grants of less than £5,000 each were awarded totalling £20,000.

The trust states that while there is no strict yearly quota, it aims for a 'liberal geographical distribution throughout the UK' of its grants.

Exclusions Grants are only given to charities recognised in Scotland or charities registered in England and Wales. The fund says that it does not consider:
• unsolicited applications
• applications from individuals.

Applications In writing to the correspondent, however, see exclusions above.

Mrs J C Dunn's Trust

General

About £8,000

Beneficial area UK, with a preference for Scotland.

Gillespie Macandrew, 25 George IV Bridge, Edinburgh EH1 1EP

Tel. 0131 225 4001 **Fax** 0131 225 1107

e-mail elspeth.paget@gillespiemacandrew.co.uk

Correspondent Mrs Elspeth M Paget, Trustee

Trustees *J S F MacGregor; E M Paget; J B Stirling.*

Scottish Charity No. SC009243

Information available No recent information was available.

General The trust has a net annual income of about £8,000, all of which is given in grants. Beneficiaries include the Salvation Army and the Royal Society for the Relief of Indigent Gentlewomen of Scotland. The trustees prefer to support charities in which the settlor was interested.

Applications Unsolicited applications are not invited.

W J & Mrs C G Dunnachie's Charitable Trust

World War Two veterans

£50,000 a year to individuals and organisations

Beneficial area Preference for Scotland.

Low Beaton Richmond, 20 Renfield Street, Glasgow G2 5AP

Tel. 0141 221 8931

Correspondent The Trustees

Scottish Charity No. SC015981

Information available Information was provided by the trust.

General The trust supports World War Two charities which assist people who are experiencing sickness, infirmity or other disadvantages as a result of the war. Individuals are also supported. There is a preference for assisting organisations connected with Scotland. Grants to individuals and organisations total about £50,000 a year.

Applications In writing to the correspondent at any time.

The Erskine Cunningham Hill Trust

Church of Scotland, general

£48,000 (2004)

Beneficial area Scotland.

Department of National Mission, Church of Scotland Offices, 121 George Street, Edinburgh EH2 4YN

Tel. 0131 225 5722 **Fax** 0131 220 3113

e-mail fmarsh@cofscotland.org.uk

Correspondent Fred Marsh, Secretary

Trustees G W Burnett; H Cole; R M Maiden; Very Revd Dr A McDonald; Very Revd Dr H R Wyllie; I W Grimmond; The Church of Scotland Trust.

Scottish Charity No. SC001853

Information available Information was provided by the trust.

General The object of the trust is stated as making grants in approximately equal proportions to Church of Scotland schemes and Scottish registered charities, particularly those largely administered by voluntary or honorary officials.

In awarding grants to the schemes of the Church of Scotland, the trustees make these to the central funds of the church, not to individual congregations.

In making grants to non-Church of Scotland charities, the trustees normally give priority to organisations working with older people, young people, ex-service personnel and seafarers.

In 2004 the trust had assets of £1 million, an income of £49,000 and made grants totalling £48,000. Previous beneficiaries include ChildLine and Cruse Bereavement Care.

Exclusions No grants to individuals.

Applications In writing to the correspondent at the above address. There is a two-year time bar on repeat grants.

Elizabeth Hardie Ferguson Charitable Trust Fund

Children, medical research, health, hospices

About £50,000

Beneficial area UK, with some interest in Scotland.

c/o 27 Peregrine Crescent, Droylsden, Manchester M43 7TA

Tel. 0161 371 7146

e-mail paul.hardman@btinternet.com

Correspondent Paul Hardman, Trustee

Trustees Sir Alex Ferguson; Cathy Ferguson; Huw Roberts; Ted Way; Les Dalgarno; Paul Hardman; Jason Ferguson.

Scottish Charity No. SC026240

Information available Limited information was provided by the trust.

General This trust was created by Sir Alex Ferguson in 1998 in memory of his mother. It supports a range of children's and medical charities. Grants range from £250 to £10,000 and can be recurrent. Various high-profile events have contributed to the trust's income in recent years. Grants are distributed in the areas where the income is raised. No recent financial information was available from the correspondent, although previous research indicates that grants total around £50,000 each year.

Charities supported by the founder in his home town of Govan will continue to be supported through the trust. Recent beneficiaries have included the Govan Initiative and Harmony Row Boys' Club.

Exclusions Non-registered charities and individuals are not supported. The trust does not make grants overseas.

Applications An application form and guidelines should be requested in writing from the correspondent. The committee meets to consider grants at the end of January and July. Applications should be received by December and June respectively.

The J & C Fleming Trust

Religion, medical research, refugees, older people

About £10,000

Beneficial area Scotland.

MacRoberts Solicitors, 152 Bath Street, Glasgow G2 4TB

Tel. 0141 332 9988 **Fax** 0141 332 8886

Correspondent James Inglis

Scottish Charity No. SC010026

Information available No recent information was available.

General The trust supports religious causes, medical research and the welfare of refugees and older people in Scotland.

Previous research indicates that the trust distributes about £10,000 each year in grants. No further information was available from the correspondent.

Applications In writing to the correspondent.

The Row Fogo Charitable Trust

Medical research, older people

£289,000 (2003/04)

Beneficial area Edinburgh, Lothians and Dunblane.

Brodies LLP Solicitors, 15 Atholl Crescent, Edinburgh EH3 8HA

Tel. 0131 228 3777 **Fax** 0131 228 3878

e-mail andrew.dalgleish@brodies.co.uk

Correspondent Andrew M C Dalgleish

Trustees E J Cuthbertson; A W Waddell; Dr C Brough.

Scottish Charity No. SC009685

Information available Accounts were provided by the trust, without a list of grants.

General This trust makes grants for medical research projects, with particular emphasis on the neurosciences, smaller local charitable projects and the care of older people.

In 2003/04 the trust had assets of £2.8 million and an income of £129,000. Grants were made totalling £289,000.

The main beneficiary of the trust is SHEFC Brain Imaging Centre for Scotland, which receives £64,000 a year until 2007 to establish the Row Fogo Charitable Trust Lectureship in Medical Image Analysis.

Previous beneficiaries include Macmillan Cancer Relief, RNLI, Alzheimer's Scotland Action on Dementia, Age Concern, Salvation Army, Multiple Sclerosis Society, Muscular Dystrophy Campaign, Wishbone Trust, Drum Riding for the Disabled, Invalids at Home and Stobhill Kidney Patients' Association.

Exclusions No grants to individuals.

Applications In writing to the correspondent.

W G Forsyth Fund

Children and young people, disability

About £5,000

Beneficial area UK, with a preference for Scotland.

Turcan Connell WS, Princes Exchange, 1 Earl Grey Street, Edinburgh EH3 9EE

Tel. 0131 228 8111 **Fax** 0131 228 8118

e-mail enquiries@turcanconnell.com

Correspondent Niall Stringer

Scottish Charity No. SC011564

Information available Accounts are available from the correspondent for £10.

General The trust supports children, young people and disability causes. Grants are not given for other causes. No further information was available.

Previous research indicates that grants are made totalling about £5,000 each year. Previous beneficiaries include Montrose YMCA and Kincardine & Mearns Special Needs Forum. One-off or recurrent grants can be given.

Exclusions No grants to individuals.

Applications In writing to the correspondent.

The Gordon Fraser Charitable Trust

Children, young people, environment, arts

£134,000 (2004/05)

Beneficial area UK, with a preference for Scotland.

Holmhurst, Westerton Drive, Bridge of Allan, Stirling FK9 4QL

Correspondent Mrs Margaret A Moss, Trustee

Trustees Mrs Margaret A Moss; William F T Anderson.

Charity Commission no. 260869

Information available Accounts were provided by the trust.

General Currently the trustees are particularly interested in supporting children/young people in need, the environment and visual arts (including performance arts). Most grants are given within these categories. The trust states that 'applications from or for Scotland will receive favourable consideration, but not to the exclusion of applications from elsewhere'.

In 2004/05 the trust had assets of £2.3 million and an income of £132,000. Grants were made to 139 organisations totalling £134,000. Most grants were for less than £1,000, with 41 for £1,000 or more.

The largest grant was given to MacRobert Arts Centre – Stirling University (£7,000). Other grants included those to Aberlour Child Care Trust and Scotland International Piano Competition (£5,000 each), Artlink Central – Stirling (£4,500), Girlguiding Scotland (£4,000), Edinburgh International Festival Society (£3,000) and National Galleries of Scotland (£2,000).

Beneficiaries receiving £1,000 each included Advocacy Partners, Council for Music in Hospitals, Edinburgh Headway Group, Hebridean Trust, Maggie's Highlands, National Library of Scotland, Shelter Scotland and St Serf's Residential Home.

Smaller grants of less than £1,000 were given to a wide range of charities, both national and local, throughout Scotland. Beneficiaries included Aberdeen International Children's Festival, Action of Churches Together in Scotland, Craighalbert Centre, Dyslexia in Scotland, Edinburgh Young Carers Project, Glasgow Children's Holiday Scheme, Montrose YMCA, Ocean Youth Trust, Perth Festival of the Arts, Scottish Amateur Music Association, St Magnus Festival and Venture Scotland.

Exclusions No grants are made to organisations which are not recognised charities, or to individuals.

Applications In writing to the correspondent. Applications are considered in January, April, July and October. Grants towards national or international emergencies can be considered at any time. All applicants are acknowledged; an sae would, therefore, be appreciated.

The Hugh Fraser Foundation

General

About £2 million (2004/05)

Beneficial area UK, especially western or deprived areas of Scotland.

Turcan Connell WS, Princes Exchange, 1 Earl Grey Street, Edinburgh EH3 9EE

Tel. 0131 228 8111 **Fax** 0131 228 8118

e-mail lnk@turcanconnell.com

Correspondent ~~Heather Thompson~~ *Katrina Muir*, Trust Administrator

Trustees *Dr Kenneth Chrystie, Chair; The Hon. Miss Ann Fraser; Miss Patricia Fraser; Blair Smith.*

Scottish Charity No. SC009303

Information available Information was provided by the trust. Annual report and accounts are available for £10.

General The foundation makes around 800 grants each year, with most for around £3,000.

The trustees' policy is to pay special regard to applications from the west of Scotland and from parts of Scotland where the local economy and/or other circumstances make it more difficult to raise funds for charitable purposes.

The trustees consider that grants to large highly publicised national appeals are not likely to be as effective a use of funds as grants to smaller and more focused charitable appeals.

The trustees also consider that better use of the funds can be made by making grants to charitable bodies to assist them with their work, than by making a large number of grants to individuals.

The trustees are prepared to enter into commitments over a period of time by making grants in successive years, often to assist in new initiatives which can maintain their own momentum once they have been established for a few years.

The foundation makes grants in many different areas, including medical facilities, education, organisations working with older people, people who are disabled or underprivileged, environmental and youth groups.

Previous beneficiaries include Scottish Science Trust and Capability Scotland.

Exclusions Grants are not awarded to individuals nor to organisations that are not registered charities. Non-profit making organisations, although not normally registered charities, may apply.

Applications In writing to the correspondent. The trustees meet on a quarterly basis to consider applications, in January, April, July and October.

The Emily Fraser Trust

Specific trades, older people

£36,000 to organisations (2003/04)

Beneficial area UK, with a preference for Scotland.

Turcan Connell WS, Princes Exchange, 1 Earl Grey Street, Edinburgh EH3 9EE

Tel. 0131 228 8111 **Fax** 0131 228 8118

e-mail lnk@turcanconnell.com

Correspondent Heather Thompson, Trust Administrator

Trustees *Dr Kenneth Chrystie, Chair; The Hon. Miss Ann Fraser; Miss Patricia Fraser; Blair Smith.*

Scottish Charity No. SC007288

Information available Information was provided by the trust. Annual report and accounts are available for £10.

General The trust makes grants mainly to people in Scotland and their dependants who were or are engaged in the drapery and allied trades and the printing, publishing, books and stationery, newspaper and allied trades. Preference is given to people who are or were employed by House of Fraser Limited, Scottish Universal Investments Limited and Paisleys.

Grants are also made to Scottish organisations caring for older and infirm people with connections in the fields described above. It prefers to support small, community organisations which find it difficult to raise funds. It also prefers to support organisations in areas where there is little local funding available. The trustees 'consider that grants to large highly publicised national appeals are not likely to be as effective a use of funds as grants to smaller and more focused charitable appeals'.

In 2003/04 it had assets of £1.8 million and an income of £67,000. Grants to 16 organisations totalled £36,000, with a further £43,000 given to individuals.

The largest grant was £15,000 to Camphill Village Trust. Other grants included those to Brainwave (£3,000) and James Powell (UK) Trust, Wheelchair Sports Club, Maggie's Cancer Caring Centre – Fife and Combat Stress (£2,000 each).

Exclusions   Applicants already receiving grants from the Hugh Fraser Foundation (see separate entry) will not be eligible.

Applications   In writing to the correspondent. The trustees meet quarterly to consider applications, in January, April, July and October. The trustees of this trust are also the trustees of the Hugh Fraser Foundation and applications are allocated to one or other of the trusts as appears appropriate.

Gaelic Language Promotion Trust

Gaelic language education projects
About £7,000 each year

Beneficial area UK.

Medrox Villa, Gain Road, Annathill, by Coatbridge ML5 2QG

Tel. 01236 879460 **Fax** 0141 779 1470

e-mail uist1@aol.com

Correspondent   Mrs Margaret Callan, Secretary

Scottish Charity No. SC004414

Information available   Information was provided by the trust.

General   This trust encourages and promotes teaching, learning and the use of the Gaelic language, and the study and cultivation of Gaelic literature. The main deciding factor at all times shall be any given project's contribution towards increasing the number of Gaelic speakers.

Support may be given to projects/individuals in the following categories:

- Gaelic education, particularly courses leading to Gaelic teaching qualifications
- Gaelic drama
- publications – particularly books in relation to GME
- croileagain/sradagan
- major projects contributing towards increasing the number of Gaelic speakers.

The amount available to fund projects is dependent upon the performance of investments in the previous year. The grant total quoted above should, therefore, only be taken as a guide. No grant given to any single project may come to more than 40% of the total cost and, in general, no applicant/project will receive funding on more than one occasion for that project.

Students studying Gaelic may receive grants of up to £500 a year for a maximum of four years unless in exceptional circumstances (the only instance where grants are awarded recurrently). Publication grants of no more than £500 will be allocated to any single project, ordinarily on receipt of the final product. New croileagain/sradagan will normally receive £200 start-up funding subject to conforming to CNSA guidelines. No major project funding (i.e. with a trust contribution of over £2,000 or lasting more than two years) will be entered into until all previous long-term projects have been satisfactorily completed.

Exclusions   No grants for travel to/from mods (a competition-based festival which celebrates the Gaelic language and culture through music, dance, drama, arts and literature).

Applications   In writing to the correspondent requesting detailed funding policy guidelines. The trustees meet at least twice a year to consider funding applications and may be called to meet at fourteen days' notice if the need arises.

Agnes Gallagley Bequest

Roman Catholic charities, education, social welfare
See below

Beneficial area Not known, possible preference for Scotland.

Grant Thornton Accountants, 196 Clyde Street, Glasgow G1 4JY

Tel. 0141 223 0000

Correspondent   Mrs Patricia Munroe

Scottish Charity No. SC016337

Information available   Accounts were available at a cost of £20.

General The trust's main concern appears to be to support Roman Catholic causes and it also supports education and social welfare. The trust has previously provided no additional information regarding its finances or charitable activities. It is known that during one particular year the trust gave grants totalling £30,000. The trust has previously returned its entries unamended, which we take as tacit agreement to its content.

Applications Unsolicited applications are not invited.

The Gamma Trust

General

About £60,000

Beneficial area UK, with a possible preference for Scotland.

Clydesdale Bank, Trust & Executry Unit, Brunswick House, 51 Wilson Street, Glasgow G1 1UZ

Tel. 0141 223 2507

Correspondent The Manager

Scottish Charity No. SC004330

Information available Information was provided by the trust.

General This trust has general charitable purposes. It appears that new grants are only given to UK-wide organisations although most grants are ongoing commitments to local organisations in Scotland. It has a grant total of about £60,000 a year.

Previous beneficiaries include British Red Cross, British Heart Foundation, Cancer Research Campaign and Erskine Hospital.

Exclusions No grants to individuals.

Applications In writing to the correspondent for consideration quarterly.

The Gannochy Trust

General

£2.5 million (2003/04)

Beneficial area Scotland, with a preference for the Perth area.

Kincarrathie House Drive, Pitcullen Crescent, Perth PH2 7HX

Tel. 01738 620653

Correspondent Murdoch MacKenzie, Administrator

Trustees Dr Russell Leather, Chair; Mark Webster; Dr James H F Kynaston; Dr James Watson; Ian W McMillan; Stewart N Macleod.

Scottish Charity No. SC003133

Information available Annual report and accounts, with a full list of beneficiaries were provided by the trust.

General The trust concentrates on the needs of 'youth and recreation', but supports a wide range of causes. It had an endowment of £104 million in 2003/04, derived from the personal fortune of Arthur Kinmond Bell, whisky distiller, and produced an income of £4.2 million. It makes a large number of grants, 213 of them in 2003/04 totalling £2.5 million, of which 110 were for amounts of £5,000 or less. They were classified as follows, with the percentages referring to the value of the grants:

Arts	32%
Health	19%
Recreation	16%
Education	14%
Social welfare	12%
Environment	7%

Major grants were:

- £900,000 to Perth & Kinross Leisure – £800,000 by way of the final installment towards the establishment of the new Perth Concert Hall, £100,000 towards the renovation and repair of community facilities in the Perth area and £90,000 towards sports coaching for young people.
- £300,000 to University of Edinburgh Research Institute for Medical Cell Biology Project towards the provision of an imaging suite.
- £250,000 to Kelvingrove Art Galley & Museum.
- £204,000 to the Royal Society of Edinburgh to cover the cost establishing the Gannochy Trust

Innovation Award.

- £135,000 to the Perth & Kinross Countryside Trust over two years for the development and upkeep of the rural heritage of the Perth countryside.
- £132,000 to the Kincarrathie Trust towards refurbishment and maintenance at Kincarrathie Home for the Elderly – Perth.
- £100,000 to Perth & Kinross Heritage Trust for the upkeep and preservation of local heritage.
- £100,000 to the University of Glasgow – British Heart Foundation Cardiovascular Research Centre.

Other larger grants over £10,000 each included £50,000 to Auchterarder Gymnastics Trust, £30,000 to Guide Association Scotland, £25,000 to Compass Christian Centre Ltd, £20,000 to Children First, £18,000 to DEBRA, £15,000 to Fairbridge in Scotland, £12,000 each to Portessie Public Hall and RSNO Junior Choir and £10,000 each to British Sports Trust, Craignish Village Hall, Leonard Cheshire Foundation in Scotland, Perth & Kinross Music Foundation, Scottish Motor Neurone Disease Association and Scottish Sports Futures.

Other beneficiaries included Scottish Huntingdon's Association (£8,000), Fife Folk Museum Trust (£7,500), Abbeyfield Ballachulish Society and National Youth Choir of Scotland (£7,000 each), Perth Choral Society (£6,000), Cornerstone Community Care and Move On Limited (£5,000 each), YMCA Coupar Angus (£4,000), Mull & Iona Community Trust (£3,000), Aberdeen International Children's Festival (£2,000), Kilmadock Development Trust Limited – Doune (£1,500) and Moray & Nairn Sea Cadets (£1,000).

Exclusions   No grants to individuals. Donations are confined to organisations recognised by the Inland Revenue as charitable.

Applications   In writing to the correspondent, confined to two pages of A4 including:

- a general statement on the objects of the applicant's charity
- the specific nature of the application
- the estimated cost and how this is arrived at
- the contribution of the applicant's charity towards the cost
- the contributions of others, actual and promised
- estimated shortfall
- details of previous appeals to the trust –

whether accepted or rejected
- a copy of the latest audited accounts.

It will be helpful to extract the following information from the accounts:

- income
- expenditure
- reserves (committed and uncommitted).

Auditors' reservations, if any, should be explained. 'It is the practice of the trustees to scrutinise accounts before making donations.' Time rarely permits visits either to the trust office or to the charity concerned. The trustees meet frequently, generally monthly, to consider appeals.

The G C Gibson Charitable Trust

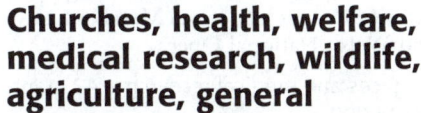

Churches, health, welfare, medical research, wildlife, agriculture, general

£574,000 (2003/04)

Beneficial area UK, with interests in Suffolk, Wales and Scotland.

Deloitte & Touche, Blenheim House, Fitzalan Court, Newport Road, Cardiff CF24 0TS

Tel. 029 2048 1111

Correspondent   Karen Griffin

Trustees   R D Taylor; Mrs J M Gibson; George S C Gibson.

Charity Commission no. 258710

Information available   Annual report and accounts on file at the Charity Commission.

General   In 2003/04 the trust had assets totalling £10.6 million and an income of £400,000. A total of £574,000 was donated to 155 charities during the year under the following headings:

- art, music and education
- health, hospices and medical research
- community and other social projects
- religion.

The trust stated of its grantmaking policy that the 'majority of donations have been made towards the annual expenditure of the charities concerned. Whilst the trustees will consider donations for capital projects, the average donation of £5,000 is more suited for meeting the revenue commitments of the donees'.

'Applications have been considered from charities working throughout the UK. Preference has been given to applications from charities who have already received donations from the trust as the trustees recognise the importance of providing recurring donations whenever possible.'

Grants were broken down as follows, shown here with examples of beneficiaries in each category:

Art, music and education – 23 grants totalling £102,000

By far the largest donation in this category was £20,000 to Royal Welsh College of Music and Drama. Other grants included £5,000 each to Cardiff Bay Chamber Orchestra, British Youth Opera, Papworth, Royal National College for the Blind – Hereford and Stefan Batory Trust; £3,000 each to Christ College Brecon Appeal Fund, St David's Hall Trust and St Michael's College – Llandaff and £2,000 each to Royal Merchant Navy School and Welsh National Opera.

Health, hospices and medical research – 42 grants totalling £174,000

Grants of £10,000 each went to King Edward VII Hospital, St Michael's Hospice – Hereford and St Nicholas's Hospice – Bury St Edmunds. Other grants included £6,000 to Marie Curie Cancer Care, £5,000 each to Haven Trust – London, Cancer Research Campaign Scotland, Cystic Fibrosis Research Trust, Jersey Hospice Care, National Ankylosing Spondylitis Society, Seeability, St Francis's Hospice, Sue Ryder Old Palace Project and Winston's Wish, £3,000 to East Anglia Children's Hospice, the Alzheimer's Disease Society, Kidney Research Unit for Wales Foundation Appeal, Mental Health Foundation, National Society for Epilepsy and Starlight Children's Foundation and £2,000 each to the Arthritis and Rheumatism Council – Newmarket, The Evelina Children's Hospital Appeal, International Spinal Research Trust, Llangasty Retreat House Appeal, Tommy's Campaign, West Suffolk Association for the Blind, Muscular Dystrophy Group and Vision Foundation.

Community and other social projects – 65 grants totalling £226,000

The largest grant in this category was £10,000 to Weston Spirit. Other grants included £7,000 to the Wildfowl and Wetlands Trust, £6,000 to Astley Institute – Newmarket, £5,000 each to Appledore Lifeboat Crew Account, British Red Cross Society, Bury St Edmunds Volunteer

Centre, Gwent Wildlife Trust, Kiloran Trust, Penarth Gymnastics Club, Salvation Army, Royal Star and Garter Home and Shelter Cymru; £4,000 each to Sail Training Association and Wallich Clifford Community Roath; £3,000 each to Age Concern Wales, Anti-Slavery Society, Kidsactive, Prospect Burma, Relate, Toynbee Hall and Worshipful Company of Farriers' Charitable Trust and £2,000 each to Army Benevolent Fund, Cardiff Young Men's Christian Association, Blue Cross Animal Welfare Charity, Frontier Youth Project, Hertfordshire Association for Young People, NSPCC – Saundersfoot, Sailors' Children's Society and Wales in Trust and £1,000 to Hampshire Garden Trust.

Religion – 21 grants totalling £72,000

Grants included £5,000 each to Ely Cathedral Restoration Trust, Llandaff Cathedral Restoration Appeal, Hereford Cathedral Appeal, Ousden Village Church, St David's Cathedral, St Mary's Church – Newmarket, Venerable Order of St John of Jerusalem and Vicar & Churchwardens – Church of the Resurrection; £3,000 to Bishopswood Parish Church Council, Christian Children's Fund of Great Britain and Walford Parish Church Council, £2,000 each to Canynges Society and Scripture Union and £1,000 to St Mary's – Old Harlow.

Exclusions No grants to individuals. Only registered charities are supported.

Applications In writing to the correspondent by October each year. Trustees meet in November/December. Successful applicants will receive their cheques during January.

Organisations that have already received a grant should re-apply describing how the previous year's grant was spent and setting out how a further grant would be used. In general, less detailed information is required from national charities with a known track record than from small local charities that are not known to the trustees.

'Due to the volume of applications, it is not possible to acknowledge each application, nor is it possible to inform unsuccessful applicants.'

The Helen and Horace Gillman Trusts

Protection of birds and birds' habitat

About £20,000 each year

Beneficial area Great Britain and Northern Ireland, with a special interest in Scotland.

Drummond Miller, 32 Moray Place, Edinburgh EH3 6BZ

Tel. 0131 226 5151 **Fax** 0131 225 2608

e-mail tbell@drummond-miller.co.uk

Correspondent Mrs T K M Bell

Trustees *J K Burleigh; F Hamilton; I Darling.*

Information available Information was provided by the trust.

General The trusts, which were set up in 1982, are valued in total at about £415,000. In 2004/05 their joint income was about £25,000.

The trusts support the protection of birds and their habitat. Grants range between £500 and £10,000. Past recipients have included RSPB, Scottish Wildlife Trust, Fife Bird Club and John Muir Trust.

Applications In writing to the correspondent. Trustees meet twice a year, usually including January/February time, and September/October time. Applications should be received in the preceding month.

The Gough Charitable Trust

Youth, Episcopal and Church of England, preservation of the countryside, social welfare

About £36,000 (2003/04)

Beneficial area UK, with a possible preference for Scotland.

Lloyds TSB Private Banking Ltd, UK Trust Centre, 22–26 Ock Street, Abingdon OX14 5SW

Correspondent Mrs E Osborn-King, Trust Manager

Trustees *Lloyds Bank plc; N de L Harvie.*

Charity Commission no. 262355

Information available Accounts were on file at the Charity Commission.

General The trust has previously shown a preference for Scotland, however it is not clear if this is still the case.

In 2003/04 the trust had an income of £36,000 and a total expenditure of £77,000. Grants were made totalling about £36,000. Although submitted by the trust to the Charity Commission, the accounts for that year had not made it to the public files for inspection.

Previous beneficiaries include St Luke with Holy Trinity Charlton, RNLI, Wykeham Crown, Manor Trust, 999 Club, National Army Development Trust, Lifeboat Service, Trinity Hospice, Household Brigade Lodge Benevolent Fund, Prince of Wales Lodge Benevolent Fund, Irish Guards' Fund, Lloyds' Benevolent Fund and Lloyds' Charities Fund.

Exclusions No support for non-registered charities and individuals including students.

Applications In writing to the correspondent at any time. No acknowledgements are sent. Applications are considered quarterly.

Dr Guthrie's Association

Children and young people

Around £47,000 a year

Beneficial area Scotland, with a preference for Edinburgh.

PO Box 23533, Edinburgh EH4 1YL

Tel. 07729 018214

e-mail drguthrie@tiscali.co.uk

Correspondent The Grant Administrator

Scottish Charity No. SC009302

Information available Information was provided by the trust.

General The trust exists for the betterment of children and young people through the financial support of not–for–profit organisations which care for economically and socially disadvantaged children and young people in Scotland, giving preference to those residing in the Edinburgh area. Small local organisations are more likely to receive grants than national organisations. Priority will be given to:

- young people aged 10–21 inclusive
- creative and outdoor pursuits for young people
- young unemployed people
- post-school education and training of young people.

In 2004/05 grants totalled £47,000. Grants are generally one–off and usually in the range of between £300 and £1,000 each.

No information was available on beneficiaries.

Exclusions Individuals; projects of an environmental nature; mainstream activities and statutory requirements of schools, universities and hospitals; large-scale building projects; historic restoration; retrospective funding.

Applications Applications are considered by the trustees three times a year (approximately) in February, June and October.

The Susan H Guy Charitable Trust

(same trustees as KPMG)

General, environment, animal welfare

£27,500 (2003/04)

Beneficial area UK, with a strong preference for Scotland.

KPMG, 24 Blythswood Square, Glasgow G2 4QS

191 W George St

G2 2U

Tel. 0141 226 5511

Correspondent Mrs Margaret-Jane McColl

Trustees *Joy Travers; Campbell Denholm; Management Trust Company Limited.*

Scottish Charity No. SC000393

Information available Accounts were provided by the trust.

General The trust has general charitable purposes with some preference for environment, animal welfare and health charities. In 2003/04 it had assets of £504,000, an income of £22,000 and gave £27,500 in grants. No information on beneficiaries was available.

Previous beneficiaries have included Marie Curie Cancer Care, RNLI, RSPB and Salvation Army. It prefers to give to Scottish branches of national charities.

Exclusions No grants to individuals.

Applications In writing to the correspondent. Trustees normally meet to consider grants in April and November.

The Harbour Trust

Evangelical Christian work

£6,000 (2004/05)

Beneficial area Unrestricted, but with some preference for Scotland.

4 St Augustine Close, Little Dunmow, Essex CM6 3FP

e-mail alanandrona@msn.com

Correspondent Dr Alan McCormick, Trustee

Trustees *Dr A H I McCormick; Mrs R McCormick.*

Scottish Charity No. SC002764

Information available Information was provided by the trust.

General The trust mainly supports evangelical Christian work. It only gives grants to individuals and organisations which are personally known or recommended to the trustees.

In 2004/05 it had an income of £7,000 and gave 6 grants totalling £6,000, including 5 grants that were recurrent from the previous year. Grants ranged from £50 to £3,300. The large grants were given to Broomfield Evangelical Church – Chelmsford (£3,300) and International Fellowship of Evangelical Students (£1,000). Other beneficiaries included New Tribes Mission (£600), Operation Mobilisation (£500) and Sudan Emergency Fund (£250).

Applications Applications are not invited and unsolicited appeals do not receive a response.

Mrs D L Harryhausen's 1969 Trust

Animal welfare, David Livingstone Centre

£6,000 (2004)

Beneficial area UK, with an interest in Scotland.

Turcan Connell WS, Princes Exchange, 1 Earl Grey Street, Edinburgh EH3 9EE

Tel. 0131 228 8111 Fax 0131 228 8118

website www.harryhausen.org.uk

Correspondent S A Mackintosh, Trustee

Trustees *Miss Vanessa Harryhausen; Simon Mackintosh; George Menzies.*

Scottish Charity No. SC015688

Information available Accounts were available from the trust.

General The trustees' priorities are to support applications concerned with either animal welfare or the activities of the David Livingstone Centre (the settlor's great-grandfather).

In 2004 the trust had assets of £294,000 and an income of £24,000. Administration charges of £5,500 were made to a firm of solicitors of which one of the trustees is a partner. Whilst wholly legal, these editors always regret such payments unless, in the words of the Charity Commission, 'there is no realistic alternative'.

The trust gave four grants totalling £6,000. Beneficiaries were International League for the Protection of Horses and National Canine Defence League (£2,000 each) and Redwings Horse Sanctuary and Scottish Castles Association (£1,000 each).

Exclusions Grants are not normally given to individuals.

Applications In writing to the correspondent, however please note the trust states that applications are not invited as the income is fully committed.

Howard Hatton Charitable Trust

General
Around £2,000 a year

Beneficial area Mostly Kidderminster, Scotland and southern England.

Carlton House, Worcester Street, Kidderminster, Worcestershire DY10 1BA

Tel. 01299 402221

Correspondent Mrs F M Swain

Trustees *Mrs Alexa Catherine Collis; Justin Forbes; The Dowager Lady Suzanne Rollo.*

Charity Commission no. 214325

Information available Information obtained from Charity Commission website, accounts on file for 1994 only.

General The trust supports projects in areas where the trustees are based, namely Scotland, Kidderminster and southern England. In practice the same organisations are supported each year. In 2003/04 the trust had an income of £2,600 and a total expenditure of £2,800. Further information for this year was not available.

In 1994/95, the most recent year for which further information was available, it had assets of £50,000 and an income of £3,400. Grants to 15 organisations ranged from £15 to £350 and totalled £1,500. Beneficiaries included Dunning Parish Church (£350), Aston Church (£250), Macmillan Cancer Relief and Samaritans (£100 each), NSPCC (£30), Barnardo's (£20) and Oxfam (£15).

Applications In writing to the correspondent at any time.

Help the Aged

Welfare, for older people
£2 million (2004/05)

Beneficial area UK.

207–221 Pentonville Road, London N1 9UZ

Tel. 020 7278 1114 Fax 020 7278 1116

e-mail info@helptheaged.org.uk

website www.helptheaged.org.uk

Correspondent Michael Lake, Director General

Trustees *Mrs Jo Connell, Chair; Dr Beverly Castleton; Ms Anna Coote; Dr June Crown; Brian Fox; Prof. Leslie Iversen; Prof. Oliver James; William Barry Keates; Mrs Rosemary Kelly; Trevor Larman; John D Mather; William Menzies-Wilson; Michael Curig Roberts; Len Sanderson; Kevin Williams; Gillian Wilmot; Christopher Woodbridge; Angus G F Young.*

Charity Commission no. 272786

Information available Report and accounts. Grants, guidance and project fundraising information.

General The most important form of support for other charities by Help the Aged is best described as 'support in kind'. For example, its staff carry out training fundraising for 'other UK charities which share the objectives of Help the Aged'.

Help is, nevertheless, also given in the more traditional form of grants. In 2004/05, grants were made totalling £2 million.

Generally small, and made through four departments or schemes, grants in 2004/05 were categorised as follows:

Research	£1,466,000
Day centres, social clubs and initiatives	£339,000
Gardening project	£86,000
Senior mobility projects	£58,000
Campaigning for older people	£128,000

There are also extensive grantmaking programmes overseas, of just over £5.8 million, which are not covered here.

'Local committees raise and distribute funds to local older people. Local committees were formed in 1986 and are a key part of Help the Aged's strategy. They have given grants to pensioners forums, HandyVans, lunch clubs and other local causes. We have established clear procedures with Community Services to ensure that grants are given according to need. During 2004/05 Local Committees distributed grants to the value of £68,000.'

Help the Aged 'is primarily a fundraising organisation' . The charity raises money, some of which is given in grants, through its Community Services division. They are usually small, and go to community-based groups for projects such as building and equipping day centres, setting up lunch clubs or buying minibuses, under a range of programmes and schemes as follows, with figures for 2004/05.

Community support general grants (£672,000)

We give support to community groups through support and guidance, information, training and in grants. In deciding where we can give support two factors will be uppermost, namely that the projects in question

1 meet needs that have been defined by older people themselves

2 clearly target disadvantage.

Due to the large demand on funds, Help the Aged are currently running a more strategically focussed grant making programme. Also though they may not be able to offer financial support at this time, the following could be available:

- help with developing your service, and in setting goals and standards for it

- help with setting up a group and with constitutions
- guidance on developing a business plan
- guidance on involving older people, and in running a group
- guidance on fundraising
- guidance on legal requirements
- guidance on certain technical matters such as vehicle specifications
- grants, whether revenue or capital, to develop a service (if applicable)
- grants for capital projects (if applicable).

It may well be that the best way to help, given the limited funds available, will be through guidance and information to your organisation. In the case of larger projects, such as significant capital programmes, our involvement could be considerable and spread over a period of time. In these situations, we ask that the organisation take part in a full feasibility study.

We may agree that the best way of helping you with a large project may be to second one of our regional development officers to you for a period of their time. They are fully trained and their expertise can help you turn your project into reality.

Criteria for supporting projects

Any project which we assist must meet all the following criteria:

- be able to demonstrate that the highest percentage of their use is by older people or their carers
- be managed by properly constituted voluntary organisations, or those working towards that status. Charitable status is not strictly necessary
- reach local communities and target vulnerable or disadvantaged older people
- produce evidence that older people have identified or support this particular way forward, and will be involved in its development
- meet a need where there is a clearly defined gap in available services and opportunities
- have a clear idea of what you are trying to achieve, so that later on we can together see how much has been achieved
- have a clear idea of how you are going to build on what you have achieved and keep it going
- be able to demonstrate that assistance is towards a new project or service, or a development of an existing one.

Not more than two applications will normally be considered within a five-year period.

Projects recently supported include:

- advocacy projects
- training and awareness programmes
- social research
- conferences and events

- assistance with mobility, sometimes involving minibuses and other forms of transport
- daily living activities, such as day care centres and lunch clubs
- older People's Community Groups
- refurbishment costs
- home care support.

£672,000 was given in grants under this scheme in 2004/05, categorised as follows:

Specialist care services	£124,000
Projects for preserving independence	£91,000
Advice/information/advocacy/research	£42,000
Access to buildings	£88,000
Access to transport	£164,000
Access to opportunities	£45,000
Empowerment	£119,000

The 282 new grant awards in 2004/05 ranged from around £50 to £25,000.

The geographical spread of grants in England vary with the South of England receiving 46% of the money and the Midlands and North of England receiving 39%. Wales received 5% and Scotland 10%. There is a separate grants programme in Northern Ireland of about £48,000 a year.

In 2003/04 grants were made to SeniorSafety (£2,000), community projects (£1,500), community services (£530), innovation and development (£250) and other projects (£460).

Exclusions   The charity does not support:

- Funding for loans, or to reduce deficits already incurred by projects, or to make up a shortfall due to underbidding for a service contract
- commercial companies or statutory agencies
- organisations artificially created as trusts, designed to meet the needs of community care proposals or to realise European funding
- holidays
- residential or nursing homes, except to support independent living of older people and where the benefits extend to the wider community
- registered social landlords except where there is a clearly defined project focusing on a vulnerable group, for example, homeless older people
- fabric appeals for public buildings, including churches.

'Grants towards individuals, outings, general entertainment, leisure clubs and festive celebrations are generally excluded except where they may be supported with funds specifically donated to us for that particular purpose or within a geographical area.'

Applications   In the first instance contact the regional distributions department on 020 7253 0253 or by fax on 020 7239 1849. The distributions committee meets approximately every other month, usually in March, June, September and December. In between meetings, grants can be agreed for up to £5,000, but only out of funds earmaked for specific local areas or subjects.

The Christina Mary Hendrie Trust for Scottish & Canadian Charities

Youth, people who are elderly, general
See below

Beneficial area Scotland and Canada.

Anderson Strathern Solicitors, 1 Rutland Court, Edinburgh EH3 8EY

Tel. 0131 270 7700 **Fax** 0131 270 7788

e-mail george.russell@andersonstrathern.co.uk

Correspondent   George R Russell, Secretary

Trustees   Mrs A D H Irwin; C R B Cox; J K Scott Moncrieff; Miss C Irwin; Maj. Gen. A S H Irwin; R N Cox; A G Cox.

Scottish Charity No. SC014514

Information available   Information was provided by the trust.

General   The trust was established in 1975 following the death in Scotland of Christina Mary Hendrie. The funds constituting the trust originated in Canada. Grants are distributed to charities throughout Scotland and Canada, although the majority is now given in Scotland. There is a preference for charities connected with young or older people, although other groups to receive grants include cancer charities.

Exclusions   Grants are not given to individuals. Only organisations known to the trustees can be considered.

Applications   No unsolicited applications can be considered as all funds are fully committed.

The Anne Herd Memorial Trust

Visual impairment

£21,500 (2003/04)

Beneficial area Scotland, with a preference for Tayside, the City of Dundee and Broughty Ferry.

Bowman Scottish Lawyers, 27 Bank Street, Dundee DD1 1RP

Tel. 01382 322267

Correspondent The Trustees

Trustees *B Neil Bowman; Mrs Pamela M M Bowman; Mrs Elizabeth N McGillivray; Rory W H Hudson; Mrs Elizabeth M Breckon; Robert J Wild.*

Scottish Charity No. SC014198

Information available Accounts were provided by the trust.

General The trust supports both individuals who are visually impaired and organisations working with them in the beneficial area. Most grants to individuals are given through an organisation.

In 2003/04 it had assets of £742,000 and an income of £51,000. The grant total for the year was £21,500, almost all of which was given to Dundee Society for the Visually Impaired (£20,000). The remaining £1,500 was awarded to High School of Dundee in three instalments for the benefit of an individual.

Applications In writing to the correspondent. Trustees meet once a year to consider grants, usually in June. Applications should be received by March/April.

The Highgate Charitable Trust

General

£10,500 (2004/05)

Beneficial area Primarily Scotland.

Miller Beckett & Jackson Solicitors, 190 St Vincent Street, Glasgow G2 5SP

Tel. 0141 204 2833 **Fax** 0141 248 7185

e-mail mail@millerbj.co.uk

Correspondent G A Maguire, Trustee

Trustees *G A Maguire; N A Fyfe; Mrs E A Thomson.*

Scottish Charity No. SC008130

Information available Information was provided by the trust.

General The trust will consider supporting:
- education/training
- medical and health, including hospitals/ hospices and medical research
- religion
- social welfare.

The trust has only a very small amount available each year to distribute to new applicant organisations, as most funds are already allocated to organisations known to the settlor.

In 2004/05 the trust gave grants totalling £10,500. Regular beneficiaries include High School of Glasgow Educational Trust, Highgate Hall, Park Church and Uddingston Congregational Church.

Applications In writing to the correspondent, although the above should be noted. Trustees meet once a year in November to consider grants. Applications should be received by September.

The L E Hill Memorial Trust

General

About £20,000

Beneficial area UK, with a preference for Scotland.

Turcan Connell WS, Princes Exchange, 1 Earl Grey Street, Edinburgh EH3 9EE

Tel. 0131 228 8111 **Fax** 0131 228 8118

Correspondent The Secretary

Trustees *Turcan Connell Trustees Ltd; J Ivory; M H H Hill.*

Scottish Charity No. SC003454

Information available Accounts are available from the correspondent for £10.

General This trust has general charitable purposes, with grants ranging between £200 and £4,000.

Grants are made totalling about £20,000 each year. Previous beneficiaries in Scotland include the Sandpiper Trust. No further information was available.

Exclusions The trust does not support non-registered charities or individuals.

Applications In writing to the correspondent.

The Hope Trust

Temperance, Reformed Protestant churches

£164,000 (2003)

Beneficial area Worldwide, with a preference for Scotland.

Drummond Miller, 32 Moray Place, Edinburgh EH3 6BZ

Tel. 0131 226 5151 **Fax** 0131 225 2608

e-mail rmiller@drummond-miller.co.uk

Correspondent Robert P Miller, Secretary

Trustees *Prof. G M Newlands; Prof. D A S Ferguson; Revd G R Barr; Revd Dr Lyall; Carole Hope; Revd Gillean McLean.*

Scottish Charity No. SC000987

Information available Information was provided by the trust.

General This trust was established to promote the ideals of temperance in the areas of drink and drugs, and Protestant church reform through education and the distribution of literature. In 2003 its income was £164,000. Grants towards temperance causes totalled £13,500, and other grants to causes related to the Protestant Reformed tradition in Scotland and worldwide totalled £150,500. PhD students of theology studying at Scottish universities were also supported.

Previous beneficiaries include Church of Scotland Priority Areas Fund, World Alliance of Reformed Churches, National Bible Society for Scotland, Feed the Minds and Waldensian Mission Aid.

Exclusions No grants to gap year students, scholarship schemes or to any individuals, with the sole exception of PhD students of theology studying at Scottish universities. No grants for the refurbishment of property.

Applications In writing to the correspondent. The trustees meet to consider applications in June and December each year. Applications should be submitted by mid-May or mid-November each year.

Howman Charitable Trust

Conservation, medical, education

Not known

Beneficial area Scotland and overseas.

William Thomson & Sons, 22 Meadowside, Dundee DD1 1LN

Tel. 01382 201534 **Fax** 01382 227654

e-mail bmckernie@wtandsons.co.uk

Correspondent Brian McKernie, Trustee

Trustees *Mrs M J B Howman; K C R Howman; B J C McKernie*

Scottish Charity No. SC001387

Information available Limited information was provided by the trust.

General Mrs M J B Howman set up this trust in 1977 and is still one of the trustees.

The trust makes grants to organisations working in nature conservation. The trust has previously informed us that it makes mainly recurrent grants with recipients including World Pheasant Association, Salmon and Trout Association Charitable Trust and St Mary's Church of Scotland – Kirriemuir.

Exclusions No grants are made to individuals.

Applications The trust states that no applications will be considered or acknowledged.

The Hunter Foundation

Education, young people, children

£1.4 million (2003/04)

Beneficial area Scotland.

Marathon House, Olympic Business Park, Drybridge Road, Dundonald, Ayrshire KA2 9AE

e-mail info@thehunterfoundation.co.uk

website www.thehunterfoundation.co.uk

Correspondent   Tom Hunter, Trustee

Trustees   *Tom Hunter, Chair; Marion Hunter; Jim McMahon; Robert Glennie; Vartan Gregorian.*

Scottish Charity No. SCO27532

Information available   Information was provided by the trust.

General   The Hunter Foundation (THF) is committed to venture philanthropy, investing capital and intellect into tackling the root causes of societal problems through holistic and systemic interventions.

Our focus in the developed world is to invest in national educational programmes that challenge stubborn, system wide issues that prevent children from achieving their potential.

In the developing world we largely invest in holistic developments that embed solutions within communities and countries, again with education being central to our programmes.

Our aim is to act as a catalyst for change by investing in pilot programmes with strategic partners and often alongside government that, if proven, are then adopted by government or the community for embedding nationally where possible.

The foundation also offers an overview of its charitable investment policy:

Objective
Effect positive, long-term cultural change to deliver a 'can do' attitude initially in Scotland via major investment in, largely, educational programmes.

Why?
The more enterprising the nation, the more economically stable it becomes providing the necessary funds to deliver for all. Education is the ultimate change agent in achieving this end goal.

Principles of Investment
- proactive identification of investments via definitive research and analysis
- active investment management against targets
- Joint ventures & partnerships dominate
- measurable ROI via definitive analysis
- exit strategies predominate – invest against target adoption of programmes by government.

Investment Profile
Four distinct profiles across short, medium or long-term objective impact:

- national educational programmes or pilots therein to deliver on our objective
- policy influence to support delivery & Government investment

- advocacy to secure extended investor base and support
- support for disenfranchised or suffering children.

Investments to Date
- over £35 million committed from THF to date
- this has leveraged £175 million of public and private sector additional investment (5x multiplier effect)
- three to five per cent of all investment funds are applied to independent research and evaluation of programme impacts
- educational investments matched funded by Government with clear policy adoption a pre-requisite outcome of measured programme success.

In 2003/04 the trust had assets totalling £2.4 million and an income of £166,000. Twenty grants were made totalling £1.4 million.

Beneficiaries were Schools Enterprise Scotland (£550,000), Head Teachers' Programme (£330,000), Determined to Succeed (£190,000 in total), Rainbow Trust (£175,000), Make a Wish Foundation (£66,000), Clyde Action (£60,000), Sargent Cancer Care for Children – Scotland (£58,000), Maggie's Cancer Care Centre and Hansel Foundation (£25,000 each), Save the Children (£24,000), West Action and Balance Charitable Foundation (£20,000 each), Columba 1400 Research (£19,000), Cash for Kids at Christmas Charitable Trust (£16,000), Teachers for a New Era (£14,000), Royal National Institute for the Blind (£12,000), Jamie Andrew Charity Account (£11,500) and Mark Scott Foundation and Prince and Princess of Wales Hospice (£5,000 each).

More recent grants include, for example, £1 million over 10 years to Radio Clyde's Cash for Kids, which commenced in 2004/05.

Applications   In writing to the correspondent.

Miss Agnes H Hunter's Trust

Social welfare

£141,000 (2003/04)

Beneficial area Scotland (apart from specified medical research).

Robson McLean WS, 28 Abercromby Place, Edinburgh EH3 6QE

Tel. 0131 538 5496 (mornings only)

Correspondent Mrs Jane Paterson, Grants Administrator

Trustees N D S Paterson; W F MacTaggart; A P Gray

Scottish Charity No. SC004843

Information available Information was supplied by the trust. An explanatory leaflet is also available from the correspondent.

General The trust was established in 1954. Its main aims are to support:

- charities for people who are blind in Scotland
- people who are disabled
- training and education for people who are disadvantaged
- research on the cause, relief or cure of cancer, tuberculosis or rheumatism.

These aims are currently being pursued in the following areas: children and family support, youth development, older people, homelessness, disability and mental illness.

The trustees are highly selective and can only consider projects in Scotland, apart from relevant medical research where applications can be made for centres of excellence throughout the UK.

In 2003/04 the trust had assets of £11 million and an income of £476,000. Grants range from £500 to £8,000, although they are usually not higher than £5,000, and during the year the trust approved 44 grants totalling £141,000. This is around £100,000 less than in previous years although the trust informed us that this was due to a reorganisation of trustees' meeting dates and published closing dates for applications and that the grant total would revert to more normal levels in future years.

The largest grants were £8,000 to Lintel Trust, £7,000 to Arthritis Care in Scotland and £6,000 to Sargent Cancer Care for Children – Scotland. The remaining grants were for between £1,000 and £5,000 and included Alzheimer's Research Trust, Cancer Bacup, Dementia Services Development Trust, Fairbridge in Scotland and Penumbra (£5,000 each), Macmillan Cancer Relief, RNIB, Shelter and Waverley Care (£4,000 each), Age Concern Scotland, CLIC, Epilepsy Action for Scotland and Lothian Autistic Society (£3,000 each), Cystic Fibrosis Trust, Edinburgh Sitters and Homelink (£2,000 each) and Angus Special Playscheme, Canniesburn Research Trust, Colon Cancer Concern, Edinburgh Family Service Unit and Scottish Adoption Association (£1,000 each).

Exclusions No grants to individuals, or to organisations under the control of the UK government.

Applications Applicants should write, in the first instance, to request the trust's guidance notes.

The following information is required in any application to the trust:

- a brief background to the organisation
- a full description of the project requiring funding, backed by a detailed budget clearly identifying funding already secured, items still outstanding and items for which you are applying to the trust (the trust does not provide grants for general funding)
- details of funding received from statutory sources (the trust can only assist those aspects of an organisation's work that have to be funded from voluntary income)
- your latest annual report and full audited accounts
- details of an independent referee unconnected to your organisation.

The trustees meet twice a year to allocate grants and the closing dates for final applications are 1 April for the summer meeting and 1 October for the spring meeting.

The Mrs E Y Imrie's Trust

Older people who are blind or visually impaired

About £6,000

Beneficial area Scotland.

Archibald Campbell & Harley, 37 Queen Street, Edinburgh EH2 1JX

Tel. 0131 220 3000

Correspondent Fiona Hutchison

Trustees *D W Cockburn; K W Dunbar.*

Scottish Charity No. SC002709

Information available Limited information was provided by the trust.

General This trust supports visual impairments and older people. Donations usually total around £6,000 but it does not distribute grants every year as it does not always have sufficient funds.

Previous beneficiaries have included Fife Society for the Blind, Royal Blind Asylum and School and Society for Welfare and Teaching of the Blind.

Applications In writing to the correspondent. The trust has previously stated that it tends to support the same organisations each year and its funds are fully committed.

The Inchrye Trust

Health, older people, medical research

About £20,000

Beneficial area Mainly Scotland.

Turcan Connell WS, Princes Exchange, 1 Earl Grey Street, Edinburgh EH3 9EE

Tel. 0131 228 8111 **Fax** 0131 228 8118

Correspondent The Trustees

Trustees *Miss R Finlay; Mrs J David; I R Clark*

Scottish Charity No. SC013382

Information available Accounts are available from the correspondent for £10.

General The trust's charitable objects are wide but it is particularly concerned with relieving ill-health and the care of older people, as well as training and research.

No recent financial information was available from the correspondent, although previous research indicates that grants are made totalling around £20,000 each year. Previous beneficiaries include Bield Housing Trust, Contact the Elderly and North Edinburgh Arts.

Exclusions No funding for expeditions, scholarships, large existing charities, animal charities or campaigns.

Applications In writing to the correspondent.

Miss P M Ireland's Charitable Trust

General

£11,500 (2005)

Beneficial area Scotland, especially local to Dundee.

c/o Messrs Lawson, Coull & Duncan, Solicitors, 136 Nethergate, Dundee DD1 4PA

Tel. 01382 227555 **Fax** 01382 200978

Correspondent Mrs McDonald

Trustees *D G Lawson; H D McKay.*

Scottish Charity No. SC003560

Information available Information was provided by the trust.

General The trust supports general charitable purposes in Scotland, particularly in the Dundee area. In 2005 grants totalled £11,500. All grants were for £275 and 42 charities were supported. All the grants were recurrent.

Beneficiaries have included Church of Scotland, National Trust for Scotland, Dovetail Enterprises, Dundee Disabled Children's Association, Oxfam and Pestalozzi Children's Village Trust.

New charities are not often supported. When new grants are awarded they are added to the list of annual grants, the trust therefore must ensure it will be able to continue to support them.

Exclusions Grants are not made to individuals.

Applications Applications are not encouraged.

The Annie Jack Memorial Trust

Disability, disadvantaged people, heritage

About £12,000 (2003/04)

Beneficial area Scotland.

Bourne Mill Cottage, Hadlow, Kent TN11 0EX

Correspondent D F Stirling, Trustee

Trustees *D F Stirling; P J Stirling; G D Stirling.*

Charity Commission no. 1026512

Information available Accounts are on file at the Charity Commission.

General The trust's objects are 'to promote the preservation, restoration and the public display of items which demonstrate the social, industrial and cultural heritage of Scotland and in addition assists other charities, principally in Scotland who care for those who may be physically, mentally or otherwise disadvantaged'.

In 2003/04 the trust had an income of £12,000, most of which is usually given in grants.

Recent beneficiaries include Sense Scotland, Strathcarron Hospice, Scottish Veteran's Residences and Royal British Legion Scotland.

The trust owns the only surviving Beardmore Taxicab built by William Beardmore in Glasgow, which remains on loan to the Glasgow Transport Museum.

Applications Unsolicited applications are not considered.

Lady Eda Jardine Charitable Trust

General

£50,000 to £60,000 a year

Beneficial area Scotland.

Anderson Strathern, 1 Rutland Court, Edinburgh EH3 8EY

Tel. 0131 220 2345

Correspondent Mrs L E Pennell, Trustee

Scottish Charity No. SC011599

Information available Limited information was available on this trust.

General This trust has general charitable purposes in Scotland, with no preferences or exclusions. A total of between £50,000 and £60,000 is distributed each year. There are no minimum or maximum grants.

Applications In writing to the correspondent by the end of April for consideration in July.

The Jeffrey Charitable Trust

Medical research, disability, children

£74,000 (2004/05)

Beneficial area Scotland and elsewhere.

29 Comrie Street, Crieff, Perthshire PH7 4BD

Tel. 01764 652224 **Fax** 01764 653999

Correspondent Robert B A Bolton, Trustee

Trustees *R B A Bolton; R S Waddell; Mrs M E Bolton; Dr A C MacCuish.*

Scottish Charity No. SC015990

Information available Accounts were provided by the trust.

General Although the trust states that it supports a wide range of charitable activities, most grants are made for medical research and, to a lesser extent, to children's charities.

In 2004/05 the trust had assets totalling £1.4 million and an income of £64,000. There were 28 grants made totalling £74,000, with two being to individuals.

The largest beneficiary during the year was Morrison's Academy Foundation, which received £21,000. Other larger grants were made to University of Dundee – Breast Cancer Imaging Research (£6,500), Daisy Chain Trust (£4,000), Bobath Scotland and Breast Cancer Care Scotland (£3,000 each) and British Heart Foundation and Sailors' Families Society (£2,500 each).

Organisations receiving typical grants of £2,000 each included Arthritis Care in Scotland, Impstart Trust, Whizz-Kidz Scotland, Epilepsy Scotland and Bethany Christian Trust.

Small grants included those to Nangchen Children's Trust, Canniesburn Research Trust and Tullochan Trust.

Exclusions Animal-related charities, medical electives and projects eligible for statutory support are not considered.

Applications In writing to the correspondent, although due to continuing support to long-term projects and anticipated repeat grants to other organisations, new requests for assistance are unlikely to be successful.

JTH Charitable Trust

General

£173,000 to organisations (2004/05)

Beneficial area Scotland, in particular west Scotland and Glasgow.

Biggart Baillie, Dalmore House, 310 St Vincent Street, Glasgow G2 5QR

Tel. 0141 228 8000 **Fax** 0141 228 8310

e-mail jlane@biggartbaillie.co.uk

Correspondent Mrs Jean Lane

Trustees *Leslie J Duncan; James Thom Howat; Russell W Howat; Gordon M Wyllie; Mrs Christine C Howat.*

Scottish Charity No. SC000201

Information available Accounts were provided by the trust.

General The trust states that it has 'continued to address real needs in the community and it is their policy to maintain this in the future'. Primarily it supports projects which are for the benefit of 'Glasgow and her citizens' but Scottish and UK-wide projects will be considered for small grants if they can be applied locally.

In 2004/05 it had assets of £4.3 million and an income of £174,000. Payments totalling £51,000 were made to partnerships in which a trustee is a partner. Whilst wholly legal, these editors always regret such payments unless, in the words of the Charity Commission, 'there is no realistic alternative'.

Grants totalled £184,000 and were broken down as follows:

- general – £173,000
- educational – £11,000

Beneficiaries included Crossroads (Scotland) Care Attendance Scheme and East Park (£10,000 each), Royal Scottish Academy of Music and Drama (£8,300), University of Glasgow and University of Strathclyde (£8,000 each) and Royal Blind Asylum and School (£5,000). 14 grants of £4,000 each were made to beneficiaries including Aged in Distress, Quarriers and Yorkhill Hospital for Sick Children.

39 grants were made to individuals totalling £11,000 ranging between £100 and £500.

Exclusions The following are not usually supported: medical electives, second or further qualifications, payment of school fees or costs incurred at tertiary educational establishments.

Applications In writing to the correspondent. There is no application form for organisations. Applications should contain a summary not longer than one side of A4, backed up as necessary with schedules. A copy of the latest accounts and/or business plan should be included. Costs and financial needs should be broken down where possible. It should be clear what effect the grant will have and details of other grants applied for or awarded should be given. Evidence that the project will enhance the quality of life of the clients and that they are involved in the decision making must be included.

'Applications should include evidence of charitable status, current funding, and the use you are making of that. Projects should be demonstrated to be practical and business-like. It is a condition of any grant given that a report be made as to how the funds have been used. Grants not used for the purposes stated must be returned.'

Successful applicants should not reapply in the following year. Unsuccessful applicants are not acknowledged due to the large number of applications received by the trust. The trustees meet to consider grants in March, June, September and December. Applications should be received in the preceding month.

The Kinpurnie Charitable Trust

General

See below

Beneficial area Scotland.

Kinpurnie Estate, North Street, Newtyle PH12 8TT

Tel. 01828 650500

e-mail enquiries@kinpurnie.co.uk

Correspondent The Estate Officer

Scottish Charity No. SC003986

Information available Up-to-date information on this trust was not available.

General The last information we have for this trust showed an annual grant total of £43,000 (1996/97). The trust would not provide up-to-date information.

Previous beneficiaries included Royal Marsden Hospital Cancer Fund, Pushkin Prizes, National Galleries of Scotland, National Symphony Orchestra of Scotland and SSAFA Dundee branch.

Exclusions Only registered charities are supported.

Applications In writing to the correspondent. This trust has previously stated that it does not respond to unsolicited applications.

The Kintore Charitable Trust

Environment, young people, general

See below

Beneficial area Scotland with a preference for Grampian.

Turcan Connell WS, Princes Exchange, 1 Earl Grey Street, Edinburgh EH3 9EE

Tel. 0131 228 8111 **Fax** 0131 228 8118

Correspondent The Trustees

Trustees *The Earl of Kintore; Turcan Connell Trustees Ltd.*

Scottish Charity No. SC000702

Information available Accounts are available from the correspondent for £10.

General The trust supports environmental causes, young people and local projects in the Grampian area.

During the past few years the trust's annual grant total has ranged from £10,000 to £40,000. Recent beneficiaries include Centre for Second World War Studies, Mackie Academy for the Earl of Kintore, Council for Music in Hospitals, Prince's Scottish Youth Business Trust, Aberdeen Foyer, University of Edinburgh and National Galleries of Scotland.

Exclusions No grants to individuals.

Applications In writing to the correspondent.

The Laidlaw Youth Project

Children and young people

£1 million (2005)

Beneficial area Scotland.

Abbey House, 83 Princes Street, Edinburgh EH2 2ER

Tel. 0131 247 6801 **Fax** 0131 247 6710

e-mail mmcginn@abbeyoffices.com

website www.laidlawyouthproject.org

Correspondent Maureen McGinn, Chief Executive

Information available Information is available on the organisation's website.

General This new organisation was established by Irvine Laidlaw, now Lord Laidlaw of Rothiemay, one of Scotland's richest men, as a vehicle for his charitable donations. It began operating in January 2004, initially as a one-year pilot project, with a view to continuing if its approach is a success. Its original focus was projects in Scotland aimed at children and young people which operate as collaborative activities, or as a befriending or mentoring project. Funding of up to £75,000 is available but average awards are closer to £25,000. It continued to operate in 2005 with a similar level of funding but with an additional focus on education. Around 50% of funds (£500,000) was available for new projects in 2005.

The following information is taken from the organisation's website:

What is the Laidlaw Youth Project?

The Laidlaw Youth Project is aimed at translating good ideas for collaborative working into reality through encouragement and funding. These projects must be aimed at supporting vulnerable children and / or young people in Scotland.

The Project has been set up through the donation of £1 million from Irvine Laidlaw and a contribution of £250,000 from the Scottish Executive, announced by Jack McConnell, First Minister, in November 2003.

Similar levels of funding were available in 2005, but around 50% was set aside for continuation funding of a number of existing projects to enable relationships to be developed between the funder and recipient charities.

Applications

All requests for funding will be expected to demonstrate need and also explain how these will deliver improved services for vulnerable children and young people in Scotland aged up to 25.

We are willing to consider the following:

- partnership applications to improve service delivery (2 or more organisations, at least one of which should be a registered charity)
- applications with a proposal for capacity building
- applications from a single organisation or more than one organisation for funding of mentoring (and /or befriending) services. Where we use the term 'mentoring', this can be taken to include befriending as well.

Applicant Bodies

We will accept applications from voluntary sector and public organisations. Applications from private sector bodies working in partnership with a charity or public sector body will be considered.

Where the application is for joint working, it must be accompanied by evidence of the other partners' willingness to participate in the activity for which funding is being sought. The application should also explain what role partners will play. We will expect a senior executive from each partner to be appointed as 'responsible owners' of the joint working proposal.

Organisations' operations do not need to be solely based in Scotland but they do need to deliver support to vulnerable children and young people in Scotland.

What we see as a priority

We will prioritise bids because we know that the total amount of funding sought will exceed the overall budget available. We will give priority to proposals which focus on improving outcomes for the most disadvantaged, and excluded children and young people. This will include young homeless people; cared for children and those leaving care; young carers; those at risk of offending or ex offenders; and the young unemployed. This list is not exhaustive nor is it set out in any particular order; but it is offered to demonstrate an intention to focus aid on areas of greatest need.

In addition, we will give priority to befriending and mentoring schemes which involve continuing support after major assistance/help/intervention. We are also likely to give priority to applications intended to deliver strategic improvements to befriending and mentoring services across Scotland.

Overall, we will give priority to proposals which use partnership working and / or mentoring to deliver improved continuity of care for the client groups.

All applications need to show how their proposals will deliver improved continuity of support from end to end within the system for the individual young people involved.

What we will not fund

We will not fund applications where the bid is largely for capital (refurbishing accommodation, contributing towards buying: buildings; motor vehicles; or boats).

We wish to concentrate most of our funding in the pilot year so we are unlikely to offer funding for periods longer than 12 months (some projects starting now will run into 2006). We may consider funding longer pieces of work but these will be the exception (and form a very small minority) because we need to review the Laidlaw Youth Project itself at the end of 2005. [Contact the organisation directly for up-to-date information.]

We will not fund individuals. We are unable to fund posts in local authorities.

We are unlikely to fund one-off events such as seminars and conferences for staff involved in service delivery.

Because of the anticipated pressure on funds, we may also prioritise support for mentoring and befriending around schemes for the most disadvantaged young people. So mentoring of the general school age population or young people in general is unlikely to be funded.

Timescales

We are willing to offer revenue funding (for up to 12 months). We will also be prepared to offer funding for specific packages of work lasting up to 12 months. Because we cannot be clear about the future direction of the Laidlaw Project at this point (and are unable to commit for longer periods than 12 months), applications will need clearly to demonstrate an exit strategy for the end of funding.

Funding Limits

We had £500,000 for new work in 2005. In order to be able to fund a range of proposals, we had set an upper limit of £75,000 for any single piece of work or scheme. There is no lower limit. However, given pressure on funding in 2005, smaller bids are more likely to be successful. That could be the sole funding or could be a contribution towards a piece of work costing more than that. We will not require match funding as a condition of funding but we will be interested to hear about other possible funders.

We will also limit the funding of any single organisation to £75,000: for example, if a charity submits a series of proposals, then we would provide no more than £75,000 of support in total. The same may apply to a charity which is involved in a number of partnership bids, even if it is not the lead partner in every one; in such circumstances, we will examine each case on its merits, as it is not our intention to discourage joint working.

Coverage

We are willing to fund organisations working in any part of Scotland. We expect the client groups to be children and young people in Scotland. We are willing to support local organisations as well as national ones. Where pieces of work have a local focus (e.g. clients are drawn from, or activities based in, a disadvantaged neighbourhood), we will be interested to hear whether there might be any positive outcomes for the wider community, as well as the young clients.

Evaluation of support

We will expect to see evidence that applicants have considered not only how improved outcomes will be achieved but also how they will be measured. We are happy that applicants include financial support to cover the costs of evaluation. Evaluation costs can be included in budgets for applications. That might be carried out externally, when appropriate; for example, for some of the largest pieces of work. We expect to agree evaluation arrangements with applicants as a condition of funding. However, we are likely to ask for some surveying of clients as part of all final evaluation packages.

Other issues

As part of our objective is to learn about what works, we expect to have some contact with the activities we fund throughout the year. This will not lead to onerous demands on bodies involved. But it may involve some visits and / or meetings with lead contacts and, where possible and appropriate, some clients.

Reporting arrangements – we may require some interim reports on larger pieces of work. We expect to agree reporting and contact arrangements as a condition of funding.

Grants first made in 2004

The following are examples of projects supported during the year taken from Laidlaw's website, which does not include the amount given to each project:

Befriending and mentoring projects

• Aberdeen Foyer: Supported Move-On Project

Aberdeen Foyer provides supported accommodation to 70 disadvantaged 16–25 year olds in Aberdeen / Aberdeenshire. While staying in the Foyer, support is provided through the individual action planning process to enable young people to move on to independent living.

In addition the Foyer Move-On initiative provides a mentoring / befriending service to help those young people with the practicalities of independent living such as moving into a new home, establishing social networks and encouraging them to continue with employment / training.

The befrienders are mainly volunteers although there are two members of staff working on this project – one in Aberdeen and one in North Aberdeenshire. The Laidlaw Youth Project has played a large part in funding this service whose aim is to help 25- 30 young people per year in transition.

• Crossroads Young Carers' Project, Sutherland

This is a local charity, which offers support to children with caring responsibilities. Many clients are referrals from social work. The project uses outreach workers to travel to some of the young carers, to take them for breaks out of the caring situation, to meet with their peers and others involved in the project, to have fun, and to feel more part of the project.

The workers are providing a supportive framework, developing existing good practice between agencies, providing a range of support to the young carers and empowering them to realise their full potential, by giving them the same opportunities as their peers.

Funds from Laidlaw Youth Project are being used to allow this scheme to make more effective use of existing sessional and outreach workers to befriend and offer a more reliable service to the children who have caring responsibilities.

• LINK – East Fife Mental Health Adolescent
  Befriending Project

LINK – the East Fife Mental Health Adult Befriending
Project launched the Adolescent Project in January
2003. The project works with 12 – 18 year olds with
mental health issues in East Fife who have a Key
Worker from Playfield House, Stratheden. Playfield
receive on average 35 new referrals a month.

The young people currently in the Project have a
variety of mental health issues, including; – suicide
attempts, self-harm, eating disorders, Asperger's,
ADHD, depression, Autism etc. These are often
combined with other problems in their lives, such as
alcohol, drugs, sexual abuse, school refusal, dyslexia,
bullying, family breakdown and pregnancy.

Laidlaw Youth Project funding is providing core support
for six months. This will enable LINK to consolidate
existing services and expand into the Levenmouth
area, as this has been identified as an area of high
need.

Other partnership projects

• Citylife, Edinburgh

This pilot project is for teenage mums who are no
longer in education, are unemployed and live in the
Wester Hailes and Sighthill areas of Edinburgh. These
are areas of social and economic deprivation with
teenage pregnancies in the Wester Hailes area four
times the city average. Citylife is aware of the
challenges and difficulties facing many teenage mums
and is developing this project to provide support and
befriending. The project will consist of group sessions
twice a week.

One session will be a mums and baby / toddler group
where mums can meet together, interact and play with
their children plus take part in some practical
workshops, e.g. infant massage, story telling. Some
workshops will be reinforced with outings to
encourage outdoor activities. Other sessions will take
the form of parenting courses and specialist
workshops for teenage mums, covering topics such as
children's health, child development, nutrition, healthy
eating, benefits, and budgeting.

One Parent Families Scotland, local community
dieticians and other agencies will facilitate the
specialist workshops and resources while Citylife staff
will co-ordinate activities and provide ongoing
friendship and support to help the mums with practical
issues.

• Hope To Oban (H2O) with Oban Youth Café;
  Atlantis Leisure; and Stramash: 'Detached Youth
  Worker pilot.'

Oban faces problems of remoteness and
unemployment. As jobs for school leavers diminish,
along with opportunities to become self reliant, an
increasing number of young people are on the street
and in danger of becoming 'at risk'.

This project funding will increase the contact between
the existing youth workers of H2O and the Oban Youth
café with the young people in and around the Oban
Youth Café and to develop and extend further
mentoring and guidance. It will allow the Youth Café to
open for longer periods of time which will improve the
deliverance of mentoring and guidance to the target
group. This part of the project is jointly coordinated by
Oban Youth Café and H2O

The rest of the funding is for a new pilot initiative.
Currently, many young people at risk are unable to
access sport activities in the town although they do
gather outside the buildings. A youth worker on the
street will work with this group to assist them in
accessing sport and other services that are available.
The worker will also advise Atlantis Leisure, a
community enterprise, on how to tailor its services to
meet the needs of young people who are at risk. This
part of the project will be co-ordinated by H2O who
will also mentor and train the person appointed.

The project welcomes informal discussions about
potential projects it might be interested in.
Contact the project directly for up-to-date
information on its plans for continuation and
future funding programmes.

Exclusions   No grants to individuals or capital
projects.

Applications   In writing to the correspondent,
although at the time of writing formal
applications were not being accepted. Informal
discussions about potential future projects were,
however, being welcomed: 'We will be pleased to
hear from bodies that have spotted opportunities
for improving the way that services and support
are delivered'.

Russell Lang Charitable Trust

General

About £15,000

Beneficial area UK, with a preference for Scotland.

GL, 23 Polwarth Street, Hyndland, Glasgow G12 9UD

Tel. 0141 337 2949

Correspondent David F Crichton, Administrator

Scottish Charity No. SC015665

Information available Information was provided by the trust.

General This trust was originally established with general charitable purposes to support causes of particular interest to the Lang family, such as charities, churches and hospitals. Initially it gave mainly in Scotland but it now gives more generally throughout the UK, giving around 15 grants of £1,000 each a year.

Applications The trust stated that unsolicited applications are not considered.

The R J Larg Family Charitable Trust

Education, health, medical research, arts – particularly music

About £100,000

Beneficial area UK but generally Scotland, particularly Tayside.

Thorntons Law LLP, 50 Castle Street, Dundee DD1 3RU

Tel. 01382 229111 **Fax** 01382 202288

e-mail nbarclay@thorntons-law.co.uk

Correspondent Nick Barclay

Trustees R W Gibson; D A Brand; Mrs S A Stewart.

Scottish Charity No. SC004946

Information available Information was provided by the trust.

General The trust has an annual income of approximately £127,000. Grants, which total about £100,000 each year, range between £250 and £6,000 and are given to a variety of organisations.

These include organisations concerned with cancer research and other medical charities, youth organisations, university students' associations and amateur musical groups. No further recent information was available.

Previous beneficiaries include High School – Dundee, Whitehall Theatre Trust, Macmillan Cancer Relief – Dundee and Sense Scotland Children's Hospice.

Exclusions Grants are not available for individuals.

Applications In writing to the correspondent. Trustees meet to consider grants in February and August.

The Lethendy Charitable Trust

General

£27,000 to organisations (2005)

Beneficial area Scotland, predominantly Tayside and north Fife.

Henderson Loggie, Chartered Accountants, Royal Exchange, Panmure Street, Dundee DD1 1DZ

Tel. 01382 200055 **Fax** 01382 221240

e-mail ghay@hendersonloggie.co.uk

Correspondent George Hay

Trustees N M Sharp, Chair; W R Alexander; D L Laird; I B Rae; A Thomson.

Scottish Charity No. SC003428

Information available Accounts were provided by the trust.

General The trust was established in 1979 to support general charitable purposes in Dundee. It has since widened its geographical area to include Angus, Perthshire and Fife. The trustees have a preference for education, health, the development of young people and religious organisations. Grants normally range from £100 to £10,000, with the trust preferring to make a small number of larger donations.

In 2005 it had assets of £1.4 million and an income of £40,000. Grants were made to five organisations and 36 individuals totalling £37,500.

Beneficiaries during the year were High School of Dundee (£10,000), The Attic – Brechin Youth Project and Ninewells Cancer Campaign (£5,000 each), Dundee Repertory Theatre Ltd youth programme (£4,000) and 1st Kirriemuir Company Boys' Brigade (£2,000).

Exclusions No grants are given to individuals for purely academic purposes such as school, university or college fees.

Applications In writing to the correspondent. Trustees meet once a year in July to consider grants.

Lindsays' Charitable Trust

Conservation, the environment, arts, medical research

£5,000 (2004)

Beneficial area Scotland.

Lindsays WS Solicitors, 11 Atholl Crescent, Edinburgh EH3 8HE

Tel. 0131 477 8713 **Fax** 0131 229 5611

e-mail csk@lindsays.co.uk

Correspondent Callum S Kennedy

Trustees *Lindsays' Trustees Ltd.*

Scottish Charity No. SC002014

Information available Accounts were provided by the trust.

General The trust supports conservation, the environment, wildlife, the arts and medical research. Preference is given to smaller, less well-known organisations which work in specialist areas.

In 2004 grants were made to nine organisations totalling £5,000. Beneficiaries were Friends of Greyfriars International Appeal and Guide Association Scotland 'Big C' Appeal (£1,000 each), Crighton Collegiate Church Trust, Edinburgh Green Belt Trust, Macmillan Fund for Nurses, Edinburgh Direct Aid, Alba Conservation Trust and Mansfield Traquair Trust (£500 each) and Youth Sport Trust (£150).

Applications In writing to the correspondent. Applications should arrive by January for consideration in March.

The Lintel Trust

Housing and community projects in Scotland

£95,000 (2004/05)

Beneficial area Scotland.

38 York Place, Edinburgh EH1 3HU

Tel. 0131 473 6240 **Fax** 0131 557 6028

e-mail pbarbour@linteltrust.org.uk

website www.linteltrust.org.uk

Correspondent Pauline Barbour, Director

Trustees *Andrew Robertson; Neil Hall; Robert McDowall; David Chalmers; Kate Dewar; Alan West; Eileen Shand; Lynn Carr; Dinesh Joshi; Isabel Moore; John Kernahan; David Orr.*

Scottish Charity No. SC006002

Information available Information was provided by the trust.

General The trust's broad aim is to encourage and enable individuals to live as independent a life as possible in their homes and to play an active part in their communities.

The trust works under the premise that the main aim of any funding should concentrate on the benefits to the eventual grant recipient. This has been achieved over the last 23 years through the operation of the trust's General Grants Programme.

What we fund

The trust recently consulted widely on where it allocates grants. As a result of this review we have established three core funding themes [until 2006], these are:

- Mainstreaming Equalities Programme
- Older People's Programme
- General Grants Programme.

The trust funds organisations in Scotland which work with:

- single homeless people
- older people
- people with support needs or disabilities of all kinds
- people of ethnic minorities
- refugees.

It makes grants or interest-free loans to:

- provide or promote accommodation and support for people in housing need
- promote volunteering in housing-related projects
- promote participation in housing activities within communities
- help social housing providers with activities which benefit their tenants and local communities
- promote innovative ideas in housing provision
- promote research into the provision of housing for the public.

The trust raises its income from donations from the voluntary housing sector, the corporate sector, individuals, events and it also manages funds on behalf of other charitable trusts. In 2004/05 it an income of £102,000 and made grants totalling £95,000.

Previous beneficiaries include Milan (Senior Welfare Council), Glasgow Old People's Welfare Association, North and West Sutherland Alliance, Western Isles Care and Repair, Answer Project, Age Concern Scotland, Senior Action Group, Greater Easterhouse Foyer Service, East Lothian Care and Repair and Sustainable Communities Initiatives.

Exclusions The trust does not fund individuals, large capital projects, large UK organisations, holidays, vehicles or projects that are not housing related.

Applications On a form available from the correspondent. The trustees meet four times a year. Applicants are encouraged to telephone the administrator beforehand for a general discussion.

Lloyds TSB Foundation for Scotland

Social and community needs, education and training, scientific, medical and social research

£5.3 million (2004)

Beneficial area Scotland and overseas.

Riverside House, 502 Gorgie Road, Edinburgh EH11 3AF

Tel. 0870 902 1201 **Fax** 0870 902 1202
e-mail enquiries@fundingthefuture.org.uk
website www.fundingthefuture.org.uk
Correspondent Andrew Muirhead, Chief Executive
Trustees *Revd Norman Drummond, Chair; Prof. Sir Michael Bond; Mrs Sandra E Brydon; Mrs Fiona Crighton; Ms Rani Dhir; James G D Ferguson; Revd Ronald Ferguson; Ms Elaine Ross; Ms Susan Robinson; Prof. Joyce Lishman; John D Scott; C M Anne Simpson.*
Scottish Charity No. SC009481
Information available Criteria, priorities and principles booklet. Exemplary annual reviews and application packs. Full report and accounts. Comprehensive information is also available on the foundation's fine website.

General The foundation allocates its funds in support of the Scottish community, to enable people, primarily those in need, to be active members of society. Although the majority of awards are for local charities, the foundation does consider larger appeals where benefit is provided across Scotland. There is no minimum or maximum sum granted, with awards ranging from a few hundred to tens of thousands of pounds.

Lloyds TSB Foundation for Scotland not only offers support under the main grant scheme but also provides funding under two other grant schemes:

- Capacity Building Grant scheme
- Partnership Drugs Initiative.

About two in three grants are for amounts between £2,000 and £10,000. Most are one-off, but grants can be spread over two or three years. Capital, running and project costs can all be supported.

In 2004 the foundation had assets of £3.6 million and an income of £8 million. Grants were made or approved totalling £5.3 million.

Background

The foundation was formed in 1986 as one of four independent trusts established by the then TSB Group. Collectively they receive 1% of the bank's pre-tax profits for distribution. The Foundation for Scotland receives 19% of this amount. Since the merger between Lloyds Bank and the TSB Group in December 1995, and in common with the Foundations for England and

Wales, Northern Ireland and the Channel Islands, income to this foundation has grown significantly.

This foundation has also developed partnerships with other bodies, including the Scottish Executive, for particular programmes and over £1.5 million of its income came from such sources in 2004.

There are 17 staff including seven grant assessors.

Besides its regular programme of 'surgeries' throughout Scotland, the foundation also runs an annual forum at which all applicants, whether successful or not, are invited to discuss their views of the foundation's work.

Lloyds TSB staff can claim £400 annually for fundraising or for volunteering their time. In 2004 this initiative, and further funds raised by staff themselves, amounted to £716,000 for charities in Scotland.

Grantmaking practice

The foundation's own excellent descriptions of its grantmaking are reprinted in full below, following a few brief introductory notes.

Success rates

The foundation estimates that about 40% of applications are successful, but that collectively they only get, on average, one-third to a half as much money as they had requested.

Reasons for rejection

The foundation has published the following note on this:

The trustees regret that demands made on the foundation's funds always outstrip the funds available and this means that many good applications, whilst meeting criteria, cannot be supported. Owing to the high quality of applications in general, there is often a narrow margin between success and failure.

In assessing past applications, there were a few recurring features in those which were unsuccessful:

- lack of clear plans for other fundraising
- insufficient detail on potential benefits a project would create
- 'all or nothing' requests for large appeals. (The foundation would prefer to see a part-funding option)
- inadequate explanation about the financial position of an applicant, e.g. policy on reserves, reasons for changes in level of costs year on year, etc.
- no clear strategy on safety/security, particularly important where a group are working with children or vulnerable adults, or engaged in transport
- multi-year funding:
  - lack of strategy for the period beyond which funding was being sought
  - vague objectives.

It should be stressed that applications are generally of a very high quality, however applicants may find the above to be a helpful checklist.

Earlier, but still useful, advice is as follows:

In particular the foundation emphasises the following, to be remembered when completing the application form:

- keep it simple – be concise and direct
- stress the difference our support will make – facts and figures are important
- always provide a detailed breakdown of costs
- tell us about other fundraising – we will be particularly interested to learn of local community fundraising as well as approaches to other charitable trusts
- it is essential that objectives relating to revenue funding are 'SMART' – Specific, Measurable, Achievable, Realistic and Testing.

Criteria, Priorities and Principles 2006–08

Criteria

Lloyds TSB Foundation for Scotland will accept applications for the Standard Grants Scheme that meet the following requirements:

Charities that are focused on improving quality of life and creating equality or opportunity for people in Scotland. This applies particularly to those who are disadvantaged or marginalised.

This criteria has been set in a way that attempts to include a wide variety of charitable activity. Applicants are advised to consult the Outwith Criteria section (below) for specific areas of work that the trustees will not consider for support.

Priorities

Services/initiatives must fit in with the general criteria outlined above to be eligible for consideration for funding. In addition, every three years the trustees establish priority areas within the general criteria which are set in consultation with charities throughout Scotland. Applications seeking to achieve the outcomes detailed in the priorities below will take precedence over those that do not.

Priority status will be attributed to initiatives/services targeted at disadvantaged and/or marginalised groups which:

- address poverty
- reduce isolation
- promote family welfare
- increase life skills
- promote citizenship and social responsibility
- empower under-represented or socially excluded groups
- promote independence
- de-stigmatise and challenge prejudice.

Principles

The following statements set out the foundation's principles of effective governance, transparency and good practice. It is expected that charities acknowledge the importance of the following and can demonstrate commitment to those that are relevant:

- evidencing need for new and existing services
- operating with openness and clear accountability
- complying with relevant regulation/inspection as required
- caring for the safety of vulnerable groups via effective vetting procedures including 'Disclosure Scotland' checks
- implementing equal opportunities particularly with regard to recruitment
- fulfilling duties as a responsible employer
- consulting and involving users
- collecting information through contacts or research to establish, consolidate and promote good practice
- adopting sound evaluation and monitoring procedures
- encouraging the involvement of volunteers
- recognising cultural diversity and particular needs that may arise
- on-going staff/volunteer/organisational development.

Points to note

- applicant organisations must be registered as a charity
- awards are made on merit to charities for work in Scotland with no geographical bias
- trustees are committed to considering support for unpopular/under-funded areas of work with vulnerable client groups
- support is available for new initiatives as well as established services/projects. Both are seen as having equal value
- funding for capital and/or running costs is available
- six closing dates for applications are set in line with six trustees' meetings which take place per annum. There is a three month period between the closing date by which you choose to submit and a decision being taken on your application
- submissions must be presented on the application form; comprehensive guidance notes are available

to assist with its completion

- two categories of application are available – a very brief application form for awards under £2,500. Applicants must choose one or the other.
- applications are invited seeking awards over one, two or three years. Where an award is made over one year, re-application is not possible until at least 12 months has elapsed from the date that the original grant was awarded. Where a multi year award has been granted no further applications will be considered until 12 months has elapsed from the date of the final scheduled payment.

From time to time, grants may be awarded to groups of charities engaged in genuine partnership initiatives. Charities that receive funding via such collaborations may also be eligible to apply for a grant in isolation for their own activities. Early contact with the foundation prior to applications of this nature being developed is required.

Outwith criteria [Exclusions]

- organisations that are not registered charities
- individuals, including students
- environment – projects entirely of an environmental nature, e.g. geographic and scenic, conservation and protection of flora and fauna
- mainstream activities and statutory requirements of hospitals and medical centres, schools, universities and colleges
- sponsorship and marketing appeals
- establishment/preservation of endowment funds
- organisations that collect funds for subsequent grant making to other organisations and/or individuals
- expeditions or overseas travel
- building projects for places of worship, other than where such buildings provide accommodation for community groups
- building projects for heritage centres, visitors centres, museums and theatres
- historic restoration/historic publications
- retrospective funding
- promotion of religion
- initiatives that are focused on development of excellence or elitism in sport or the arts
- charities that have paid employees who also hold a position as director/member on the board or management committee of the employing charities. The principle also applies to charities operating as collectives.

Other programmes

Although each charity can only make one application and hold one award at a time under the Standard Grant Scheme, this foundation operates a range of programmes to which charities are eligible to apply simultaneously. A summary of each is provided below:

Capacity Building Programme

Phase One – Organisational Review

This programme has been designed to help your charity build its capacity by helping identify strengths and opportunities for development. An independent adviser will spend the equivalent of two days evaluating where you are and giving pointers on the way forward, culminating in the provision of a report.

Phase Two – Development Support

Once you have completed an 'Organisational Review'. you have the option to engage an adviser again to develop some of the improvement areas which have been identified. An allocated number of days will be agreed with your organisation in which the developments can be implemented. An independent adviser will be allocated to work with you over that period, the cost of which will be awarded to your charity for onward payment to your adviser at a pre-agreed set rate.

Partnership Drugs Initiative (PDI)

The PDI encourages and enables charities to work in partnership with other agencies (both voluntary and statutory) to ensure a holistic approach to meeting the needs of children and young people affected by substance misuse. This programme encourages charities to form a relationship with relevant staff within this foundation to be guided through the process of forming local partnerships and making an application. There are two opportunities to apply to this programme per annum and a two stage application process operates. An outline bid is submitted and approved prior to a full application being made.

Overseas Programme

The Overseas Programme makes awards to charities with a base in Scotland that work overseas in fragile communities. Awards are made for development of charities at home and for the initiation or continuation of sustainable indigenous services abroad.

Research Initiative

The foundation makes awards for medical, scientific and social research through partner organisations specialising in such work. The aim of this programme is to help inform the work of charities in a range of fields tackling social disadvantage and improving quality of life. The trustees review research themes every three years.

Grantmaking in 2004

During the year there were 297 single year awards totalling almost £1.4 million, with the average award being £4,600. Seventy multi-year awards were made, typically for three years, with the average grant being for £17,000. There was a 47% success rate on applications, salary funding made up 36% of all awards, 36% were for running costs and 28% were for capital funding. Conditional/multi-year awards totalled £1.7 million; grants from the Partnership Drugs Initiative totalled £651,000; overseas grants totalled £336,000; the Staff Matched Giving Scheme awarded a contribution to staff fundraising totalling £197,000; Capacity Building Grants Scheme awarded £65,000; and Organisational Reviews amounted to £37,000.

Exclusions The trustees regret they cannot support all fields of voluntary and charitable activity. To focus funding on the foundation's priority areas, the following purposes will not be considered:

- organisations which are not recognised as a charity by the Inland Revenue/Charity Commission
- individuals – including students
- animal welfare
- environment – projects entirely of an environmental nature, e.g. geographic and scenic, conservation and protection of flora and fauna
- mainstream activities and statutory requirements of schools, universities and colleges
- mainstream activities and statutory requirements of hospitals and medical centres
- sponsorship or marketing appeals
- activities which collect funds for subsequent redistribution to others
- the establishment/preservation of endowment funds
- expeditions or overseas travel
- building projects for places of worship, other than where such buildings provide accommodation to community groups
- building projects for visitor centres, heritage centres, museums and theatres
- historic restoration
- retrospective funding
- the one year rule – applicants will not be eligible for further consideration until at least one year has elapsed from their original application. In the case of a multi-year award having been granted, no further application will be considered until 12 months has elapsed from the final scheduled payment.

Applications Application forms for all grants schemes, complete with comprehensive guidance notes, are available from the foundation. These can be requested by telephone, by e-mail, or through the website. Foundation staff are always willing to provide additional help.

Closing dates for applications to our Standard Grant and Capacity Building programmes in 2006 are as follows:

Closing Date	Board Meeting
20th March 2006	8th June 2006
15th May 2006	3rd August 2006
17th July 2006	5th October 2006
18th September 2006	7th December 2006

The Logie Charitable Trust

General

About £10,000

Beneficial area Mainly the north of Scotland, particularly Morayshire.

Turcan Connell WS, Princes Exchange, 1 Earl Grey Street, Edinburgh EH3 9EE

Tel. 0131 228 8111 **Fax** 0131 228 8118

Correspondent The Secretary

Trustees *Colin Baxter; Mrs Graeme Laing; Earl of Leven and Melville.*

Scottish Charity No. SC011176

Information available Limited information was provided by the trust.

General The trust supports local community organisations. There is a preference for organisations which are known to the trustees and local branches of UK-wide organisations. The trust has previously stated that about £10,000 is given in grants each year. Grants range from £25 to £5,000. Details of the beneficiaries were not available.

Applications In writing to the correspondent. The trustees distribute grants once a year, between November and January.

Mrs M A Lumsden's Charitable Trust

General

About £15,000 each year

Beneficial area Scotland.

Turcan Connell WS, Princes Exchange, 1 Earl Grey Street, Edinburgh EH3 9EE

Tel. 0131 228 8111 **Fax** 0131 228 8118

e-mail kjp@turcanconnell.com

Correspondent Kenneth J Pinkerton

Scottish Charity No. SC005176

Information available Limited information was provided by the trust

General The trust supports general charitable purposes, with an annual grant total of about £15,000. No further information was available.

Applications In writing to the correspondent. Unsolicited applications are not acknowleged

The R S Macdonald Charitable Trust

Visual impairment, cerebral palsy, children, animal welfare

£357,000 (2003/04)

Beneficial area Scotland.

27 Cramond Vale, Edinburgh EH4 6RB

Tel. 0131 312 6766

Correspondent Richard K Austin, Trustee

Trustees *Eric D Buchanan; David W A Macdonald; Ms Sheila C Macdonald; Donald G Sutherland; Richard K Austin.*

Scottish Charity No. SC012710

Information available Accounts were provided by the trust.

General The trust supports charities concerned with the following:

- the care and welfare of people with visual impairment or cerebral palsy
- research into the causes, prevention or treatment of visual impairment and cerebral palsy

- the prevention of cruelty to children
- the prevention of cruelty to animals.

Six organisations are mentioned in the trust deed and these are often, but not always, supported. The trust is prepared to give very large grants to enable organisations to carry out major projects or develop ideas. Average grants are about £30,000.

In 2003/04 the trust had assets of over £27.2 million and an income of £428,000. (The value of the trust's assets increased at the end of the 2004/05 financial year. *See below*) Grants were made to 17 organisations totalling £357,000.

The beneficiaries were SSPCA (£40,000), RNIB Scotland (£38,000), Flight for Sight (£31,000), Capability Scotland and Royal Blind Asylum and School (£30,000 each), Children 1st and Princess Alexandra Eye Pavilion (£25,000 each), Deafblind Scotland, Sense Scotland and Dystonia Society (£20,000 each), Glasgow and West of Scotland Society for the Blind, Highland Society for the Blind and Atavia UK (£15,000 each), Scottish Motor Neurone Disease Association and Multiple Sclerosis Society Scotland (£10,000 each), Henshaw's Society for Blind People (£8,000) and Action for the Blind (£5,000).

The trust's newly published 2004/05 accounts (November 2005) show a similar grant total to the previous year (£351,000), but also an income of £22 million from the sale of shares. As a result of the increased income, the trustees intend to review their awards policy accordingly. Contact the trust for up-to-date information on any change in policy or focus.

Exclusions Grants are not given to non-registered charities or individuals.

Applications In writing to the correspondent, including a copy of the latest audited accounts and constituting documents. Applications should be received by March/April to be considered in the summer. Trustees usually want to meet new applicants requesting a larger grant. Successful applicants are asked for a follow-up report and are often visited by a trustee.

The N S Macfarlane Charitable Trust

General, see below

Not known

Beneficial area Mainly Scotland.

Wright Johnston & Mackenzie, 302 St Vincent Street, Glasgow G2 5RZ

Tel. 0141 248 3434 **Fax** 0141 221 0432

e-mail im@wjm.co.uk

Correspondent Ian Macdonald

Trustees *Lord Macfarlane of Bearsden; Hon. Hamish Macfarlane; Lady Macfarlane of Bearsden; Hon. Mrs Fione McNaught.*

Scottish Charity No. SC010834

Information available Information, but with no financial details, was provided by the trust.

General The trust will support a wide range of organisations. It will consider the following causes:

- arts
- buildings
- children and young people
- disability
- environment, conservation, heritage
- education/training
- medical/health, including medical research
- older people
- religious appeals.

It gives grants mostly ranging from £100 to £1,000 except for a small number of major awards each year. Unfortunately no financial information was available.

Exclusions Grants are not normally given to individuals. Overseas projects and political appeals are not supported.

Applications In writing to the correspondent, giving details of the organisation or project and financial information. Trustees usually meet twice a year to consider applications.

M L MacIntyre Begonia Trusts

Research, education and publications on begonias

About £17,000 each year

Beneficial area UK (see below).

Glasgow Botanic Gardens, 730 Great Western Road, Glasgow G12 0UE

Correspondent Dr C T Wheeler, Hon. Secretary

Scottish Charity No. SC022500

Information available Information was provided by the trust.

General The trusts were established in 1994 to promote and encourage the furtherance of research and education in any sphere relating to begonias, including the writing or publication of works on begonias and subsidy of the costs for competent persons to travel and collect begonias plants.

Funds available are limited. Preference is given normally to the financial support of postgraduate students with excellent academic records. Prospective students must register for a higher degree at the University of Glasgow.

Postgraduate studentships (Ph.D or M.Sc only) total around £12,000 a year plus Glasgow University fees. Small grants total around £5,000 a year.

Exclusions Funding is confined without exception to applications for support of work on begonias.

Applications In writing to the correspondent.

Catherine Mackichan Trust

Education and research in archaeology and history

About £1,500 (2004/05)

Beneficial area Scotland, especially the West Highlands.

Aros, Towerside, Whittingham, Alnwick NE66 4RF

Tel. 01665 574335

Correspondent The Honorary Secretary

Scottish Charity No. SC020459

Information available Information was provided by the trust.

General The trust funds research into various aspects of Scottish history including archaeology, genealogy and language studies. Schools and individuals (including people who are unemployed, senior citizens or have disabilities) can also receive grants towards work involving archaeology or history.

It prioritises the West Highlands, followed by Scotland, and then causes outside Scotland that have connections with Scotland. Grants range from £50 usually up to £600.

Applications Applications are welcome from academic institutions as well as individuals or groups not in the academic field.

Application forms are available from Mr I Fraser, Vice Chair, The Catherine Mackichan Trust, 21 Cowan Road, Edinburgh, EH11 1RL. Apply between the start of January and 15 April each year.

The Mackintosh Foundation

Performing arts, general

£385,000 (2003/04)

Beneficial area UK, with an interest in western Scotland, and overseas.

1 Bedford Square, London WC1B 3RB

Tel. 020 7637 8866 **Fax** 020 7436 2683

Correspondent Nicholas Mackintosh, Appeals Director

Trustees *Sir Cameron Mackintosh, Chair; Nicholas Mackintosh; Nicholas Allott; D Michael Rose; Patricia Macnaughton; Alain Boublil; Robert Noble.*

Charity Commission no. 327751

Information available Information was provided by the trust.

General In 2003/04 the foundation had an income of £948,000 mostly in donations from Sir Cameron Mackintosh, the settlor. Grants to 214 organisations were made totalling £385,000.

During the 15 years since it was set up, the foundation has made over 3,600 separate grants (including repeats) totalling nearly £15 million to over 1,100 different charities or charitable objects. It has endowed Oxford University at a cost of well over £1 million with a fund known as *The Cameron Mackintosh Fund for Contemporary Theatre*, part of which has been used to set up a Visiting Professorship of Contemporary Theatre at the University. It also provided a fund of £1 million over a period of 10 years to the Royal National Theatre, for revivals of classical stage musical productions under the auspices of the RNT. It has provided financial support to a number of projects in the United states [...] This includes a major grant of US$1.5 million over 5 years to The Alliance of New American Musicals to foster, encourage and promote the creation and production of new dramatico-musical plays by American writers and artists. The foundation also paid £500,000 of 'partnership funding' over 5 years in respect of selected applications by theatres and others under the Art Council's *Arts for Everyone* scheme of National Lottery Funding.

The foundation classifies its grants in the following way:

- theatre and the performing arts
  - theatre building projects
  - theatre company development
  - promotion of new theatrical works and classical music repertoire
  - theatrical training and education
  - theatre-related pastoral care
- the homeless
- children's projects and children's education
- medical – including hospices, alternative, therapies and rehabilitation
- community projects – including adult education
- environment
- overseas.

Grants in 2003/04

Grants were distributed by size as follows:

Grant total	2003/04	(2001/02)
£50,000–£99,999	–	(1)
£20,000–£49,999	2	(1)
£10,000–£19,999	4	(5)
£5,000–£9,999	9	(12)
£1,000–£4,999	85	(79)
Less than £1,000	145	(116)

Exclusions Religious or political activities are not supported. Apart from the foundation's drama award and some exceptions, applications from individuals are discouraged.

Applications In writing to the correspondent outlining details of the organisation, the project you're seeking funding for and a breakdown of the costs involved. Keep supporting documents to a minimum and enclose a sae if materials are to be returned. The trustees meet in May and October in plenary session, but a grants committee meets weekly to consider grants of up to £10,000. The foundation responds to all applications in writing and the process normally takes between 4–6 weeks.

The Maclay Murray & Spens Charitable Trust

Health and social welfare
About £10,000

Beneficial area Scotland.

c/o Maclay Murray & Spens, 151 St Vincent Street, Glasgow G2 5NJ

Tel. 0141 248 5011 **Fax** 0141 248 5819

e-mail jennifer.johnson@mms.co.uk

Correspondent Ms Jennifer Johnson, Trustee

Trustees *Ms Jennifer Johnson.*

Scottish Charity No. SC012364

Information available Accounts are available from the correspondent for £10.

General The trust supports the following causes:

- children/young people
- older people
- people who are disabled
- social welfare causes
- health and medical causes, including hospices, hospitals and medical research.

The trust's income totals about £10,000 each year, all of which is given in grants. Grants usually range from £200 to £500. Most grants are recurrent and the following organisations receive regular support: ChildLine Scotland, Macmillan Cancer Relief, Prince and Princess of Wales Hospice and St Columba's Hospice.

Applications In writing to the correspondent. The trustees meet irregularly to consider grants.

The MacLennan Trust

Homelessness, children, young people, education

About £25,000

Beneficial area UK, with a strong preference for Scotland.

Royal Bank of Scotland plc, Trust & Estate Services, 2 Festival Square, Edinburgh EH3 9SU

Tel. 0131 523 2658 **Fax** 0131 228 9889

Trustees *The Royal Bank of Scotland plc*

Scottish Charity No. SC010562

Information available Accounts are available from the trust for the prohibitive cost of almost £30.

General The trust supports homelessness projects, children and young people. Education and religious appeals are also considered. Grants total about £25,000 each year and usually range between £500 and £1,500.

Previous beneficiaries include Girls' Brigade, Church of Scotland, Glasgow City Mission and Perth & District YMCA.

Exclusions No grants to individuals.

Applications On an application form available from the correspondent. Trustees meet in April to consider grants.

The MacRobert Trust

General

£467,000 (2004/05)

Beneficial area UK, mainly Scotland.

Cromar, Tarland, Aberdeenshire AB34 4UD

Tel. 01339 881444

website www.themacroberttrust.org.uk

Correspondent Air Comm. R W Joseph, Administrator

Trustees *R M Sherriff, Chair; Mrs C J Cuthbert; Keith Davis; D M Heughan; J Mackie; W G Morrison; Group Capt. D A Needham; A M Summers; Mrs J C Swan; H B Woodd.*

Scottish Charity No. SC031346

Information available Good website featuring guidelines and a full grants list.

General Originally several trusts established by Lady MacRobert in memory of her three sons who were all killed as aviators, the eldest in a civil air accident in 1938 and the middle and youngest as officer pilots in the Royal Air Force on operational sorties in 1941.

This trust was established on 6 April 2001 when the assets of the no longer operating MacRobert Trusts, a collection of four charitable trusts and two holding companies were merged into the new, single MacRobert Trust. The merging of these trusts has led to a decrease in management and administration cost and a general increase in grantmaking.

The trust has assets totalling around £50 million, comprising of Douneside House (a holiday country house for serving and retired officers of the armed forces and their families) and an estate of 1,700 acres of woodland and 5,300 acres of farmland and associated residential properties let by the trust. The surplus income generated from these assets, following management and administration costs, is donated in grants.

Guidelines for applicants

The following guidelines are taken from the trust's website:

Lady MacRobert recognised that new occasions teach new duties and therefore the new Trust deed gives wide discretionary powers to the Trustees. The Trust is reactive so, with very few exceptions, grants are made only in response to applications made through the correct channels.

The Trustees reconsider their policy and practice of grant giving every five years. The beneficial area is United Kingdom-wide but preference is given to organisations in Scotland. Grants are normally made only to a recognised Scottish Charity or a recognised charity outside Scotland.

Trust's Categories of Interest

Currently, the major categories under which the Trustees consider support are:

- science and technology
- youth
- services and sea
- ex-servicemen's hospital and homes
- education
- disabled and handicapped
- community welfare

The minor categories are:

- agriculture and horticulture
- arts and music

- medical care
- Tarland and Deeside.

The Trustees look for clear, realistic and attainable aims. Grants vary but most lie between £5,000 and £10,000. Occasionally the Trustees make a recurring grant of up to three years.

The Trustees recognise the need to assist voluntary organisations which need funds to complement those already received from central government and local authority sources. However, this is not to say that the Trust makes a grant where statutory bodies fail to provide.

The Trustees are prepared to make core/revenue grants where appropriate but favour projects.

The Trustees recognise that, at present, experiment and innovation are much more difficult to fund and the Trust's role in funding them the more significant.

Grantmaking in 2004/05

During the year the trust made grants totalling £467,000. Grants were broken down as follows:

Agriculture and horticulture – 5 grants totalling £108,000

The largest grant made, as in previous years, was to Royal Highland & Agricultural Society of Scotland, which received £100,000. Other beneficiaries included Worshipful Company of Farmers (£2,500), Royal Scottish Agricultural Benevolent Institution and Scottish Association of Young Farmers' Clubs (£2,000 each) and Scotland Gardens Scheme (£1,500).

Youth – 16 Grants totalling £81,000

Beneficiaries included Girlguiding, Scottish Headquarters (£12,000), British Sports Trust and Perth & District YMCA (£10,000 each), Glencoe Trust (£7,000), Barnardo's (£6,000), Prince's Scottish Youth Business Trust (£5,000), Tullachan Trust (£4,000) and the Scouts' Association – Scottish headquarters (£2,000).

Education – 5 grants totalling £56,000

Beneficiaries included University of Edinburgh – Royal (Dick) School of Veterinary Medicine (£15,000), Woodland Trust (£10,000), Napier University (£8,000) and British Schools' Exploring Society (£2,500).

Disabled and Handicapped – 9 grants totalling £54,000

Beneficiaries included Hansel Foundation (£12,000), Scottish Centre for Children with Motor Impairments (£8,000), Scottish Spina Bifida Association (£4,000) and Alzheimer's Scotland and Defeating Deafness (£3,000 each).

Community Welfare – 8 grants totalling £36,000

Beneficiaries included Lamp of Lothian Collegiate Trust (£7,000), International Voluntary Service (£6,000), Federation of City Farms & Community Gardens and Harmony Education Trust Ltd (£5,000 each) and Aberdeen Samaritans (£1,700).

Services and Sea – 10 grants totalling £32,000

Beneficiaries included Armed Forces Memorial Trust and Imperial War Museum – Duxford (£10,000 each), Lord Roberts' Workshops (£5,000), Gordon Highlanders Museum Appeal (£4,000), Royal Airforce Cranwell – the MacRobert Prize (£1,000) and North East Scotland Branch Korean Veterans (£300).

Arts & Music – 9 grants totalling £29,000

Beneficiaries included Scottish Chamber Orchestra (£5,000), North East of Scotland Music School (£4,000), Aberdeen International Children's Festival (£3,000) and Poetry Association of Scotland (£500).

Science & Technology – 4 grants totalling £26,000

Beneficiaries were National Maritime Museum (£10,000), the Royal Institution (£7,500), Satrosphere (£5,000) and Institute of Nanotechnology (£3,000).

Medical Care – 8 grants totalling £24,000

Beneficiaries included the Prince & Princess of Wales Hospice (£8,000), Epilepsy Scotland (£5,000), Lee Smith Foundation (£4,000) and Marie Curie Cancer Care (£500).

Ex-Servicemen's Hospitals and Homes – 2 grants totalling £10,000

Beneficiaries were Ex Services Mental Welfare Society (£10,000) and Windmill Court Residents' Association (£120).

The trust also made non-monetary donations to the Royal Air Force Benevolent Fund for Alastrean House, which it leases from the MacRobert Trust (£140,000), Tarland Gold Club (£5,000) and Scottish Agricultural College – Walton Farm (£4,000). Further grants were made to Douneside House (£123,500) Alastrean House (£67,000) and Horticulture/Gamekeeping Training Scheme (£43,000).

Exclusions Grants are not normally provided for:

- religious organisations (but not including youth/community services provided by them,

or projects of general benefit to the whole community)
- organisations based outside the UK
- individuals
- endowment or memorial funds
- general appeals or mail shots
- political organisations
- student bodies (as opposed to universities)
- fee-paying schools (apart from an educational grants scheme for children who are at, or need to attend, a Scottish independent secondary school and for which a grant application is made through the headteacher)
- expeditions
- retrospective grants
- departments within a university (unless the appeal gains the support of, and is channelled through, the principal).

Applications   The application form and full guidelines can be downloaded from the website, although applications must be posted.

The trustees meet to consider applications twice a year in March and October. To be considered, applications must be received for the March meeting by the end of October previously and for the October meeting by early June previously.

Applicants are informed of the trustees' decision, and if successful, payments are made immediately after each meeting.

Ian Mactaggart Trust

Education & training, culture, welfare and disability

About £200,000

Beneficial area UK, with a preference for Scotland.

c/o Breeze Paterson & Chapman, 257 West Campbell Street, Glasgow G2 4TU

Correspondent   The Trustees

Trustees   *Sir John Mactaggart; P A Mactaggart; Jane L Mactaggart; Fiona M Mactaggart; Lady Caroline Mactaggart; Karin T Woodcock; Leora J Armstrong.*

Scottish Charity No. SC012502

Information available   No recent information was available.

General   The trust supports education and training, culture, the relief of people who are poor, sick, in need or disabled. No recent

financial information was available from the correspondent, although previous research indicates that grants are made totalling around £200,000 each year.

Previous beneficiaries in Scotland include Bobath Scotland, Cantilena Festival on Islay, Royal One Scotland, Glasgow Social Work Department, Islay Pipe Band and Greater Glasgow Health Fund.

Applications   In writing to the correspondent, although unsolicited requests are discouraged.

W M Mann Foundation

The arts, education, medical research, music

£100,000 (2004/05)

Beneficial area Scotland.

201 Bath Street, Glasgow G2 4HY

Tel. 0141 248 4936 **Fax** 0141 221 2976

Correspondent   Bruce M Mann, Trustee

Trustees   *W M Mann; B M Mann; A W Mann; S P Hutcheon.*

Scottish Charity No. SC010111

Information available   Accounts were provided by the trust.

General   Grants are generally given to organisations based in Scotland or serving the Scottish community, in the fields of music, arts, education, medical research and care and so on.

In 2004/05 the trust had assets of £2.6 million and an income of £485,000. Grants to 95 organisations totalled £100,000; donations were in the range of £100 to £10,000.

The largest grants were £10,000 each to Special Olympics – Glasgow 2005 and Marie Curie Centre and £5,000 each to City of Glasgow Chorus and Tullochan Trust. Other beneficiaries include RSNO (£3,000), East Park and Scottish Ballet Ltd (£2,500 each), Glasgow Academicals' War Memorial Trust, Maxie Richards Foundation and St John's Renfield Church (£2,000 each).

Smaller grants in the range of £100 to £500 include Alzheimer's Research Trust, Fisherrow Community Centre, Action for Kids and Great Ormond Street Hospital.

Applications   In writing to the trustees.

The Martin Charitable Trust

General

About £75,000

Beneficial area Scotland, particularly Glasgow and the west of Scotland.

Miller Beckett & Jackson Solicitors, 190 St Vincent Street, Glasgow G2 5SP

Tel. 0141 204 2833 **Fax** 0141 248 7185

e-mail mail@millerbj.co.uk

Correspondent Norman A Fyfe, Trustee

Trustees *A C Fyfe; N A Fyfe; G H W Waddell.*

Scottish Charity No. SC028487

Information available Brief information was provided by the trust.

General The trust supports general charitable purposes in Scotland, particularly Glasgow and the west of Scotland. In previous years grants were made totalling around £75,000. No further information was available.

Exclusions No grants to individuals.

Applications In writing to the correspondent, including up-to-date accounts.

The Nancie Massey Charitable Trust

Education, medical research, the arts, young and older people

About £130,000

Beneficial area Scotland, particularly Edinburgh and Leith.

Chiene & Tait, Cairn House, 61 Dublin Street, Edinburgh EH3 6NL

Tel. 0131 558 5800 **Fax** 0131 558 5899

Correspondent James G Morton, Trustee

Trustees *J G Morton; M F Sinclair; Ann Trotman.*

Scottish Charity No. SC008977

Information available No recent information was available.

General The trust was established in 1989 to help organisations supporting older people, young people, medical research, education and the arts. Assistance is primarily given to projects established in the Edinburgh and Leith areas.

'Donations generally range from £500 to £2,000; larger donations may be made on the basis that the trustees may wish to verify how the donation has been spent.'

In previous years the trust made grants totalling around £130,000. Several years ago the trustees indicated that funds may be accumulated to donate to a single large project – at that time no suitable project had been identified, however it may be the case that the trust's funds are now committed to a single large project. No further information was available.

Previous beneficiaries of typical grants include Donaldson's Trust, Royal Zoological Society of Scotland, Edinburgh Community Trust, Children's Society, SSAFA Forces Help, Royal Artillery Charitable Fund, Marie Curie Memorial Foundation, St Columba's Hospice and Greenbank Parish Church.

Exclusions Grants are not given to individuals.

Applications Write to the correspondent requesting an application form. Trustees meet three times a year in February, June and October. Applications need to be received by January, May or September.

Gwen Mayor Memorial Trust

Primary schools

About £6,000

Beneficial area Scotland.

46 Moray Place, Edinburgh EH3 6BH

Tel. 0131 225 6244 **Fax** 0131 220 3151

Correspondent The Secretary

Trustees *President, vice-president and past president of the Educational Institute of Scotland; Mrs Claire McLeod; Mrs Deborah Buchanan.*

Scottish Charity No. SC025852

Information available Brief information was provided by the trust.

General The trust gives donations to primary schools and 'departments' in Scotland for projects in the area of the arts, culture, music and sport. It gives a maximum of £750 to a single project.

Exclusions Projects which cost in excess of £2,000 will generally not be supported.

Applications Applications to be made by September annually via schools. Each primary school in Scotland is sent information on the trust.

The McCorquodale Charitable Trust

Children, health, heritage, wildlife

About £14,000 (2003/04)

Beneficial area UK, particularly Scotland.

Coutts & Co., Trustee Department, P O Box 1236, 6 High Street, Chelmsford, Essex CM1 1BQ

Correspondent The Trust Manager

Trustees *C N McCorquodale; Coutts & Co.*

Charity Commission no. 297697

Information available Accounts were on file at the Charity Commission.

General The trust mainly supports charities concerned with children, health and heritage. Wildlife organisations are also supported.

Grants can be given for building costs, core costs, projects and research. They generally range from £100 to £1,000, although most grants are for £300. In 2003/04 the trust had an income of £5,500 and a total expenditure of £15,000, most of which is likely to have been given in grants. Information on beneficiaries was not available.

In previous years beneficiaries included Scotland's Churches Scheme, National Trust Scotland and Imperial Cancer Research Campaign.

Applications In writing to the correspondent.

The McGlashan Charitable Trust

Educational including undergraduates and postgraduates

£11,000 to organisations (2004/05)

Beneficial area Mostly Scotland.

PO Box 16057, Glasgow G12 9XX

Correspondent The Administrator

Trustees *Iain McGlashan; Ian Mackenzie; Catherine Scott; Andrew Lockyer; Burns Shearar; Dr Catherine Pickering.*

Scottish Charity No. SC020930

Information available Information was provided by the trust.

General In 2004/05 the trust had a total expenditure of £42,000 of which 26% went to organisations specified by the trustees. 43 grants were made to individuals, all of whom had to be aged between 18 and 30, born or living/studying/working in Scotland.

The usual range of educational grants is between £250 and £1,000 and may be, subject to satisfactory annual reports, repeated for subsequent years.

Applications In writing directly to the administrator for trustees' consideration to decide whether to issue a formal application form. The trust responds only to applications in which the trustees might be interested.

The Meyer Oppenheim Trust

Jewish organisations, arts, education, social welfare

£2,700 (2003/04)

Beneficial area UK, but mainly Scotland.

c/o KPMG, 191 West George Street, Glasgow G2 2LJ

Tel. 0141 226 5511

Correspondent Mrs M J McColl

Trustees   *P Oppenheim; Mrs E Kornberg; The Management Trust Company Limited.*

Scottish Charity No. SC004976

Information available   Information was provided by the trust.

General   The trust supports the arts, Jewish organisations, education and social welfare. In 2003/04 the trust had assets totalling £121,000 and an income of £5,000. Grants were made totalling £2,700. Beneficiaries were UFIA (£500), Ben Uri Gallery and MDA UK (£300 each), Aish, Barnardo's, Salvation Army, Jewish Care Scotland and Nightingale House (£250 each), Jewish Child's Day (£200) and Edinburgh Hebrew Congregation (£125).

Applications   In writing to the correspondent.

The Mickel Fund

General

About £50,000

Beneficial area UK, with a preference for Scotland.

Mactaggart & Mickel Ltd, 126 West Regent Street, Glasgow G2 2BH

Tel. 0141 332 0001 **Fax** 0141 248 4921

e-mail alan.hartley@macmic.co.uk

Correspondent   Alan Hartley

Trustees   *J C Craig; D A Mickel; B G A Mickel; A Smith; A L Bassi.*

Scottish Charity No. SC003266

Information available   Limited information was provided by the trust.

General   This trust distributes charitable donations from Mactaggart & Mickel Ltd house builders. Grants are made each year totalling around £50,000. No further information was available.

Previous beneficiaries have included Bo'ness Old Kirk, Cancer Research, Dunbar John Muir Museum, National Trust for Scotland and Scottish Sports Aid Trust.

Exclusions   Unsolicited applications from individuals will not be acknowledged.

Applications   In writing to the correspondent.

The Hugh and Mary Miller Bequest Trust

Disability

About £90,000

Beneficial area Mainly Scotland.

Maclay Murray & Spens, 151 St Vincent Street, Glasgow G2 5NJ

Tel. 0141 248 5011 **Fax** 0141 271 5319

e-mail andrew.biggart@mms.co.uk

Correspondent   Andrew S Biggart, Secretary

Trustees   *G R G Graham; H C Davidson.*

Scottish Charity No. SC014950

Information available   Accounts are available from the correspondent for £10.

General   The trust supports disability causes, with the same 18 organisations receiving the majority of funding each year. Grants of £6,000 each are made to 11 of these organisations with the remaining 6 receiving donations between £1,000 and £500 each. Consequently the trust's funds are usually fully committed.

No recent financial information was available, although previous research indicates that grants are made to regular beneficiaries totalling around £90,000 each year.

Exclusions   Only registered charities are supported. No grants to individuals.

Applications   In writing to the correspondent, although the trust's funds are usually fully committed. Trustees meet in October; applications should be received by September.

The Miller Foundation

General, animal welfare

About £150,000

Beneficial area UK, with a preference for Scotland, especially the west of Scotland.

Maclay Murray & Spens, 151 St Vincent Street, Glasgow G2 5NJ

Tel. 0141 248 5011 **Fax** 0141 248 5819

e-mail andrew.biggart@mms.co.uk

Correspondent   Andrew S Biggart, Secretary

Trustees *C Fleming-Brown; G R G Graham; J Simpson; G F R Fleming-Brown.*

Scottish Charity No. SC008798

Information available No recent information was available.

General The trust supports a wide range of charities in Scotland, as well as animal welfare charities throughout the UK. Grants range from £500 to £2,000, with the majority of them recurrent.

No recent financial information was available, although previous research indicates that grants are made totalling around £150,000 each year. A list of beneficiaries was not available.

Exclusions No grants to individuals.

Applications On a form available from the secretary, although the trust has previously stated that its funds were fully committed. Trustees meet once a year to consider grants in October. Applications should be received by the end of September.

The Mitchell Trust

General

£47,000 (2003/04)

Beneficial area Scotland and the developing world.

c/o Pagan Osborne, 12 St Catherine Street, Cupar KY15 4HN

Tel. 01334 653777 **Fax** 01334 655063

Correspondent The Trustees

Trustees *Mrs M A Lascelles; C W Pagan.*

Scottish Charity No. SC003495

Information available Information was provided by the trust.

General The accounts of this trust have previously been in the name of Mrs M A Lascelles' Charitable Trust, but publicly it is known as the Mitchell Trust. The trust gives for general charitable purposes to recognised Scottish charities.

In 2003/04 it had assets of £1.6 million and an income of £55,000. Grants were made totalling £47,000.

Beneficiaries who received £1,000 or more included Seer Centre (£2,000), Voluntary Services Overseas and Intermediate Technology (£1,500 each), Oxfam (£1,200), Marie Stopes International and Save the Children (£1,100 each) and Children 1st, Interact Worldwide and Playfair Project (£1,000 each).

Exclusions Recognised Scottish charities are the principal beneficiaries.

Applications In writing to the correspondent. Applications should be received by 30 November.

Monamy Trust

See below

£11,000 (2003/04)

Beneficial area Principally, but not exclusively, Scotland.

The Courtyard, 130 Constitution Street, Leith, Edinburgh EH6 6AJ

Tel. 0131 553 6848 **Fax** 0131 553 4813

e-mail ndk.ltd@ukgateway.net

Correspondent J Norman, Trustee

Trustees *John Norman; Jack Kerr; Richard Burrell; David Tippett.*

Scottish Charity No. SC024267

Information available Accounts were provided by the trust.

General The objects of the trust are:
- alleviation of poverty generally, and among homeless and unemployed people
- research into the causes of poverty
- conservation and protection of the environment
- promotion of good race relations
- alleviation and care for those with disability or infirmity
- rehabilitation of former prisoners and relief of stress among prisoners' families
- educational activity associated with peace and non-violence.

Grants are only given to constituted groups and organisations and are to a maximum of £500 each.

In 2003/04 it had assets of £181,000, which generated an income of £16,500. Grants were made totalling £11,000. As in previous years, the beneficiary of the largest grant was L'Arche (£6,500). There were 10 further donations, mainly for £500 each. Recipients included Scottish Centre for Nonviolence, Crisis Recovery, Ayrshire

Rolling Cougars, Lothian Shopmobility and St James the Great Parish Church.

Exclusions No grants to individuals.

Applications On a form available from the correspondent. The trustees meet in March and September to award grants; applications must arrive by the end of February and August.

The Stanley Morrison Charitable Trust

Education, general, sports for young people

£32,000 (2004)

Beneficial area The west coast of Scotland, with a preference for Glasgow and Ayrshire.

O'Connell Consulting, McGregor House, Southbank Business Park, Kirkintilloch, Glasgow G66 1XF

Tel. 0141 578 2252 **Fax** 0141 578 2248

e-mail tom@oconnell-consulting.com

Correspondent Tom O'Connell, Trustee

Trustees S W Morrison; J H McKean; Mrs M E Morrison; T F O'Connell; A S Dudgeon.

Scottish Charity No. SC006610

Information available Information was provided by the trust.

General The trust states that grants are awarded to:

- sporting activities in Scotland, with particular emphasis on the encouragement of youth involvement
- charities which have as their principal base of operation and benefit the west coast of Scotland, and in particular the Glasgow and Ayrshire areas
- those charities whose funds arise from or whose assistance is provided to people having connection with the licensed trades and in particular the whisky industry
- scottish educational establishments.

In 2004 it had assets of around £2 million and an income of £40,000. Grants were made totalling £32,000. No information was available on beneficiaries during the year.

Previous beneficiaries include Scottish Cricket Union, Princess Royal Trust for Carers, Riding for the Disabled, Mark Scott Foundation, Glasgow University Sports Sponsorship, Grange Cricket Club – Youth Section, Cancer UK Scotland and Scottish Schools' Badminton Union.

Applications In writing to the correspondent. Applicants should include details on the purpose of the grant, what funding has already been secured and the actual sum that they are looking for.

The Morton Charitable Trust

General

About £90,000

Beneficial area Scotland, especially the Lothian region.

Turcan Connell WS, Princes Exchange, 1 Earl Grey Street, Edinburgh EH3 9EE

Tel. 0131 228 8111 **Fax** 0131 228 8118

Scottish Charity No. SC004507

Information available Limited information was provided by the trust.

General This trust gives about £90,000 each year in two or three grants to charitable organisations at the trustees' discretion. Unfortunately, no further information was available on the size or number of grants made, or beneficiaries.

Applications In writing to the correspondent. The trust stated it is not in a position to acknowledge individual applicants or consider unsolicited applications.

The Mugdock Children's Trust

Children up to the age of about 14 who are ill or disabled

£39,000 (2004/05)

Beneficial area Scotland.

Wylie & Bisset Accountants, 168 Bath Street, Glasgow G2 4TP

Tel. 0141 566 7000 **Fax** 0141 566 7001

Correspondent   Leslie J McIntyre

Trustees   *Graham A Philips; Rosamund Blair; Moira Bruce; Dr Anne Cowan; Joyce Duguid; Avril Meighan; Alastair J Struthers; Christine Brown; James Morris.*

Scottish Charity No. SC006001

Information available   Accounts were provided by the trust

General   The trust makes grants for the welfare of children up to the age of about 14 within the following categories:

- poor children from Glasgow or other districts of Scotland who are in need of convalescent treatment for sickness or any other disability
- organisations of a charitable nature whose objects either consist of or include the provision in Scotland of rehabilitation, recreation or education for children convalescing or still experiencing the effects of illness, injury or disability
- organisations of a charitable nature whose objects either consist of or include the provision in Scotland of accommodation or facilities for children who are in need of care or assistance.

It tends to support organisations rather than individuals. In 2004/05 it had assets of £944,000 and an income of £37,000. Grants totalled £39,000 and were divided as follows:

Charities regularly supported without specific application

Grants, ranging from £1,000 to £6,000, were made to seven organisations and totalled £18,500. Beneficiaries were Riding for the Disabled – St Mungo Group (£6,000), Braendam Family House – Thornhill (£4,000), Camphill Foundation, Children First and City of Glasgow Society of Social Service (£2,000 each), Children's Classic Concerts (£1,500) and Salvation Army (£1,000).

Charities sent application forms without request

Grants, ranging from £500 to £3,000 were given to four organisations and totalled £4,500. Beneficiaries were Sighthill Youth Centre (£3,000), Boys' Brigade – Glasgow Battalion and Ruchill Parish Council (£1,000 each) and Stepping Stones for Families (£500).

Other applications

Grants, ranging from £250 to £2,000 were made to 26 organisations and totalled £16,000. The largest grant was made to FARE (£2,000). Donations of £1,000 each went to Barnado's, Cancer & Leukaemia in Childhood, Home Start Denny and Sargent Cancer Care for Children. Other beneficiaries included Abercorn School, Ark Trust, Children's Heart Federation, Glasgow Children's Holiday Playscheme, Hopscotch Holidays Ltd, Sense, Wanderers Youth Club and West Scotland Deaf Children's Society.

Applications   On a form available from the correspondent. Trustees meet in March and November.

Murdoch Trust

Christian religion

Not known

Beneficial area Scotland.

c/o Cook and Co., Suite 525, Baltic Chambers, 50 Wellington Street, Glasgow G2 6HJ

Tel. 0141 226 4100

Correspondent   A S Cunningham

Trustees   *W A T Murdoch; N B Rankine; A S Cunningham*

Scottish Charity No. SC007591

Information available   Limited information was available on this trust.

General   The trust supports mainly Christian agencies and charities as well as individuals involved in worldwide missionary endeavour.

Applications   The trust has previously stated that unsolicited applications are not accepted as all funds are committed

The James & Elizabeth Murray Charitable Trust

General

About £1,500 a year

Beneficial area Scotland, but mostly Aberdeenshire.

Adam Cochran Solicitors, 6 Bon-Accord Square, Aberdeen AB11 6XU

Tel. 01224 588913 **Fax** 01224 581149

e-mail dgmorgan@adamcochran.co.uk

Correspondent   The Trustees

Trustees *D G Morgan; Miss Dorothy Walker*

Scottish Charity No. SC012263

Information available Information was provided by the trust.

General This small trust receives about 50 applications a year, although it only gives three grants each year totalling £1,500. Previous beneficiaries have included Aberdeen Hospitals Relay Association, Grampian Tape Services for the Blind, Salvation Army and Voluntary Services Aberdeen Fuel Fund.

Exclusions No grants to individuals.

Applications The trust is receiving far too many appeals for the small number of grants available and can no longer consider unsolicited applications.

Mrs Jean Murray's Charitable Trust

General

About £15,000 a year

Beneficial area Scotland.

Mitchells Roberton Solicitors, George House, 36 North Hanover Street, Glasgow G1 2AD

Tel. 0141 552 3422 **Fax** 0141 552 2935

e-mail jamc@mitchells-roberton.co.uk

Correspondent John A M Cuthbert, Trustee

Trustees *J A M Cuthbert; D A R Ballantine; Revd P D Thomson; Mrs A D S Bell.*

Scottish Charity No. SC020144

Information available Limited information was provided by the trust.

General This trust gives about £15,000 each year for general charitable purposes. No further information was available.

Applications In writing to the correspondent.

The Bill and Margaret Nicol Charitable Trust

General

£60,000 (2005)

Beneficial area Scotland.

Messrs MacRoberts, 152 Bath Street, Glasgow G2 4TB

Tel. 0141 332 9988 **Fax** 0141 332 8886

Correspondent David MacRobert, Trustee

Trustees *Mrs Margaret Nicol; David Nicol; David McRobert.*

Scottish Charity No. SC007516

Information available Limited information was available from the trust.

General This trust supports a wide variety of organisations in Scotland. Grants in 2005 totalled £60,000.

Applications Unsolicited applications are unlikely to be successful.

Noble Resolve Gospel and Temperance Mission Auxiliary

Temperance movement, religion, welfare

£22,000 (2004)

Beneficial area Scotland, some preference for Kilmarnock and Ayrshire.

c/o Carruthers Curdie Sturrock & Co, 1 Howard Street, Kilmarnock KA1 2BW

Tel. 01563 572727 **Fax** 01563 527901

e-mail ccsandco@aol.com

Correspondent A A Stewart

Trustees *James McBroom; John Reddox Dick; Mrs Agnes Thompson; Mrs Eleanor Hamilton.*

Scottish Charity No. SC010270

Information available Accounts were provided by the trust.

General 'The purposes of the Auxiliary are the promotion of temperance; the prevention and lessening of intemperance, gambling, drugs and other evils; the promotion of the Christian Gospel, especially among the young; the circulation and teaching of educational literature in schools, societies, homes etc., so as to educate and stimulate interest in the foregoing objects.'

In 2004 it had assets of £184,000 and an income of £30,000. Grants were made to 24 organisations totalling £22,000. Grants ranged from £500 to £3,000, although 19 grants were for £750 each.

Larger grants were made to Ayrshire Council on Alcohol (£3,000) and Park School, Woodstock School and Witchhill School – Kilmarnock (£1,500 each). Beneficiaries receiving £750 each included Alzheimer's Scotland, Barnardo's, Church of Scotland Board of Social Responsibility, Macmillan Cancer Relief, Samaritans of Kilmarnock and Ayrshire, Scottish Spina Bifida Association and Westpark Education Centre Language Unit. Henderson Parish Church of Scotland received £500.

Applications Applications are not invited.

The North British Hotel Trust

Welfare, health

£390,000 (2004/05)

Beneficial area UK, but mainly Scotland.

1 Queen Charlotte Lane, Edinburgh EH6 6BL

Tel. 0131 554 7173

Correspondent The Trustees

Trustees *W G Crerar, Chair; I C Fraser; Dr R L Frew; J R M MacQueen; P Crerar; G Brown; Mrs J Crerar; M Still.*

Charity Commission no. 221335

Information available Information was provided by the trust.

General The trust makes over 50 grants a year. Giving is concentrated in areas where the North British Trust Hotels company operates (a holding of shares in that company constitutes the charity's endowment). There are hotels in Scotland covering much of the country.

Most identifiable grants are for welfare purposes, especially those benefiting older or disabled people, or for health.

In 2004/05 the trust made grants totalling £390,000. Beneficiaries included the Duke of

Edinburgh's New Start scheme (£100,000), Scarborough & District Search and Rescue (£48,000), South Edinburgh Amenities Group Ltd (£37,000), Chapelton Farm Riding for the Disabled Association (£25,000), Carrick Group Riding for the Disabled (£20,000), Old People's Welfare Association (£19,000) and Highland Homeless Trust and HIT Scotland (£10,000 each).

Exclusions No grants to individuals.

Applications An application form is available from the correspondent.

The Northwood Charitable Trust

Medical research, health, welfare, general

Around £1.5 million (2004/05)

Beneficial area Scotland, especially Dundee and Tayside.

William Thomson & Sons, 22 Meadowside, Dundee DD1 1LN

Tel. 01382 201534 **Fax** 01382 227654

e-mail bmckernie@wtandsons.co.uk

Correspondent Brian McKernie, Secretary

Trustees *Brian Harold Thomson; Andrew Francis Thomson; Lewis Murray Thomson.*

Scottish Charity No. SC014487

Information available Brief annual report and accounts, with a list of the 50 largest donations only, available from the trust for £10.

General The Northwood Trust is connected to the D C Thomson Charitable Trust, D C Thomson & Company and the Thomson family. It was established by Eric V Thomson in 1972 and has received additional funding from other members of the family.

The brief annual report notes that 'the trustees have adopted the principle of giving priority to assisting Dundee and Tayside based charities' and says 'unsolicited applications for donations are not encouraged and will not normally be acknowledged'. Other than this there is little indication of the trust's grantmaking policy, beyond what can be deduced from the partial, uncategorised grants lists, and there was no review of the trust's grantmaking in previous reports.

Grants total around £1.5 million each year. No recent information was available.

Previous beneficiaries include Tenovus Medical Projects, Tayside Orthopaedic and Rehabilitation Technology Centre, Macmillan Cancer Relief Scotland, Brittle Bone Society, Dundee Repertory Theatre, Dundee Samaritans, Dundee Age Concern, Couple Counselling Tayside and Tayside Association for the Deaf.

Applications The trust's funds are fully committed and it states that no applications will be considered or acknowledged.

Novum Trust

Church of Scotland

£6,500 (2005)

Beneficial area UK and overseas, with a preference for Scotland.

Mission and Discipleship Council, Church of Scotland Offices, 121 George Street, Edinburgh EH2 4YN

Tel. 0131 225 5722 **Fax** 0131 226 6121

e-mail amillar@cofscotland.org.uk

Correspondent Revd Alex M Millar, Applications Secretary

Scottish Charity No. SC021277

Information available Information was provided by the trust.

General 'The Novum Trust provides small short-term grants to initiate projects in Christian research and action which cannot be readily financed from other sources. Special consideration is given to proposals aimed at the welfare of young people, the training of others associated with the church and new ways of communicating the faith.'

Examples of areas the trust are likely to support include:

- research into and application of ideas for the maintenance and improvement of the spiritual and moral welfare of young people in the United Kingdom
- research into and application of new methods and improvements in existing methods of communicating the Christian message

- work in association with overseas churches or on behalf of immigrants in Scotland
- Christian education and training for ministers and laymen of the Scottish churches.

At the May 2005 trustees' meeting six grants were approved totalling £6,500. Beneficiaries included: Newhaven Church – Edinburgh for the Community Cafe Project in the redeveloped church (£1,500); Dundas Foundation for an open air production of 'The Life of Jesus Christ' (£1,000); and the Old Kirk – West Pilton for new ways of teaching the Christian faith to young people using computer technology (£750).

Exclusions 'It is not intended that the trust should simply supplement funds already available from church or state resources. Primarily it is intended that the trust should provide funds for projects that cannot readily be financed from other sources. If such projects after a year or two still need money, this would normally be obtained elsewhere; the Novum Trust would by then have primed the pump and allow a new enterprise the chance to prove itself.'

Applications On a form available from the applications secretary, or by e-mail from the trust. The trustees meet twice a year, applications should normally arrive by 1 April for the May meeting and 1 October for the November meeting.

The Harold Oppenheim Charitable Trust

General

£7,000 (2003/04)

Beneficial area Unrestricted.

16 Rutland Square, Edinburgh EH1 2BB

Tel. 0131 229 8751

Correspondent Miss Linda Millar, Secretary to the Trustees

Trustees *Mrs Enid M Oppenheim Sandelson; Mrs Jane P Prevezer; Mrs Rosemary S Bello; Mrs Fiona L Arghebant.*

Scottish Charity No. SC008028

Information available Accounts are available from the trust.

General It has been a policy of the trust to support charities known personally to the trustees and whose charitable activities the trustees admire and consider worthy of support. In 2003/04 the trust had assets of £222,000 and an income of £8,500. Grants were made totalling £7,000.

Applications In writing to the correspondent but note the above.

Orrin Charitable Trust

General

£48,000 (2003/04)

Beneficial area Scotland.

c/o Hedley Foundation Limited, 9 Dowgate Hill, London EC4R 2SU

Correspondent P T Dunkerley

Trustees *Mrs E Y MacDonald-Buchanan; H J MacDonald-Buchanan; A J MacDonald-Buchanan.*

Charity Commission no. 274599

Information available Information was provided by the trust.

General The trust makes grants mainly to Scottish organisations, including conservation charities, galleries, hospitals and community projects.

In 2003/04 it had assets of £492,000, an income of £38,000 and made 33 grants totalling £48,000.

Beneficiaries included National Galleries Scotland (£7,500), Wester Ross Fishing Trust (£6,000), Atlantic Salmon Conservation Trust (£5,000), Inverasdale Primary School and Poolewe Primary School (£3,000 each).

Exclusions Grants are not given to individuals.

Applications The trust will not accept any unsolicited appeals.

The P F Charitable Trust

General, particularly arts/ heritage, health, welfare, education

£5.3 million (2003/04)

Beneficial area Unrestricted, with local interests in Oxfordshire and Scotland.

Ely House, 37 Dover Street, London W1S 4NJ

Tel. 020 7409 5685

Correspondent D H Pocknee, Secretary, or Geoffrey Fincham

Trustees *Robert Fleming; Valentine P Fleming; Philip Fleming; Rory D Fleming.*

Charity Commission no. 220124

Information available Brief annual report and accounts; grants list covers top 50 grants only.

General The trust states that its policy is to 'continue to make a substantial number of small grants to charitable organisations both on a one-off and recurring basis'.

In 2003/04 it had assets of £84 million and an income of £1.4 million. Grants totalled £5.3 million and went to 'a wide variety of UK charitable causes'. The 50 largest donations – those of £10,000 or more – are listed in the accounts. These account for over 80% of the total value.

By far the largest grant was £2.2 million to St Paul's Cathedral Foundation for the cleaning and restoration of the interior. There were six other grants made of £100,000 or more: £250,000 to the Oxford University Development Trust towards the establishment of a Gene Function Research Centre; £150,000 to Open Trust towards financing the work of the Rural Regeneration Unit; £115,000 to Marie Curie Cancer Care for cancer nursing services in Oxfordshire and Argyllshire; £100,000 each to Oxford Children's Hospital for building a children's hospital in Oxford, Sir John Soane's Museum towards cost of Adjacent property and Royal Marsden Cancer Campaign towards the cost of cancer research.

Other larger grants included £93,000 to Charities Aid Foundation; £80,000 to SPECAL; £75,000 to Kelvingrove Refurbishment Appeal; £60,000 each to Isaac Newton Institute for Mathematical

Science and Covent Garden Cancer Research Trust; £ 50,000 each to Scottish Community Foundation, Maggie's Centre – Inverness Branch, Prince's Trust and Artifiacila Heart Fund.

Remaining listed grants were mainly for either £25,000, £20,000 or £10,000 each and included those to British Sporting Arts Trust, Historic Churches Preservation Trust, Nettlebed Community Fund, Purley Park Trust, Roundhouse Project, Seven Springs Play and Support Centre and The Development Trust.

Exclusions No grants to individuals or non-registered charities.

Applications Applications to the correspondent in writing. Trustees usually meet monthly to consider applications and approve grants.

Miss M E Swinton Paterson's Charitable Trust

Church of Scotland, young people, general

£41,000 (2004/05)

Beneficial area Scotland.

Lindsays' Solicitors, 11 Atholl Crescent, Edinburgh EH3 8HE

Tel. 0131 477 8721

e-mail csk@lindsays.co.uk

Correspondent Callum S Kennedy, Trustee

Trustees *Michael A Noble; J A W Somerville; C S Kennedy; R J Steel.*

Scottish Charity No. SC004835

Information available Full accounts were provided by the trust.

General The trust was set up by the will of Miss M E Swinton Paterson who died in October 1989. The objectives of the trust are the support of charities in Scotland, specifically including schemes of the Church of Scotland.

In 2004/05 the trust had an income of £46,000. Administration costs were very low at just £75, although agent's revenue fees totalled £2,500. Grants totalling £41,000 were made to 47 organisations. Just one beneficiary received over £1,000, L'Arche Edinburgh Community (£2,000).

All other grants were for either £1,000 or £500. Beneficiaries receiving £1,000 included Livingstone Baptist Church, Lloyd Morris Congregational Church, Haddington West Parish Church, Acorn Christian Centre, Stranraer YMCA, Care for the Family, Boys & Girls Clubs of Scotland, Fresh Start, Friends of the Elms, Iona Community, Edinburgh Young Carers Project and Epilepsy Scotland.

Beneficiaries receiving £500 included Stoneykirk Parish Church, Scotland Yard Adventure Centre, Atholl Centre, Scottish Crusaders, Disablement Income Group Scotland and Artlink.

Exclusions No grants to individuals or students.

Applications In writing to the correspondent. Trustees meet once a year in July to consider grants.

Andrew Paton's Charitable Trust

General

See below

Beneficial area Unrestricted but with a preference for the west of Scotland.

Miller Beckett & Jackson Solicitors, 190 St Vincent Street, Glasgow G2 5SP

Tel. 0141 204 2833 **Fax** 0141 248 7185

e-mail mail@millerbj.co.uk

Correspondent G A Maguire, Trustee

Trustees *G A Maguire; N A Fyfe; R G Dingwall.*

Scottish Charity No. SC017502

Information available Limited information was provided by the trust.

General This trust has general charitable purposes with a preference for Scotland, particularly the Glasgow and west of Scotland area. In previous years grants have been made ranging from around £25,000 to £60,000 a year. Despite providing accounts in the past, the administrators now make a charge for this information. No further information was available.

Previous beneficiaries include St Andrew's Hospice, Church of Scotland Mission Aid Fund, Scottish Motor Neurone Disease Association, Abbeyfield (Glasgow) Society Ltd, Children 1st,

Glasgow Old People's Welfare Association, King George's Fund for Sailors, Sense Scotland, West of Scotland Deaf Children Society, Boys' Brigade Glasgow Battalion, Ocean Youth Trust Scotland, Paintings in Hospitals – Scotland, Royal National Mission to Deep Sea Fishermen, Scottish Adoption Association, Scottish Committee for the Hundred Languages of Children, Adam Smith Foundation, Visual Impairment Services – Scotland, West of Scotland Lung Foundation, Glasgow City Mission, Glasgow Seamen's Friend Society, Royal Society for the Relief of Indigent Gentlewomen of Scotland, Scottish Crusaders, TOCH Scotland and Gartnavel General Hospital Rheumatology Research.

Exclusions No grants to individuals.

Applications In writing to the correspondent.

Paw Print Charitable Trust

General
See below

Beneficial area Scotland.

Turcan Connell WS, Princes Exchange, 1 Earl Grey Street, Edinburgh EH3 9EE

Tel. 0131 228 8111 **Fax** 0131 228 8118

Correspondent The Trustees

Scottish Charity No. SC025671

Information available Accounts are available from the correspondent for £10.

General The trust supports a wide variety of charitable causes. No recent information was available from the correspondent, although previous research showed that the trust has an income of about £10,000 each year. Grants may not be made every year.

Applications In writing to the correspondent.

Penpont Charitable Trust

Medical research, music, visual arts
About £1,000 (2004/05)

Beneficial area Scotland.

25 Lauder Road, Edinburgh EH9 2JX

Tel. 0131 668 3378 **Fax** 0870 705 1395

e-mail jimcook@nestor15.plus.com

Correspondent James Cook, Trustee

Trustees *James Cook, Chair; Patricia Cook; Douglas Connell.*

Scottish Charity No. SC023685

Information available Information was provided by the trust.

General Grants are given to organisations working in the areas of music, the visual arts and medical research. The maximum single grant is usually £500. About £1,000 in total is available each year.

Recent beneficiaries include Council for Music in Hospitals, St Giles' Cathedral and St Mary's Music School.

Exclusions Grants are given to recognised charities only.

Applications In writing to the correspondent.

A M Pilkington's Charitable Trust

General
About £130,000

Beneficial area UK, with a preference for Scotland.

Carters, Chartered Accountants, Pentland House, Saltire Centre, Glenrothes, Fife KY6 2AH

Tel. 01592 630055 **Fax** 01592 623200

e-mail info@cartersca.co.uk

Correspondent The Trustees

Scottish Charity No. SC000282

Information available Information was provided by the trust.

General The trust supports a wide variety of causes in the UK, with few causes excluded (see below). In practice there is a preference for Scotland – probably half the grants are given in Scotland. There is a preference for giving recurring grants, which normally range from £500 to £1,500.

Around 300 grants are made each year totalling about £130,000. Most grants are made to the same organisations each year. Details of beneficiaries were not available.

Exclusions Grants are not given to overseas projects or political appeals.

Applications The trustees state that, regrettably, they are unable to make grants to new applicants since they already have 'more than enough causes to support'. Trustees meet in June and December.

The Portrack Charitable Trust

General

£28,000 (2003/04)

Beneficial area Some preference for Scotland.

Bank of Butterfield (UK) Ltd, St Helen's, 1 Undershaft, London EC3A 8JX

Tel. 020 7816 8100 **Fax** 020 7816 8206

Trustees *Charles Alexander Jencks; Keith Harold Galloway; John Keswick Jencks.*

Charity Commission no. 266120

Information available Accounts were on file at the Charity Commission.

General In 2003/04 the trust had assets of £930,000 and an income of £31,000. Grants were made totalling £28,000 in 24 grants.

The largest beneficiary, as in previous years, was the M Jencks Cancer Caring Centre, which received £15,000 in total. The Royal Institute of British Architects received £1,500; most of the remaining grants were for either £700 or £300. Some beneficiaries received more than one grant during the year.

Recipients included Centrepoint, Forum for the Future, New Horizon Youth Centre, Response International, Prison Reform Trust, Tricycle Theatre and St John's Hospice.

Exclusions Grants are not given to individuals.

Applications In writing to the correspondent.

The Priory of Scotland of the Order of St John of Jerusalem

Health, welfare, disability
See below

Beneficial area Scotland.

c/o The Moray House School of Education, Paterson's Land, Holyrood, Edinburgh EH8 8AQ

Tel. 0131 651 6026 **Fax** 0131 651 6027

e-mail info@stjohnscotland.org.uk

Correspondent Mrs Joan Blair, Administrator

Scottish Charity No. SC000262

Information available Limited information was available.

General The organisation provides the following information on its website:

In its early years, the order provided training in first aid and related subjects in Scotland, as in other parts of the United Kingdom. However, the Scottish-based St Andrew's Ambulance Association existed to undertake identical activities, both in Scotland and England. In 1908 it was agreed that St Andrew's would cease first aid training south of the border and St John north of it.

In the 1940s, some of its members felt there was scope for the order to undertake a variety of public services in Scotland. In 1947, the Scottish Priory of the Order was formed and since then, from a standing start, it has achieved remarkable success in meeting a wide diversity of need. Over the years the priory has responded to changes of some of these needs brought about by development such as the creation and evolution of the National Health Service. More recently it has extended its support to mountain rescue teams in Scotland through the provision of vehicles and bases and has funded minibuses for other needy organisations. A brief history of the priory of Scotland was published to make its 50th anniversary.

Today in Scotland the priory provides, amongst other things, a palliative care clinic and unit, sheltered and nursing residential accommodation, and holiday/respite homes for disabled people and their carers. A branch of St John Cadets provides an outlet for the enthusiasm of its younger members. Also, the priory supports many local initiatives which provide services and supplies for people of all ages who are ill, disabled, infirm or in danger. The Scottish priory has always supported the order's hospital in Jerusalem and currently sponsors its chief executive officer.

Its objectives were listed as including:

- the encouragement of all that makes for the spiritual and moral strengthening of mankind
- the encouragement and promotion of all work of humanity and charity for the relief of people in sickness, distress, suffering or danger
- the provision of assistance to the St John Eye Hospital in Jerusalem and its clinic and research projects
- the provision and maintenance of nursing homes, sheltered housing, hospices and rest and residential homes in Scotland
- the provision of a library and museum.

In previous years the organisation has had a total expenditure of around £1 million, about three quarters of which has been spent on running retirement homes and similar activities. Direct grants to other organisations have previously been for around £25,000. At the time of writing (October 2005), its website was out-of-date, with information only for the year 2001. No further information was available.

Exclusions   The trust tends not to support individuals, but if so, only through a recognised third party.

Applications   In writing to the correspondent. Trustees meet in November and December; applications should be received by early September.

Quaker Tax Witness Fund

Welfare, health, employment, general

£3,000 (2004)

Beneficial area South east Scotland (i.e. Edinburgh and the Lothians, the Borders and Fife).

Quaker Meeting House, 7 Victoria Terrace, Edinburgh EH1 2JL

Tel. 0131 225 4825

Correspondent   David Turner

Trustees   *John Phillips; Gill Reid; David Turner.*

Information available   Information was provided by the trust.

General   The fund is interested in assisting local groups working within their community supporting, amongst other projects, healthy eating schemes, health projects, community care, employment initiatives and housing repair schemes. Priority is given to organisations which 'help people to help themselves' tackle poverty. There is also a preference to support new projects which could not be established without funding from the trust. It operates in Edinburgh, the Lothians and parts of the Borders and Fife. Grants range from £25 to £500 each. In 2004 they were given to 8 organisations and averaged £400 each.

Exclusions   No grants to individuals or towards day-to-day running costs or political groups.

Applications   In writing to the correspondent for an application form. Applicants do not need charitable status, but they do need a constitution and a bank account operated by at least two signatures.

Radio Forth Help a Child Appeal

Children with special needs

About £125,000 (2005)

Beneficial area Edinburgh, Lothians and Fife.

Forth House, Forth Street, Edinburgh EH1 3LE

Tel. 0131 556 9255 **Fax** 0131 475 1221

e-mail lesley.fraser@srh.co.uk

website www.forthonline.co.uk

Correspondent   Lesley Fraser-Taylor, Charity Coordinator

Trustees   *B Malcolm; D Mackinlay; M Scott; Adam Findlay; W Hunter; L McCulloch; John McLellan.*

Scottish Charity No. SC005626

Information available   Information was provided by the trust.

General   The trust raises money for children with special needs in Edinburgh, Lothians and Fife. It organises appeals and events through the radio station and encourages listeners to hold their own fundraising events. The following are examples of the types of projects supported:

- holiday home for young people with disabilities
- minibuses for several local children's charities
- emergency equipment for special baby units
- wheelchairs and specially adapted seating
- play area for children who are blind
- modern equipment to improve the lives of children with disabilities
- help with therapies and treatment
- outdoor play e.g. toys and climbing frames
- specially adapted sensory rooms and equipment
- toys and computers
- music room for terminally ill children
- music therapy for autistic children
- riding for children with disabilities.

Both organisations and individuals are supported. Unfortunately we were unable to obtain financial information, other than that grants totalled around £125,000 in 2005.

Exclusions Capital costs, salaries and training.

Applications Contact the correspondent. Initial telephone calls are welcome and application forms and guidelines are available. No sae required.

RNVR Club (Scotland) Memorial Trust

Maritime, naval

About £7,000

Beneficial area Scotland, mainly the west coast.

The Little House, Pier Road, Rhu G84 8LH

Tel. 01436 820382

Correspondent I J Scott, Treasurer

Scottish Charity No. SC018009

Information available Limited information was provided by the trust.

General This trust was set up in memory of the Scottish officers of the Royal Navy Volunteer Reserve. The trust has a number of aims including: to educate the public in maritime and naval matters; to assist in the preservation of ships and articles of naval significance; to provide facilities for education, character training and development both on and off shore for deserving men and women; and to assist voluntary organisations with similar aims such as Sail Training Association and Outward Bound

Scheme. The trust has an annual income of around £7,000, all of which is distributed in grants.

Applications In writing to the correspondent, requesting an application form.

The Robertson Trust

General

£6.7 million (2004/05)

Beneficial area Scotland.

85 Berkeley Street, Glasgow G3 7DX

Tel. 0141 221 3151 **Fax** 0141 221 0744

e-mail admin@therobertsontrust.org.uk

website www.therobertsontrust.org.uk

Correspondent Sir Lachlan Maclean, Secretary

Trustees *John J G Good, Chair; Sir Lachlan Maclean; Richard J A Hunter; David D Stevenson; Mrs Barbara M Kelly; Ian B Curle; Shonaig A L A Macpherson.*

Scottish Charity No. SC002970

Information available Full annual report and accounts were provided by the trust. An annual review, guidelines for applicants and a biannual newsletter are also available.

General A wide range of organisations are supported each year, with grants of all sizes, although more than half the grant total reported above was spent in one of the four priority areas:

- care
- drug prevention and treatment
- education
- medical.

The trust also has a small grants programme for one-off donations of up to £5,000 for a particular project or activity. Outside this programme, there is no set minimum or maximum grant size.

The trust was established in 1961 by the Robertson sisters, who inherited a controlling interest in a couple of whisky companies (now the Edrington Group) from their father and wished to ensure the dividend income from the shares would be given to charitable purposes.

In 2004/05 the trust had an income of £7 million from assets of £261 million. Most of the assets are still in the form of shares in the private Edrington Group (which is controlled by the trust) and which cannot be freely sold under the terms of the trust.

Recently revised guidelines for the trust read as follows:

Care

Examples include residential homes and day care centres for older people, hospices, charities supporting people with disabilities or mental health problems, services for people who are homeless and local and national support organisations.

Drug prevention and treatment

For example drug and alcohol rehabilitation and/ or education programmes, projects working with children who are at risk of misusing drugs and services working with recovering drug addicts to assist them back into training and employment.

Education

This includes support for capital developments at education establishments particularly where community use is encouraged, projects for young people with special needs, informal community-based education activities including youth training and projects which encourage links between the family and school. Core revenue costs for nurseries, schools and after-school groups are not usually considered.

Medical

Medical research is no longer supported by the trust. Capital and revenue applications will be considered from Centres of Excellence and in particular where activities will be of direct benefit to the patients.

These priority areas account for a minimum of 40% of the trust's expenditure each year but applications will be considered from most fields of charitable activity. The trust is also keen to encourage community sports initiatives with capital or revenue funding. Other categories include community, which includes advice centres, youth work, community centres and transport; arts, culture and heritage; animal welfare and the environment.

The Robertson Trust currently disburses £6 million a year. There are no minimum or maximum donations. The trust does operate a small grant scheme for smaller charities to apply for one-off donations of up to £5,000 to support a particular project or activity.

The trust prefers to offer a contribution towards the total funds required for both capital and revenue requests. Core funding or specific project costs will be considered and may be for a maximum period of three years. As an example

revenue grants towards salary costs average between £5,000–£10,000 a year and capital donations may be up to 10% of total costs. Major donations over £50,000 are usually only considered in the trust's priority areas and any organisation considering applying for a major donation is advised to telephone the trust beforehand for an informal discussion.

In 2004/05, out of 738 applicants, 503 grants, totalling £6.7 million, were awarded in the following areas:

Category	No.	Total
Care	191	£1.8 million
Educational	87	£1.8 million
Medical	11	£1 million
Community	110	£800,000
Drugs	24	£299,000
Arts, culture and heritage	28	£258,000
Environment	15	£192,000
Sport	31	£150,000
Animal welfare	8	£59,500

The trustees have identified a new priority area, rural homelessness, and have developed a partnership with Shelter Scotland. A new service centred on the needs of homeless families is being developed in Dumfries & Galloway and in Argyll & Bute research is being undertaken to ascertain the needs of homeless families. In each case the appropriate local authority is also involved.

The trustees continue to fund Professor Neil McKeganey's work at the Centre for Drug Misuse at the University of Glasgow [£109,000 in 2004/05]. This research programme covers research into drug addiction and how those affected can be helped, as well as the prevention of young people becoming involved in illegal drugs. As a result of this research two new initiatives were established. The first of these is a partnership with the Scottish Executive, called Girls on the Move. This project encourages girls and young women between the ages of 9 and 25, who are currently inactive, to take part in all forms of physical activity. The second initiative aims to help drug-using prisoners to maintain contact with their families, with the aim of reducing re-offending levels on their release. In all those cases the impact of these initiatives will be externally monitored and evaluated to assess the potential for establishing similar projects elsewhere in Scotland.

As part of the education priority area, the trustees' objective of increasing the number of young people attending university with bursaries from the trust, the funding of the Robertson Scholarship Trust has increased to £484,000 in 2005, compared to

£420,000 in 2004. There are now 152 young people receiving bursaries and 13 receiving scholarships.

The trust also made major donations to the Beatson Institute for Cancer Research of £1 million, Eden Court Theatre & Cinema of £300,000, Kelvingrove Refurbishment Appeal of £300,000 and Emmaus Glasgow of £200,000.

The following are examples of more typical grants in each category:

Animal Welfare

Beneficiaries included Scottish Wildlife Trust (£15,000), International League for the Protection of Horses (£7,000), Lochaber Fisheries Trust (£5,000) and Hollyfield Wild Bird Hospital and Animal Sanctuary (£1,000).

Arts, Culture & Heritage

Beneficiaries included An Lanntair (£30,000), National Trust for Scotland (£22,000), Scottish Opera (£10,000), Children's Music Foundation in Scotland (£6,500), Council for Music in Hospitals (£5,000), Glasgow Music Festival (£4,000), Skeklers Theatre Company and Ankur Productions (£3,000 each), Perth Festival of the Arts and Aberdeen International Youth Festival (£2,000 each), Two's Company (£1,000) and Elgin and District Pipe Band (£500).

Care

Beneficiaries also included Forth Valley Sensory Centre Trust (£100,000), Medical Council on Alcohol (£55,000), Aberdeen Cyrenians (£30,000), Glasgow Old People's Welfare Association (£22,000), Capability Scotland (£20,000), Alcohol Focus Scotland (£17,000), Action for Kids (£15,000), Highland Hospice (£12,000), Spinal Injuries Scotland and Scottish Huntington's Association (£10,000 each), Royal Navy Benevolent Trust and Headway Ayrshire (£8,000 each), Angus Carers' Association (£7,000), Motability and Arden House Project (£5,000 each), Poverty Solutions and Army Benevolent Fund (£4,000 each), Action on Elder Abuse (£2,000) and Friends of Insch Hospital & Community (£500).

Community

Beneficiaries included Guide Association Scotland (£50,000), Easthall Residents' Association (£40,000), Scottish Samaritans Trust (£30,000), St David's Cottage Day Centre (£15,000), Forth Valley Area Scout Council (£14,000), Trossachs Community Trust, Houldsworth Institute and Cromarty Action for Young People (£10,000 each), Scottish Marriage Care (£8,000), Positive Action in Housing (£7,000), Your Choice and Caithness Voluntary Group (£5,000 each), Doune and Deanston Youth Project (£2,000), Couple Counselling Borders (£1,000) and Ardgour Memorial Hall (£500).

Drugs

Beneficiaries included Scottish Drugs Forum (£18,000), Simpson House, First Base Agency and Alness Mothers Against Drugs (£10,000 each), Scottish Sports Futures and Bute Council on Alcohol & Drugs (£8,000 each), Drug Scope (£7,000) and Action Recovery Centre (£3,000).

Education

Beneficiaries included Kibble Education and Care Centre (£85,000), Prince's Scottish Youth Business Centre (£50,000), Cottage Family Centre (£40,000), Harmeny Education Trust Limited (£20,000), Right Track (£16,000), East Park (£13,000), Youth at Risk, Six Circle Arbroath Project and Dyslexia Scotwest (£10,000 each), Skill Scotland (£8,000), Befriend a Child Scheme (£6,000), South Glasgow Childcare Partnership Forum (£5,000), Gala Day Services (£3,000), Carlogie Fun Day (£2,000) and Goodtrees Neighbourhood Centre (£500).

Environment

Beneficiaries included Kintail Land Research Foundation (£88,000), RSFS Forest Trust Company (£28,000), Campbeltown Waste Watchers (£10,000), Bike Station (£8,000), Forth Environment Link (£5,000), Trees for Life (£2,500) and Loch Lomond Fisheries Trust (£500).

Medical

The trust's largest donation during the year was £1 million to Beatson Institute for Cancer Research. Other beneficiaries included Friends of Borders General Hospital (£100,000), Canniesburn Research Trust (£15,000), Kidney Dialysis Patients' Association (£2,000) and Meningitis Research Foundation (£165).

Sport

Beneficiaries included Factory Skatepark (£100,000), Scottish Sports Aid Trust (£80,000), Youth Scotland (£50,000), Ness Sports and Recreation Association (£20,000), Atlantis Leisure Fund (£11,000), Dance Base (£10,000), FARE (£7,000), Uphill Ski Club of Great Britain (£3,000), Hugh Fraser Foundation (£1,000) and Helensburgh Challenger Group (£200).

Exclusions The trust does not support:

- individuals or organisations which are not recognised as charities by the Inland Revenue or the Charity Commission
- general appeals or circulars, including contributions to endowment funds
- local charities whose work takes place outside Scotland
- projects which are exclusively or primarily intended to promote political beliefs
- organisations which have applied within the last 12 months
- students or organisations for personal study, travel, or for expeditions, whether in Scotland or not.

The trust is unlikely to support:

- projects which are properly the subject of statutory funding
- projects which collect funds to distribute to others.

Applications The trust does not have an application form. It invites application by letter to enable applicants to express themselves in their own words without the restrictions of set questions. However, there are certain details which you will need to include to enable the trust to make an informed decision on whether or not to fund an organisation:

- A brief description of the organisation.
- A description of the project – what do you want to do, where will it take place and how will the work be managed?
- How do you know there is a need for this work?
- What will be the benefits of the work?
- How do you intend to monitor and evaluate the work so that you know whether or not you have been successful?
- What is the income and expenditure budget for the piece of work, including details of funds already raised and other sources being approached?

In addition the trust will require a copy of your most recent annual report and full accounts. If the request is for a donation towards salary costs, a job description will also be required.

The trustees meet every two months in May, July, September, November, February and March. You are advised to submit your application as soon as it is ready and it would be unusual to have to wait more than three months for a decision. You may be contacted for more information or to arrange an assessment visit.

Royal Scots Benevolent Society

Services and ex-services

About £50,000

Beneficial area UK.

RHQ, The Royal Scots (Royal Regiment), The Castle, Edinburgh EH1 2YT

Tel. 0131 310 5016 **Fax** 0131 310 5019

e-mail rhqroyalscots@edinburghcastle.fsnet.co.uk

website www.theroyalscots.co.uk

Correspondent Cpt. W.G Sutherland

Trustees *D J C Meehan, Chair; C B S Richardson; G S Richardson; Henderson Logie.*

Information available Information was provided by the trust.

General The trust supports soldiers and former soldiers, and their dependants, of the Royal Scots (The Royal Regiment) who are in need. The trust will also give to organisations which help the same people. About £50,000 in total is given to individuals and organisations each year.

Applications Applications should be made via SSAFA Forces Help or British Legion.

The Hector Gordon Russell Trust

General

£8,500 (2004)

Beneficial area Greenock, Inverness and Campbeltown.

Henderson & Co., Chartered Accountants, 73 Union Street, Greenock PA16 8BG

Tel. 01475 720202 **Fax** 01475 720203

Correspondent R T Henderson, Trustee

Trustees *D Caldwell; D R Fairbairn; R T Henderson; H R Fairbairn.*

Scottish Charity No. SC000679

Information available Accounts were provided by the trust.

General   The late Hector Gordon Russell was a local Greenock businessman who had interests in a number of organisations, mainly located in Inverness, Greenock and Campbeltown.

In 2004 the trust had assets of £118,000 and an income of £15,500. Grants were made to 18 organisations totalling £8,500. The largest grant was £2,500 to Little Sisters of the Poor.

The remaining grants were for £500 or less. Beneficiaries included Hessilhead Wildlife Trust, Highland Award Project, Erskine Hospital, Inverness Hospice, Female Benevolent Society of Campbeltown and Inverness Sea Cadets.

Applications   The trust states that: 'No applications whatsoever should be made for any financial assistance, as none will be forthcoming in response to any such application.'

The Russell Trust

General

£222,000 (2003/04)

Beneficial area UK, especially Scotland.

Markinch, Glenrothes, Fife KY7 6PB

Tel. 01592 753311

e-mail russelltrust@trg.co.uk

Correspondent   Mrs Cecilia Croal, Secretary

Trustees   *Mrs Cecilia Croal; Fred Bowden; Duncan Ingram; David Erdal; Mrs Margaret Russell Granelli; Graeme Crombie.*

Scottish Charity No. SC004424

Information available   Accounts were provided by the trust, without full grants list.

General   This family trust was established in 1947 in memory of Capt. J P O Russell who was killed in Italy during the Second World War. The trustees prefer to make grants to pump-prime new projects, rather than giving on an ongoing basis. Grants of up to £10,000 can be distributed; however, generally the amounts given are for between £250 and £2,000. Three or four larger grants of up to £20,000 may be awarded annually.

In 2003/04 it had assets of £8.7 million and an income of £268,000. Grants totalled £222,000, broken down as follows:

St Andrew's University	£35,500
Archaeology	£20,000
National Trust for Scotland	£4,000
Church	£2,500
Music and the Arts	£27,000
Education	£40,500
Youth work	£8,500
Preservation work	£22,500
Local	£10,000
General	£2,500
Health and Welfare	£50,500

Exclusions   Only registered charities or organisations with charitable status are supported.

Applications   On a form available from the correspondent. A statement of accounts must be supplied. Trustees meet quarterly, although decisions on the allocation of grants are made more regularly.

The Andrew Salvesen Charitable Trust

General

About £100,000

Beneficial area UK, with a preference for Scotland.

c/o Meston Reid & Co., 12 Carden Place, Aberdeen AB10 1UR

Tel. 01224 625554 **Fax** 01224 626089

Correspondent   Mark Brown

Trustees   *A C Salvesen; Ms K Turner; V Lall.*

Scottish Charity No. SC008000

Information available   Limited information was available from the trust.

General   The trust gives grants for general charitable purposes, in particular it will support the arts, education/training, medical sciences and welfare of people who are young, elderly or ill.

In previous years grants have been made totalling around £100,000. Unfortunately we were unable to obtain further up-to-date information.

Previous beneficiaries in Scotland include Royal Zoological Society of Scotland, Scottish Down's Syndrome Association and MS Society in Scotland.

Exclusions   No grants to individuals.

Applications   The trustees only support organisations known to them through their personal contacts. The trust has previously stated that all applications sent to them are 'thrown in the bin'.

Mr & Mrs John Salvesen's Charitable Trust

General
See below

Beneficial area Unrestricted, but with a preference for Scotland.

Turcan Connell WS, Princes Exchange, 1 Earl Grey Street, Edinburgh EH3 9EE

Tel. 0131 228 8111 **Fax** 0131 228 8118

Correspondent D A Connell, Trustee

Trustees *Mrs A M Salvesen; D A Connell.*

Information available Accounts are available from the correspondent for £10.

General The trust makes general grants, with beneficiaries normally including Royal Scottish Agricultural Benevolent Institution, Mercy Corps Scotland, Princess Royal Trust for Carers and St Mary's School – Edinburgh. Typically, grants range from £1,000 to £5,000.

Grants are not made every year, as in 2002/03 for example, when funds were built up again due to a higher than normal grant total the previous year. Previous research indicates that around £100,000 is available in a typical year, although much of this is likely to be awarded to many of the same organisations.

Applications In writing to the correspondent, although note the above.

The Scotbelge Charitable Trust

Housing, arts, culture, recreation, health, conservation, community facilities

£24,000 (2002/03)

Beneficial area UK, with a preference for Scotland.

Butterfield Private Bank, 99 Gresham Street, London EC2V 7NG

Tel. 020 7776 6700 **Fax** 020 7776 6701

Correspondent Raymond A Sykes

Trustees *Mrs A Wetherall; S L Keswick; K H Galloway; A J J Stanford.*

Charity Commission no. 802962

Information available Accounts were on file at the Charity Commission.

General The trust will support organisations concerned with housing, arts and culture, recreation, health, conservation and community facilities. It will give one-off or recurrent grants for core costs and building costs and funding for up to three years will be considered. In 2003/04 the trust had an income of £25,000 and a total expenditure of £17,000. Further information for this year was not available.

In 2002/03 the trust had assets of £378,000, an income of £25,000 and gave grants totalling £24,000. Most grants were for £500 each, with a few for £1,000 or £2,000.

Beneficiaries included Council for Scottish Archaeology, Edinburgh Young Carers Project, Scottish Opera, Scottish Adoption Association, Epilepsy Action Scotland, RNIB Scotland and Innerpeffray Library.

Exclusions No grants to individuals, expeditions or travel bursaries.

Applications In writing to the correspondent. Telephone calls are not welcome.

Mark Scott Foundation

Young people

£88,000 to individuals and organisations
(2004)

Beneficial area Scotland.

McGrigors, Pacific House, 70 Wellington Street, Glasgow G2 6SB

Tel. 0141 248 6677 **Fax** 0141 221 5178

e-mail niall.scott@mcgrigors.com

Correspondent Cathie Higgins, Foundation Administrator

Trustees *J N Scott; J Scott; G Brown; Father G Tartaglia; R Woods.*

Scottish Charity No. SC025254

Information available Information was provided by the trust.

General 'From January 2005 the foundation decided to concentrate on sponsoring the Mark Scott Leadership for Life Awards Programme. This is a programme in which over 100 young people living in Scotland work together to develop their talents and to benefit local communities. The programme also addresses sectarianism.'

Applications See above.

The John Scott Trust

General

About £80,000

Beneficial area Scotland.

Kilpatrick & Walker Solicitors, 4 Wellington Square, Ayr, South Ayrshire KA7 2SW

Tel. 01292 618585

Correspondent Nicholas C Kilpatrick, Trustee

Trustees *J W Laughland; N C Kilpatrick; L Smith.*

Scottish Charity No. SC003297

Information available Limited information was provided by the trust.

General The trust supports general charitable purposes. In previous years grants were made totalling around £80,000. No further recent information was available.

Previous beneficiaries include Ayrshire Fiddle Orchestra, Barnardo's, Dumfries Area Scout Council, Marie Curie Cancer Care, National Trust for Scotland, Salvation Army and Tom Allan Centre.

Exclusions No grants to individuals.

Applications Applications are not invited.

The Scottish Chartered Accountants' Trust for Education

To promote education and research in accountancy, finance and management

£88,000 (2004)

Beneficial area UK, with a preference for Scotland.

CA House, 21 Haymarket Yards, Edinburgh EH12 5BH

Tel. 0131 347 0233 **Fax** 0131 347 0110

e-mail dwood@icas.org.uk

Correspondent David A Wood, Secretary

Trustees *Mrs V A Dickson; A M Hathorn; H M M Johnston; I M Stubbs; Prof. J P Percy; M Darroch; G S Johnston; Prof. V Beattie.*

Scottish Charity No. SC008368

Information available Information was provided by the trust.

General The trust was established in 1977 from contributions from members of the Institute of Chartered Accountants of Scotland, accountancy firms and others. The principal objects of the trust are to promote education and research in accountancy, finance and management.

The trust provides grants for education and research, scholarships and bursaries for study and research in accountancy and related subjects, and commissions and publishes books and journals on accountancy and related subjects.

In 2004 the trust had assets of £356,000 and an income of £26,000. During the year grants were made totalling £88,000 for research and for presenting papers at conferences. Beneficiaries were SATER (£38,000), ICAS Research

Committee – Taking Ethics to Heart (£36,000), Rankin & Co – Tax Reform: A Comparative Study (£13,000) and one grant of £1,000 for the presentation of papers at Conference: A Survey of Investor Relations among the top 500 European Countries.

Applications   In writing to the correspondent.

The Scottish Churches Architectural Heritage Trust

Scottish church buildings

£113,500 (2004)

Beneficial area Scotland.

15 North Bank Street, The Mound, Edinburgh EH1 2LP

Tel. 0131 225 8644 **Fax** 0131 225 8644

e-mail info@scaht.org.uk

website www.scaht.org.uk

Correspondent   Mrs Florence MacKenzie, Director

Trustees   *Lord Penrose, Chair; Magnus Magnusson; Lady Marion Fraser; John Gerrard; Revd Malcolm Grant; Ivor Guild; Revd Kenneth Nugent; Prof. Frank Willett; Revd Douglas Galbraith.*

Scottish Charity No. SC000819

Information available   Information was taken from the trust's website.

General   This trust was established 'to assist congregations of any denomination in Scotland in the preservation and upkeep of church buildings which are in regular use for public worship, principally by raising funds for their repair and restoration and by acting as a source of technical advice and assistance on maintenance and repair'. Specifically:

- Repairs to or restoration of the structure of church buildings in use for public worship;
- Other work essential to preserve or to recover the identity or continued function of the building as a place of worship within the context of an accepted religious tradition;
- Conservation work upon items of special artistic quality or having associations with the history of the building and its significance to the community.

In 2004 the trust made 31 grants totalling £113,500 as follows:

Church of Scotland	£55,500 (14)
Scottish Episcopal Church	£30,500 (11)
Roman Catholic Church	£24,500 (5)
Sikh Temple	£3,000 (1)

Exclusions   No grants are given for: repairs to halls or manse; electrical or heating work; interior decoration; disabled access or facilities; or grounds or boundary walls.

Applications   On a form available from the correspondent. The grants committee meets four times a year in February, May, October and November.

Scottish Churches' Community Trust

Community projects

£130,000 (2004)

Beneficial area Scotland.

200 Balmore Road, Possilpark, Glasgow G22 6LJ

Tel. 0141 336 3766 **Fax** 0141 336 3771

e-mail admin@scct.org.uk

website www.scct.org.uk

Correspondent   Jennifer Stuart

Trustees   *Gordon Armour; Sandra Carter; Nena Dinnes; Irene Hudson; Frank Maxwell; Robert Owens; Hilary Davis; Ruth Angove; Desmond Maguire; Ewan Aitken; Graham Bell.*

Scottish Charity No. SC030315

Information available   Full information was provided by the trust.

General   The trust provides grants, resources and support for inter–church and community initiatives which aim to relieve poverty and typically supports projects in their early stages. It is made up of nine member churches who provide the majority of the trust's income. Grants can be one-off or for up to four years.

The following is taken from the director's 2004 report:

The trust will consider applications from initiatives directly developed by local churches, which is based primarily on a partnership with local churches and the community working together to meet local needs, as well as work developed by community or non-church groups but which is actively supported by local churches.

Priority is given to churches and other organisations with minimal resources operating in areas of greatest disadvantage.

During 2004 the trust has continued to support 48 church/community projects in urban and rural areas as well as awarding funding to seven new projects. Each demonstrates a commitment to working in partnership across denominations and communities to tackle issues of poverty and disadvantage. Grants are paid annually and are normally between £3,000 and £5,000 and are available for up to four years. In addition to every grant award the trust gives a training allowance. This allowance may be used to develop the skills of those working in projects. Training allowances are worked out as 15% of the main grant award and can be up to a maximum of £750 in one year. Funding from the trust often acts as 'seed funding' enabling projects to get that first foot on the funding ladder that will attract match funding from other sources.

In 2004 the trust had an income of £161,000 and made grants totalling £130,000, of which £113,000 was awarded to new projects.

The new projects supported during the year were:

- Hot Chocolate – Dundee (£20,000 over 4 years), for a youth drop-in project with music practice facilities, gigs, 'chill' space, sports and workshops on making short films, photography and music recording, amongst others.
- The Safety Zone – Bargeddie (£20,000 over 4 years), to provide activities for children to help enhance their educational, physical and social skills, including arts and crafts, computer projects, board games, sports and discussions.
- PEEK – Glasgow (£20,000 over 4 years), to help provide a programme of activities for children in the East End of Glasgow, with emphasis on the performing arts.
- 3D Drumchapel (£20,000 over 4 years), to help provide care, help and support for parents, children and young people in the area.
- Route 81 Youth Project – Garelochhead (£20,000 over 4 years), to help provide outward bound activities for local young people to encourage their development.
- Starter Packs Inverclyde (£10,000 over 3 years), to help provide basic household goods to individuals and families taking up new tenancy to provide security and prevent poverty.
- The Glasgow Bridge (£3,000 over 3 years), to support a Christian drop-in centre which acts

as a 'bridge' between prison/community/church.

Exclusions   No funding for: work developed by organisations working in isolation from others; building work being done solely in compliance with legislation or not in direct support of a project for community benefit; one-off short-term activities such as trips or excursions, holiday clubs, mission events and festivals; work developed by organisations whose primary purpose is the promotion of abortion, euthanasia or artificial contraception; or work not carried out by recognised charities or properly constituted groups.

Applications   In writing to the correspondent. The trust produces helpful step-by-step guidelines to assist applicants which are available to download on its website.

Applications are considered in May and November.

Scottish Coal Industry Special Welfare Fund

Miners' welfare
Around £100,000 each year

Beneficial area Scotland.

c/o CISWO, Second Floor, 50 Hopetoun Street, Bathgate, West Lothian EH48 4EU

Tel. 01506 635550 **Fax** 01506 631555

e-mail ian.mcalpine@ciswo.org.uk

website www.sciswf.org.uk

Correspondent   Ian McAlpine, Secretary

Trustees   *Keith Jones, Chair; William Menzies; Robert McGill.*

Scottish Charity No. SC001200

Information available   Information was taken from the fund's website.

General   The fund was set up to improve the conditions of people employed in the mining industry and their families. It supports individuals in need and also through the provision of recreational facilities and miners' welfare schemes.

The purposes of the fund are as follows:

To improve the conditions of life of persons who are or have been employed in Scotland in the mining industry or its ancillary undertakings, their families or dependants, who have need of the facilities provided by the fund by reason of youth, age, infirmity or disablement, poverty, or social or economic purposes, for the purpose of improving their conditions of life. Without prejudice to foregoing generality the methods used to achieve these objects may include any or all of:

- the organisation and provision of outdoor and indoor recreational facilities including sports, games, pastimes, arts and crafts, holidays, excursions, outings and entertainment
- the provision and maintenance of convalescent accommodation and aid in the rehabilitation of the disabled
- the provision of comforts for the aged, sick, infirm and disabled
- the promotion and maintenance of youth clubs and youth courses
- co-operation with individual miners' welfare schemes and other centres in predominantly mining communities in promoting activities of the foregoing kinds within or including their own districts
- the relief of distress occasioned by any accident occurring in the coal mining industry in Scotland involving the loss of life or serious or permanent injury to any person employed in the said industry and the relief of distress shall include the making of provision for or towards maintenance, education and training of the dependants of any persons losing their lives or sustaining serious or permanent injury in any such accident.

Grants are made each year totalling around £100,000 to organisations and individuals. At the time of writing (November 2005) the fund's website contained only basic information – check this resource for further details on recent beneficiaries and other information as it develops.

Applications 'If you feel you, your group or organisation would qualify for some financial assistance from the fund, please write to us to request a grant.

Please include as much information as possible in your letter to avoid any delay caused by questions raised by the trustees prior to grant issue.

It is also extremely important to highlight your link to the coal mining industry in your grant request.

The trustees meet quarterly to consider grant requests.'

The fund also intends to have an application form available to download from its website in the near future.

The Scottish Community Foundation

Community development, general

£1.5 million (2003/04)

Beneficial area Scotland.

126 Canongate, Edinburgh EH8 8DD

Tel. 0131 524 0300 **Fax** 0131 524 0325

website www.scottishcommunityfoundation.com

Correspondent Giles Ruck, Chief Executive

Trustees *Anne Boyd, Chair; Alastair Balfour; Hamish Buchan; Helen Mackie; Revd Robert Anderson; John Dunsmore; Alan Harden; Colin Liddel.*

Scottish Charity No. SC022910

Information available Information was provided by the trust.

General The foundation makes small grants, of up to £5,000, for community groups in Scotland. In common with other community foundations, it makes grants from various sources – both public and private – as well as having its own endowment with which it distributes money.

The following information is taken from the foundation's 2004 yearbook:

In 2003/04, £1.5 million of Scottish Community Foundation grants were made, changing the lives of people of all ages and backgrounds. The year also saw changes within the foundation itself, with some subtle shifts in focus and direction. We are renewing our determination to forge stronger relationships with our supporters and their professional advisers, to provide a truly comprehensive service for planned charitable giving.

Strategically our role is evolving too. Every one of the world's 1,000 Community Foundations is faced with the challenge of engaging with local social issues, and we are no different. It is not enough to be simply just charitable bankers. Often we have to choose the road less travelled for our grants to really benefit a community.

In 2005 we'll become even more involved with many of the more critical concerns of Scotland today, linking with other grant makers, public bodies, our trustees and communities to agree the issues we need to address.

There will always be a place for small, quick and accessible grants for immediate results. However, in 2004 we started to make what we call strategic grants. These are larger grants designed to sustain a project for years to come. A good example is the £75,000 awarded to Venture Scotland, who run outdoor courses to help young people at a turning point in their lives. The three-year funding enabled them to appoint a director to manage and grow the charity on a professional, full time basis [...]

In 2004, Scottish Community Foundation grants reached every sector of society in every corner of Scotland; from under fives and over seventies to women's groups and disadvantaged teenagers; from the Highlands and Islands to the Scottish Borders, isolated rural areas to crowded inner cities.

The sums involved were just as far ranging; the smallest gift was £200, the largest a long term grant of £25,000 a year. In every case the money was valuable. But the result was priceless. Size is irrelevant, impact is what counts. That, and a complete absence of reverse gear [...]

In 2003/04 we received 980 applications for funding. Each one was reviewed by our staff or volunteer assessors and then passed on to the funding panel. The panel is made up of volunteers and trustees; people chosen for their hands-on experience of work in the voluntary sector [...]

Over 200 charitable funds are administered by the foundation, including Community Grants, the main programme, Women's Fund for Scotland, Your Community, Your Environment and Sport Relief on behalf of Comic Relief. Full details are available on the foundation's website or by calling one of the foundation's offices.

Grants in 2003/04

Grants of up to £5,000 each were made to organisations including Kintyre Fiddlers, Gairloch and District Development Association, Fathers First in Scotland, North Glasgow Community Food Initiative, Prison Phoenix Trust, Colston Milton Friendship Circle, Skye Old People's Welfare, Dance Base, Berneray Drama Group and North West Training Centre – Lairg.

Exclusions   We have some general rules for all our grant programmes.

We do not fund:

- individuals or groups which do not have a constitution
- groups other than not-for-profit groups
- groups whose grant request is for the advancement

of religion or a political party (this means we won't fund grant requests to support the core activities of religious or political groups)
- the purchase of second hand vehicles
- the repayment of loans, payment of debts, or other retrospective funding
- payments towards areas generally understood to be the responsibility of statutory authorities
- groups who will then distribute the funds as grants or bursaries
- applications that are for the sole benefit to flora and fauna. Applicants are invited to demonstrate the direct benefit to the local community and/or service users in cases where the grant application is concerned with flora and fauna
- projects which do not benefit people in Scotland.

Our different grant programmes have additional restrictions.

Community Grants will not fund:

- groups whose annual income is more than £250,000
- groups whose grant request is for less than 25% of the total project costs.

Sport Relief will not fund:

- groups whose annual income is more than £250,000
- groups whose grant request is for less than 25% of the total project costs
- statutory organisations (such as schools)
- trips abroad
- mini buses
- building costs or access adaptations to buildings
- projects with total costs greater than £10,000
- non-essential clothing; this includes strips or other items whose primary purpose is to identify a team (new policy from September 2005).

Women's Fund for Scotland will not fund:

- groups whose grant request is for less than 25% of the total project costs
- individual's salary costs (although help with sessional costs may be provided)
- international exchange visits
- applications for activities for people under the age of 16.

Your Community, Your Environment will not fund:

- groups whose annual income is more than £250,000
- groups whose grant request is for less than 50% of the total project costs.

Applications   (NB. The information in this section does not apply to the Your Community, Your Environment programme. Your

Community, Your Environment has a separate application form.)

How to apply

To apply for a grant you will need to complete an application form and send it to us. There are no deadlines for receipt of applications.

There are two application forms: One for Small Grants (up to £1,000) and one for Main Grants (up to £5,000). Which form you should use depends on how much money you are requesting from us. There are tick-boxes on the forms to indicate which programme you are applying to (e.g. Community Grants, Sport Relief etc.)

You can download an application form and guidelines for completing it from the foundation's website.

Please ensure you have read the information about the programme you are applying to before completing the form. Please also read the guidelines for completing the form carefully to make sure that you give us all the information we require, and make sure you send us any supporting documents requested.

Application forms should be signed and posted to our Glasgow office:

Scottish Community Foundation
Suite 3.4
Turnberry House,
175 West George Street,
Glasgow
G2 2LB

We hope to introduce 'on-line' applications in future.

Scottish Disabled Sports Trust

Sports events for people who are disabled

£4,500 (2003/04)

Beneficial area Scotland.

17 Kinkell Avenue, Glenrothes, Fife KY7 4QG

Tel. 01592 773406

e-mail userpn@aol.com

Trustees *A G Mills, Chair; W P Noble; R C Brickley; Ms J Eaglesham; A R Mitchell.*

Scottish Charity No. SC005435

Information available Information was provided by the trust.

General This trust was originally established to further the aims of Scottish Disabled Sports, although it can aid other organisations and individuals concerned with the promotion of sports for people who are disabled. The 2003/04 accounts stated:

'Donations come from many sources but donors generally indicate the area of sport they would wish to assist and are therefore retained in named funds. Money is placed on long or short term investments appropriate to the time when grants are expected to be sought. The net investment income of the trust is allocated fairly between and added to named funds.'

During the year the trust had assets of £63,000 and an income of £3,000. Grants were made to support swimmers at the British Swimming Championships (£3,000) and to assist a Scottish team to take part in a four-countries bowls international (£1,500).

Applications As the trust effectively operates as a banking house, no unsolicited applications can be considered.

The Scottish Hospital Endowments Research Trust

Medical research

£688,000 (2003/04)

Beneficial area Scotland.

Turcan Connell WS, Princes Exchange, 1 Earl Grey Street, Edinburgh EH3 9EE

Tel. 0131 659 8800 **Fax** 0131 228 8118

e-mail enquiries@shert.co.uk

website www.shert.co.uk

Correspondent The Administrator

Trustees *Prof. S Moira Brown, Chair; Prof. Margaret Alexander; Dr Graham Beastall; Prof. Jane Bower; Prof. William Bowman; Frederick Dalgarno; David Grahame; Prof. Nicol Keith; Dr Zosia Miedzybrodzka; Alan A Stewart.*

Scottish Charity No. SC014959

Information available Full accounts were provided by the trust.

General The objectives of the trust are to:

- receive and hold endowments, donations and bequests
- make grants from these to promote medical research in Scotland
- engage in fundraising activities for the purposes of the trust
- develop and exploit ideas and exploit intellectual property.

The trust aims to improve health standards by funding research of the highest quality into the cause, diagnosis, treatment and prevention of all forms of illness and genetic disorders, and into the advancement of medical technology.

The trust fulfills its objects by supporting research-minded members of the scientific, medical and allied professions by giving them the opportunity to pursue high-calibre research either independently or in collaboration with colleagues in their own or other universities, major hospitals and research units in Scotland.

The trust intends to:

- increase its provision of research support in further encouragement of young doctors, scientists, nurses and those in professions allied to medicine
- augment the funds available to it to help sustain the outstanding contributions of Scottish medical research to healthcare throughout the world.

In 2003/04 it had assets of £23 million. Total income was £1.2 million, including £134,000 in legacies and donations and £14,000 in royalties. Grants were made totalling £688,000.

During the year ten research grants were awarded. The unconditional amount awarded was in the range of £39,000 to £75,000. Six travel grants and two workshop grants were made to individuals in the range of £600 and £2,000 totalling £12,000.

Six grants were made to individuals at Edinburgh University totalling £266,000, five were made at Glasgow University totalling £229,000; three were made at Aberdeen University totalling £136,000 and one grant of £41,000 was made at Western General Hospital – Edinburgh.

Exclusions Grants are only for projects carried out in Scotland.

Applications Contact the correspondent for further information. Detailed information regarding the foundation's grant programmes, guidance notes and more is available from the foundation's excellent website. Application forms can also be downloaded from the website.

The Scottish International Education Trust

Education, the arts, economic and social welfare

£109,000 to organisations and individuals (2003/04)

Beneficial area Scotland.

22 Manor Place, Edinburgh EH3 7DS

Tel. 0131 225 1113

e-mail siet@ukonline.co.uk

Correspondent Edward C Davison, Director

Trustees Andy Irvine, Chair; Joseph Campbell; Sir Menzies Campbell; Sir Sean Connery; Tom Fleming; Lady Gibson; Prof. Sir Alistair Macfarlane; Sir Jackie Stewart; John F McClellan; Gerda Stevenson; Alex Salmond; David Michie.

Scottish Charity No. SC009207

Information available Information was provided by the trust.

General The Scottish International Educational Trust is a charitable organisation set up in 1971 on the initiative of Scottish-born actor Sir Sean Connery. The trustees regard their two primary purposes to be as follows:

- to assist young Scots who have demonstrated excellence in their initial course of higher education and wish to take their studies or professional training further
- to support projects which seem to the trustees especially valuable in contributing to the cultural or economic or social development of Scotland.

The trust gives grants to organisations and individuals contributing to the cultural, economic and social development of Scotland.

Grants, usually one-off, are given ranging from £400 to £2,000.

In 2003/04 it had assets totalling £1.4 million and an income of £74,000. Grants to organisation and individuals totalled £109,000.

A total of £15,000 was distributed in travel grants to students made through Scottish universities. Other grants included £10,000 to Royal Scottish Academy of Music and Drama, £5,000 to Scottish

International Piano Competition, £3,500 to Scottish Schools Debating Council and £2,000 to Scotland Yard Adventure Centre.

Exclusions No grants to commercial organisations, for capital work, general maintenance, or for courses (e.g. undergraduate study) for which there is support from statutory bodies/public funds.

Applications Guidelines for applicants are available from the correspondent.

Scottish Silver Jubilee & Children's Bursary Fund

Young people under 25, local community

£12,000 (2004/05)

Beneficial area Scotland.

1 Woodside Road, Tullibody, Alloa FK10 2QQ

Tel. 01259 723935

e-mail iscambus@aol.com

Correspondent Ian Sutherland, Hon. Secretary

Trustees *Mrs Alison Findlay, Chair; Hon E David Bruce; George S Geary; Ian Sutherland; Mrs Freda Cutler; Richard James Marks; Mrs Sheila Robertson; Mrs Fiona Waite; Revd Mrs Lindsey Sanderson; Douglas Gibson; Paul Robertson; John Mackie.*

Scottish Charity No. SC005154

Information available Accounts were provided by the trust.

General The trust supports projects in Scotland which are planned and undertaken by young people and which benefit the community in general. It also helps to provide play equipment to playgroups. Projects can be from an established organisation which helps communities abroad. Individuals are only supported in exceptional circumstances. Funds are sometimes available to young people undertaking voluntary work to benefit those in need overseas. Young people must be under 25 and can apply either as part of a group or on their own.

Types of projects supported include:

- help to older people and people who are disabled, e.g. letter writing, gardening,

redecoration, entertainment, company
- creating or repairing nature walks, gardens, walls, fencing
- provision of equipment to playgroups and parent and toddler groups
- youth information and resource projects
- activities for underprivileged children.

In 2004/05 the trust had an income of £4,500 and made grants totalling £12,000. Around 40 grants were made, mainly to organisations, with all but one for £500 or less (Quest Overseas, Edinburgh, received £1,000 on behalf of seven individuals).

Other beneficiaries included Edinburgh Young Carers Project, Special Needs Adventure Playground, Sounds of Progress, Strichen Playgroup, Caithness Youth Forum, Stonehaven and District Sea Cadets and Acorn Christian Centre Youth Project.

Applications On a form available from the correspondent. Applications should be countersigned by a supporter, e.g. youth leader, minister of religion, community policeman, teacher and so on. Constructive monitoring and reporting on the progress of a project is desirable but not essential. Cheques are made payable to a group bank account, local or national agency or organisation or suppliers. Trustees meet in March and October. Guidelines for applicants are available from the trust.

The Scottish Slimmers Charitable Trust

Poverty, education, health

See below

Beneficial area UK, with a preference for Scotland.

47 St Mary Court, Huntly, Aberdeen AB10 1TH

Tel. 01224 256103

Correspondent Elaine Rennie

Trustees *J L Reid; Ms Carol Polson.*

Scottish Charity No. SC021002

Information available Limited information was available from this trust.

General This trust's income is raised purely from fundraising events. In recent years the trust's support has focused on large national healthcare charities such as Cancer Relief Macmillan Fund, Breakthrough Breast Cancer and British Heart Foundation. However, Scottish hospices such as Strathcarron Hospice in Glenny, Ayrshire Hospices and Inverness Highland Hospice were also supported. Amounts given vary, but are usually to a maximum of £500 each.

No recent financial information was available from the correspondent, although in previous years the trust has raised up to £50,000, all of which was distributed in grants.

Exclusions   Grants are not awarded to animal charities nor to overseas organisations.

Applications   In writing to the correspondent.

Scottish Trust for the Physically Disabled

Disability

£2,700 (2004)

Beneficial area Scotland.

Craigievar House, 77 Craigmount Brae, Edinburgh EH12 8YL

Tel. 0131 317 7227 **Fax** 0131 317 7294

Correspondent   Peter Mountfield-Smith

Trustees   *Phillip Harris; Robin Burley; Grant Carson; David Hay; David Tares; Ron Carthy; Stephen Gallagher; Fiona Ritchie.*

Scottish Charity No. SC049682

Information available   Accounts were provided by the trust.

General   This trust promotes the welfare of people with physical disabilities in Scotland, as well as supporting the residents of the Margaret Blackwood Housing Association through the Margaret Blackwood Foundation.

The trustees have recently decided to concentrate their funding more on strategic grants rather than grants to individuals.

In 2004 it had assets of £104,000 and an income of £1,500. Just one grant was made during the year – £2,700 to Margaret Blackwood Technical Consultants, a specialist architectural design service focused on practical designs for disabled people and a subsidiary of Margaret Blackwood Housing Association.

Applications   In writing to the correspondent for consideration in March, June or September.

The Patricia and Donald Shepherd Trust

General

£68,000 to organisations (2003/04)

Beneficial area Worldwide, particularly the north of England and Scotland.

5 Cherry Lane, Dringhouses, York YO24 1QH

Correspondent   Mrs Patricia Shepherd, Trustee

Trustees   *Mrs P Shepherd; Mrs J L Robertson; Patrick M Shepherd; D R Reaston; I O Robertson; Mrs C M Shepherd; Michael James Shepherd.*

Charity Commission no. 272948

Information available   Full accounts were on file at the Charity Commission.

General   The trust makes grants through charitable organisations to benefit people in need and society in general. There is a preference for supporting charities in the north of England and Scotland, or those connected with the trustees, particularly those involving young people.

In 2003/04 it had assets of £472,000 and an income of £86,000. Grants were made to 175 organisations totalling £68,000, with a further £7,000 given in total to 25 individuals.

The following institutions received £1,000 during the year: Prostate Cancer Charity, Cancer Bridge, Lower Nidderdale Community Centre and Motability.

Other grants averaged £250. Previous beneficiaries of grants of this size are Catholic Youth Services, Dermatrust, Caring for Life, Books Abroad, Filey Sea Cadets, National Playing Fields Association and Missing Persons Helpline.

Applications   In writing to the correspondent.

The A Sinclair Henderson Trust

Visually impaired, older people, education, church of Scotland

£17,000 (2004)

Beneficial area Dundee.

Thorntons Law LLP, 50 Castle Street, Dundee DD1 3RU

Tel. 01382 229111 **Fax** 01382 228208

e-mail afmcdonald@thorntons-law.co.uk

Correspondent A F McDonald, Trustee

Trustees *J S Fair; Mrs V Oyama; A F McDonald; Mrs M S Grundberg.*

Scottish Charity No. SC016110

Information available Limited information was provided by the trust.

General In 2004 the trust had assets of £606,000 and an income of £20,000. Grants were made totalling £17,000 and ranged between £250 and £2,000. No further information was available.

Exclusions Grants are not available for individuals.

Applications In writing to the correspondent. Trustees meet in May and applications should be received by the previous month.

The Society in Scotland for Propagating Christian Knowledge

Church of Scotland, missionary work

See below

Beneficial area UK, with a preference for Scotland.

Tods Murray LLP, Edinburgh Quay, 133 Fountainbridge, Edinburgh EH3 9AG

Tel. 0131 656 2000 **Fax** 0131 656 2020

Correspondent The Trustees

Scottish Charity No. SC000270

Information available Information was provided by the trust.

General This trust supports missions in the Highlands and Islands and the work of the Church of Scotland. We were informed in January 2002 that there are no surviving trustees and as such nobody has the authority to donate funds from the trust. A few existing commitments are continuing to be paid, with the remaining funds being accumulated for such time as the trust is able to resume its grantmaking. The trust stated in December 2003 that it was still in the process of obtaining a court order to instate trustees so the 'available' funds of around £7,000 a year can be distributed.

Communication in July 2005 provided an updated address but no further comment on the trust's situation.

Applications The trust will be unable to accept any applications until its trust deed is altered.

The Souter Charitable Trust

Christian evangelism, welfare

£987,000 to organisations (2003/04)

Beneficial area UK, but with a preference for Scotland; overseas.

PO Box 7412, Perth PH1 5YX

Tel. 01738 634745 **Fax** 01738 636662

Correspondent Ramsay Gillies, Secretary

Trustees *Brian Souter; Betty Souter; Ann Allen.*

Scottish Charity No. SC029998

Information available Full accounts were provided by the trust.

General This trust is funded by donations from Scottish businessman Brian Souter, one of the founders of the Stagecoach transport company. It gives the following account of its policies:

Our stated policy is to assist "projects engaged in the relief of human suffering in the UK or overseas, particularly those with a Christian emphasis". We tend not to get involved with research or capital funding, but would be more likely to provide a contribution towards the revenue costs of a project. Grants are generally given to charitable organisations and not to individuals or in support of requests on behalf of individuals. Applications for building projects, personal educational requirements or personal expeditions are specifically excluded.'

Most grants are one-off payments of £1,000 or less; a small number of projects receive support over three years. The grants list indicates a specific interest in the support of marriage and parenting issues, and it has a preference for funding revenue rather than capital costs.

In 2004 the trust had an income of £1.3 million, assets of £10 million and a grant total of £997,000. 317 grants were made of which only 69 were for over £1,000. 240 grants of under £1,000 were made totalling £450,000 and 25 donations totalling £9,900 were made to individuals.

Over 30% of the total was accounted for by one grant, of £305,000, to Alpha International, an Anglican evangelical movement based in Knightsbridge, London which had received £360,000 in the previous year. Other large grants were made to Operation Mobilisation (£60,000), Sargent Cancer Care (£37,500) and Scripture Union (£32,000).

Smaller grants have previously been made to Prince's Trust – Scotland, Highland Theological College and Turning Point Scotland.

Exclusions Building projects, individuals, personal education grants and expeditions are not supported.

Applications In writing to the correspondent. Please keep applications brief and no more than two sides of A4 paper: if appropriate, please send audited accounts, but do not send brochures, business plans, videos and so on. The trust states that it will request more information if necessary. The trustees meet every two months or so, and all applications will be acknowledged in due course, whether successful or not. A stamped addressed envelope would be appreciated. Subsequent applications should not be made within a year of the initial submission.

The Springboard Charitable Trust

Education, young people
£10,000 to organisations (2003/04)

Beneficial area Scotland.

38 Suffolk Street, Helensburgh G84 9PD

Tel. 01436 673326

Correspondent Colin Edgar Shannon, Trustee

Trustees *Colin Edgar Shannon; Angela Mary McLeod Shannon.*

Scottish Charity No. SC013077

Information available Limited information was provided by the trust.

General 'The objective of the trust is to help individuals make the best use of their talents and resources in cases where finance would help them make significant progress towards meeting their objectives.' Emphasis is placed on helping young people.

In 2003/04 the trust had an income of £10,000, all of which was distributed in grants. A list of beneficiaries was not provided.

Exclusions No grants to: overseas students, older people, second degree or further education courses, medical research, overseas travel. People with disabilities must not be over 25 years old. Applications for the arts, expeditions, religious projects, brain injuries should not be made by individuals. Applicants must have the support of a sponsoring organisation through which any grant can be channelled. Household items, repairs, debt reduction and similar items are not eligible.

Applications Applicants must apply at least three months in advance and provide the following details:

- aims and objectives
- budget
- fundraising plans and progress
- name, address and telephone number of referee and/or sponsoring body
- documentary evidence of the project.

The Spurgin Charitable Trust

Social welfare

About £14,000

Beneficial area Scotland.

31 Fountainhall Road, Edinburgh EH9 2LN

Tel. 0131 466 0661

Correspondent Mrs Lucy C Richardson, Trustee

Trustees *Malcolm Macmillan; Mrs Lucy C Richardson.*

Scottish Charity No. SC019799

Information available Limited information was available on this trust.

General The trust has an annual income of about £14,000 to dispose of. Grants, to a maximum of £1,000, are usually awarded to people caring agencies in Scotland. Both recurrent and one-off grants are awarded.

Applications In writing to the correspondent.

St Andrew Animal Fund

Animal welfare

£26,000 (2004)

Beneficial area UK and overseas, with a preference for Scotland.

10 Queensferry Street, Edinburgh EH2 4PG

Tel. 0131 225 2116 **Fax** 0131 220 6377

e-mail info@advocatesforanimals.org

website www.advocatesforanimals.org

Correspondent Ross Minett, Secretary

Trustees *Murray McGrath; David Martin; Dr Jane Goodall; Heather Petrie; Rebecca Ford; Shona McManus; Stephen Blakeway; Emma Law, Audrey Fearn; Duchess of Hamilton; Virginia Hay; Les Ward; Sheelagh Graham.*

Scottish Charity No. SC005337

Information available Annual report and accounts were provided by the trust.

General The fund was formed in 1969 to carry out charitable activities for the protection of animals from cruelty and suffering. Grants are awarded only to fund or to part-fund a specific project, e.g. building work, renovation, repairs and so on; an animal project – spaying/neutering, re-homing and so on; animal rescue/animal sanctuary – providing care for unwanted, ill or injured animals.

The activities during 2004 included making grants and awards to further animal welfare projects in the UK and overseas. The fund continued its involvement in a project dealing with the force feeding of ducks and geese in the production of foie gras, and with Focus on Alternatives, a group promoting the development, acceptance and use of humane alternatives to animals in research.

The trustees consider that the priorities for the charity in the next few years are support for the development of non-animal research techniques, funding farm animal and companion animal and wildlife projects to improve and enhance the welfare of animals.

In 2004 the assets of the fund stood at £572,000. Income totalled £63,000, including £22,000 from donations and legacies, £20,000 from investments and £18,000 from rent. Grants totalled £26,000 with other charitable expenditure amounting to £68,000.

There were 19 grants made in the year, the largest of which was made to Lawrence & Beavan Website Project (£11,000). Other beneficiaries receiving over £1,000 were Tinto Kennels (£3,000), InterNICHE and Uist Hedgehog Rescue (£2,000 each) and Captive Animals Protection Society and Norwegian School of Veterinary Science (£1,200 each).

Beneficiaries of smaller grants included ATLA Abstracts, Friends of the Ferals – Devon, Muirhead Animal Fund – Edinburgh, Cat Register and Rescue Centre – Falkirk and The Sanctuary – Morpeth.

Exclusions No support for routine day-to-day expenses.

Applications In writing to the correspondent. The trustees meet in April and applications must reach the fund by 28 February for consideration at the next meeting. Applications should include a copy of the latest accounts, the name and address of a referee (e.g. veterinary surgeon or an animal welfare organisation), the purpose for which any grant will be used and, where relevant, two estimates. Receipts for work carried out may be requested and the fund states that visits by representatives of the fund to those organisations receiving grants will be made at random.

The Hugh Stenhouse Foundation

General

£40,000 (2004/05)

Beneficial area Mainly Scotland, with an emphasis on the west coast.

Lomynd, Knockbuckle Road, Kilmacolm, Renfrewshire PA13 4JT

Tel. 01505 872716

Correspondent P D Bowman, Secretary and Treasurer

Trustees *Mrs P R H Irvine Robertson; M R L Stenhouse; R G T Stenhouse; Mrs R C L Stewart.*

Scottish Charity No. SC015074

Information available Information was provided by the trust.

General The trust will support social welfare causes, children and young people, medical and health organisations and the environment/conservation and heritage. It supports organisations in Scotland, especially on the west coast.

In 2004/05 it had assets of £1.2 million and an income of £47,000. After administration costs of just under £11,000, grants were made totalling £40,000. By far the largest grant was £24,000 to Maxwelton Chapel Trust. Other beneficiaries included Riding for the Disabled Association (£2,500), Muscular Dystrophy Campaign, Church House Bridgeton and Helensburgh Sea Cadets (£2,000 each) and Sargent Cancer Care for Children (£1,000).

Exclusions Grants are not given for political appeals or to individuals.

Applications In writing to the correspondent. Trustees meet in March and September. Applications should be received by February and August respectively.

Alexander Stone Foundation

Social welfare

About £10,000

Beneficial area Not known.

c/o Burness, 242 West George Street, Glasgow G2 4QY

Tel. 0141 248 4933 **Fax** 0141 204 1601

Correspondent Steven Phillips

Scottish Charity No. SC008261

Information available No recent information was available.

General Established in 1967 by the late Sir Alexander Stone, the trust supports a range of charities, with a possible preference for Scotland. The most recent information available indicates that the trust distributes grants totalling about £10,000 each year.

Applications In writing to the correspondent.

The T C Charitable Trust

General, education

£9,000 (2003/04)

Beneficial area Mainly Scotland.

c/o KPMG, 191 West George Street, Glasgow G2 2LJ

Tel. 0141 226 5511

Correspondent Mrs M J McColl

Trustees *D G Coughtrie; R J Thomson; W J M Kinnear.*

Scottish Charity No. SC017335

Information available Information was provided by the trust.

General The trust supports general charitable purposes and education. Grants are usually to organisations. It tends to give fewer, larger grants. In 2003/04 it had assets of £242,000, an income of £10,000 and made six grants totalling £9,000. Beneficiaries were Angus College (£5,000), Craighalbert Centre (£1,500), Perth College (£1,000) and Music for the Deaf, Scottish Ballet and Scottish Schools Orchestra Trust (£500 each).

Applications In writing to the correspondent. Applications should be received by the end of January for consideration in February. Grants are distributed in March.

Talteg Ltd

Jewish, welfare

£275,000 (2003/04)

Beneficial area UK, with a preference for Scotland.

90 Mitchell Street, Glasgow G1 3NQ

Tel. 0141 221 3353

Correspondent F S Berkeley, Trustee

Trustees F S Berkeley; M Berkeley; A Berkeley; A N Berkeley; M Berkeley; Miss D L Berkeley.

Charity Commission no. 283253

Information available Accounts were on file at the Charity Commission, but without a grants list or a narrative report.

General In 2003/04 the trust had assets totalling £3.2 million and an income of £373,000. Grants were made during the year totalling £275,000. Unfortunately a list of grants has not been available since 1993.

Previous beneficiaries include British Friends of Laniado Hospital, Centre for Jewish Studies, Society of Friends of the Torah, Glasgow Jewish Community Trust, National Trust for Scotland, Ayrshire Hospice, Earl Haig Fund – Scotland and RSSPCC.

Applications In writing to the correspondent.

The Tay Charitable Trust

General

£178,000 (2003/04)

Beneficial area UK, with a preference for Scotland, particularly Dundee.

6 Douglas Terrace, Broughty Ferry, Dundee DD5 1EA

Correspondent Mrs Elizabeth A Mussen, Trustee

Trustees Mrs E A Mussen; Mrs Z C Martin; G C Bonar.

Scottish Charity No. SC001004

Information available Accounts were provided by the trust.

General This trust has general charitable purposes and supports a wide range of causes. Grants are generally made to UK-wide charities or organisations benefiting Scotland or Dundee, although local groups elsewhere can also be supported.

In 2003/04 the trust had assets of £4.2 million and an income of £176,000. Management and administration for the year was very low at just £2,500. Grants were made to 210 charities totalling £178,000, including 126 smaller grants of less than £1,000 totalling £62,000.

The largest grants were made to Dundee Congregational Church (£7,000) and Dundee Heritage Trust, LINK and RNLI (£5,000 each). Other beneficiaries included Dermatrust (£3,000) and Bobath Scotland, Byre Theatre, John Muir Trust, Little Sisters of the Poor and TICR (£2,000 each).

Recipients of £1,000 each included the following: Amnesty International, Alzheimer's Scotland, Breakthrough Breast Cancer, Camphill Village Trust, CSC Scotland, Drugscope, Dundee West Church, Edinburgh International Festival, Great Ormond Street Hospital, Marine Conservation, National Counselling Service Dundee, National Youth Choir of Scotland, Prison Fellowship Trust, Scottish Centre for Motor Impairments, Trees for Life and Tay Sailing Association.

Exclusions Grants are only given to charities recognised by the Inland Revenue. No grants to individuals.

Applications No standard form; applications in writing to the correspondent, including a financial statement. An sae is appreciated.

Tenovus Scotland

Medical research

£450,000 (2004/05)

Beneficial area Scotland.

234 St Vincent Street, Glasgow G2 5RJ

Tel. 0141 221 6268 or 01292 311276

Fax 01292 311433

e-mail gen.sec@talk21.com

website www.tenovus-scotland.org.uk

Correspondent E R Read, General Secretary

Trustees *The Committee: D G Brown; Mrs F Cutler; Dr S Duncan; Mary Marquis; G M Philips; Lady Arbuthnott; Prof. I H Stevenson; Prof. P W Howie; Prof. A A Calder; M McIver; P C M Roger.*

Scottish Charity No. SC009675

Information available Information was provided by the trust, and taken from the trust's website.

General The trust aims to 'assist young research staff who have yet to establish a track record, to get research programmes underway'. The full range of medical science is considered. Preference is given to innovative, patient-related projects and particularly to preliminary 'pump priming' studies, which are thought likely to lead to subsequent funding from major grant-giving bodies. Grants of up to £10,000 are available for equipment and consumables, but rarely for salaries. Larger grants may be considered.

In 2004/05 the trust had assets totalling £1.1 million and an income of £648,000, from interest, legacies, donations and fundraising events. Grants were made totalling £450,000.

Exclusions Grants are not made to individuals other than as members of institutions engaged in research approved by such institutions and by the National Scientific Advisory Committee of Tenovus Scotland.

Applications At any time on a form available via e-mail from the correspondent. Regional committees meet quarterly. Applications closing dates are 15 February or 15 August; allow three months for notification.

The Len Thomson Charitable Trust

Young people, local projects, medical research

£30,000 (2003/04)

Beneficial area Scotland.

Turcan Connell WS, Princes Exchange, 1 Earl Grey Street, Edinburgh EH3 9EE

Tel. 0131 228 8111 **Fax** 0131 228 8118

e-mail dac@turcanconnell.com

Correspondent D A Connell, Trustee

Trustees *D A Connell; Mrs E Thomson.*

Scottish Charity No. SC000981

Information available Information was provided by the trust.

General The trust supports young people, local community organisations and medical research.

In 2003/04 the trust's total funds amounted to £598,000, generating an income of £23,000. Grants to organisations totalled £30,000 and ranged between £1,000 and £5,000.

Beneficiaries included CHAS, Sick Kids Friends' Foundation and British Red Cross (£5,000 each), Maggie's Centre and The Princess Royal Trust for Carers (£3,000 each) and Outward Bound Trust (£2,500).

Applications In writing to the correspondent.

Scott Thomson Charitable Trust

Relief of poverty, education, Christian

See below

Beneficial area Scotland.

36 Norwood Drive, Glasgow G46 7LS

Correspondent R Scott Thomson, Trustee

Trustees *R H Craig; R Scott Thomson, Ms M B Thomson.*

Scottish Charity No. SC004071

Information available Limited information was available on this trust.

General The trust makes grants to organisations concerned with the relief of poverty, the advancement of education and the Christian religion.

The trust provided financial information for the year 1994/95 as an update to the entry that appeared in the previous edition of this guide, which showed a grant total of £23,000.

No further information was available.

Applications In writing to the correspondent.

Tulip Charitable Trust

Medical research, drug abuse, children, young people and older people

See below

Beneficial area Mainly Scotland, especially Edinburgh.

Anderson Strathern Solicitors, 1 Rutland Court, Edinburgh EH3 8EY

Tel. 0131 270 7700 **Fax** 0131 270 7788

e-mail george.russell@andersonstrathern.co.uk

Correspondent George R Russell, Secretary

Scottish Charity No. SC026572

Information available Limited information was available.

General The trust makes donations to smaller local charities or to other charitable organisations. It supports groups working in fields such as medical research, drug abuse, children and young people and older people. It has an interest in supporting unemployed young people through training schemes and workshops. Grants are likely to total a few thousand pounds each year. No further information was available.

Exclusions No grants are made to individuals.

Applications In writing to the correspondent. Applications are considered half-yearly.

The Tunnell Trust

Chamber music

£29,000 (2003/04)

Beneficial area UK, with a preference for Scotland.

4 Royal Terrace, Edinburgh EH7 5AB

Tel. 0131 556 4043 **Fax** 0131 556 3969

e-mail tunnelltrust@aol.com

website www.tunnelltrust.org.uk

Correspondent The Secretary

Trustees C J Packard, Chair;; T D Chadwick; M Hunter; D McLellan; D Nicholson; K Robb; D W S Todd; O W Tunnell; P Tunnell.

Scottish Charity No. SC021739

Information available Information was provided by the trust.

General The trust was set up in 1988 as a tribute to John Tunnell, who was leader of the Scottish Chamber Orchestra from its foundation in 1974 until his death in 1988.

The trust aims to promote chamber music, advance the education of young professional chamber musicians and provide performance opportunities for talented chamber musicians. Modest fees are paid to British groups of two to eight young professional chamber music players aged 27 or under.

Its main programme is to support Scottish chamber music clubs and societies for tours of Scotland. Other fees are paid, usually for residential chamber music courses and concerts elsewhere in the UK.

In 2003/04 it had an income of £52,000 and made awards totalling £29,000. Beneficiaries included Trio Belle Epoque and Pavao String Quartet. In making these awards, the trust sponsored a total of 15 concerts in 15 different music clubs and societies through Scotland and a chamber music course at Strathgarry House – Perthshire.

Exclusions Awards are not available to singers or vocal groups, nor to instrumental duos consisting of a soloist with accompanist. Duos in which the players are equal partners, for example in violin and piano, or cello and piano sonatas, are eligible.

Applications Application forms are available from the trust's website. The deadline is 30 June each year, with auditions for potential recipients held in November.

The Underwood Trust

General

See below

Beneficial area Wiltshire and Scotland and UK-wide.

32 Haymarket, London SW1Y 4TP

website www.theunderwoodtrust.org.uk

Correspondent Antony P Cox, Manager

Trustees Robin Clark, Chair; Patricia Clark; Jack C Taylor.

Charity Commission no. 266164

Information available Information was taken from the trust's website.

General 'The trust currently supports UK registered charities and other official charitable organisations which benefit society nationally or locally in Wiltshire and Scotland.

'The trustees seek to cover a wide spectrum of activities so as to benefit as many charitable causes as possible and to make donations to organisations where its contribution really can be seen to make a difference. The trust does not wish to be the principal funder of a charity. As such medium sized bodies are more likely to receive grants than either very small charities or well known large national ones.'

The trust anticipates the annual investment income available for grant making for the next few years will be around £500,000. At present applications are invited at a level between £15,000 and a maximum of £25,000.

Grants are categorised under the following headings:

- medicine and health
- welfare
- the environment
- education and sciences
- the arts.

The allocation between these headings varies from year to year. The trust's website details the specific interests in the current year (2004/05) as:

- the environment
- welfare – specifically: crime prevention, victim support and the re-education of offenders.

In 2003/04 the trust had an income of £548,000 and a total expenditure of £737,000. It gave grants totalling £711,000. Although the trust states a preference for Scotland, its latest list of beneficiaries includes relatively few Scottish charities, with little money awarded there.

Exclusions No grants to:

- individuals directly
- political activities
- commercial ventures or publications
- the purchase of vehicles including minibuses
- overseas travel, holidays or expeditions
- retrospective grants or loans
- direct replacement of statutory funding or activities that are primarily the responsibility of central or local government
- large capital, endowment or widely distributed appeals.

Applications In order to be considered for a grant applicants must complete an application form and send it by post to the correspondent. The trustees meet to consider applications regularly during the year.

In any event, all applicants should review the guidance on the trust's website and complete the application form which can be found on the website.

The Volant Charitable Trust

General

£3.7 million (2004/05)

Beneficial area UK.

Turcan Connell WS, Princes Exchange, 1 Earl Grey Street, Edinburgh EH3 9EE

Tel. 0131 228 8111 **Fax** 0131 228 8118

Correspondent Robin D Fulton, Trustee

Trustees *J K Rowling; Dr N S Murray; G C Smith; R D Fulton.*

Scottish Charity No. SC030790

Information available Accounts were provided by the trust.

General This trust was established in 2002 by the author J K Rowling for general charitable purposes.

The following guidelines were provided by the trust:

- the trustees are prepared to support charity by way of regular annual payments but only in exceptional circumstances would grants exceed five years
- the trustees will support the general purposes of a charity or specific projects
- the trustees' principal objective is to support charitable organisations whose purpose is to alleviate poverty, suffering or social deprivation with particular emphasis on children's and women's issues. Such charities may or may not be national charitable institutions
- the trustees will, as and when appropriate, support disaster appeals but will generally not support applications from individuals who are seeking assistance for a specific project which that individual may be carrying out, or to relieve a need due to illness or similar circumstances.

In 2004/05 the trust had assets of £22.5 million and an income of £8.3 million, including a donation of £7.7 million from the settlor. Grants were made to 50 organisations totalling £3.7 million.

The largest grants made during the year were £1 million donated to help the victims of the Asian Tsunami and £300,000 to One Parent Families London (which is to receive the same amount each year for five years). Other grants included those to Refuge (£195,000 in total), Terrence Higgins Trust (£192,000), Edinburgh Women's Aid and International Pen Scottish Centre (£50,000 each), Revive Scotland, Shelter Scotland and Stirling Castle Concert (£25,000 each), Prince's Trust Scotland (£15,000), Lamlash Church of Scotland and Downside Fisher Youth Club (£10,000 each), Friends of Midlothian Children (£5,000), Scottish Association of Sigh Language Interpreters (£4,000) and Starlight Children's Foundation (£1,000).

Exclusions   No grants to individuals.

Applications   In writing to the correspondent. There is at least one trustees' meeting each year, in November.

Voluntary Action Fund

Voluntary projects engaging people as volunteers

£743,000 (2004/05)

Beneficial area Scotland.

Comely Park House, 80 New Row, Dunfermline, Fife KY12 7EJ

Tel. 01383 620780 **Fax** 01383 626129

e-mail info@voluntaryactionfund.org.uk

website www.voluntaryactionfund.org.uk

Correspondent   Sandra Carter, Secretary

Trustees   *Susan Elsley; Carol Downie; Nina Giles; John Hawthorn; John Knox; Lifang Lamb; Richard Louden; Steven Marwick; Laurie Naumann; Jonathan Squire.*

Scottish Charity No. SC035037

Information available   Annual report and accounts were provided by the fund.

General   Formerly the Unemployed Voluntary Action Fund (UVAF), this new fund came into being in early 2004 after assets were transferred from the old fund. The Voluntary Action Fund

incorporated the UVAF as one strand of its activities (now closed to new applicants). The fund has a full review of its aims, objectives and recent activities, from which this entry is taken.

Its stated aims are:

1. To secure and manage funding to invest in grant schemes which reflect the principles of the Voluntary Action Fund by:

- empowering people to play an active part in their communities through volunteering
- overcoming barriers to participation in community activities
- promoting inclusion and challenging inequality;
- helping organisations respond to the needs of disadvantaged groups
- building the skills and confidence of individuals and organisations in local communities
- targeting resources at disadvantaged organisations and individuals.

2. To develop and disseminate a framework of best practice by:

- demonstrating transparency, fairness, rigour and equality in all our grant making processes
- working alongside organisations to achieve high standards
- investing in [the fund's own] learning and development
- identifying and supporting new ways of working
- being alert to activities of wider significance and sharing information
- undertaking action research and disseminating the results
- ensuring the impact and effectiveness of our funded programmes through systematic monitoring and evaluation.

3. To add value to the voluntary sector in Scotland by:

- encouraging organisations to develop networks to share their knowledge and learn from each other
- providing affordable and useful training opportunities and support
- contributing to local and national forums and networks to influence and shape policy
- proactively building relationships with other funders.

Funding programmes

The Voluntary Action Fund's main activities during [2004/05] to achieve these aims have been the delivery of three separate grants programmes funded by the Scottish Executive. These were:

- the Unemployed Voluntary Action Fund (*now closed to new projects*)

- the Ethnic Minorities Grant Scheme
- Valuing Volunteers.

Extensive promotion of the funding opportunity, assistance and support for applicants, and development and training for successful projects is fundamental to the Voluntary Action Fund's approach. In-house publications are distributed, resources available from other agencies are signposted, and opportunities for networking and sharing experiences are organised.

Grantmaking in 2004/05

The Unemployed Voluntary Action Fund programme assisted the voluntary sector in Scotland with grants and support for development and capacity building. Grants were awarded to enable voluntary organisations recognised as charitable to establish local projects. The funding created opportunities for people to be involved in projects in their local communities to meet identified needs in the fields of health, social and community development, and to develop volunteering as a means of promoting inclusion and increasing job readiness [...] In the Main Grants Programme most projects were funded for three years and monitored on a six monthly cycle. Support and training were offered during the funding period. This year [2004/05] was the last year of new grants from UVAF, but the on-going commitments for the second and third years of the three year projects approved in the year to 2004/05 funding round will be provided alongside new grant programmes.

The Voluntary Action Fund also administers the Ethnic Minorities Grant Scheme with grant-aid from the Voluntary Issues Unit of the Scottish Executive. Grants were made to voluntary organisations seeking to promote racial equality and reduce racial disadvantage by setting up projects which enable black and ethnic minority communities to access mainstream services. Support with the application process was available and continued if funding was approved.

Recommendations for grants were made by the Voluntary Action Fund's trustees to ministers at the Scottish Executive. Successful organisations were able to participate in training courses for UVAF programme projects. In addition, individual support, linked to the six monthly monitoring cycle, was provided to funded projects to build their skills and build the infrastructure of their organisations.

Valuing Volunteers is a small grant scheme which aimed to recognise, facilitate and promote volunteering and gave priority to small local groups. It was administered by the Voluntary Action Fund on behalf of the Scottish Executive. A short application form and simple monitoring process in proportion to the level of grant of £500 was applied.

Achievements and Performance in 2004/05

The UVAF was heavily oversubscribed, receiving 90 applications, of which seven were funded. A detailed analysis provided information about the geographic spread of applications across Scotland, the range of beneficiaries and activities undertaken. Existing commitments to 26 organisations in the second and third years of their funding made a total of 33 projects. Grants awarded totalled £743,000. During the funding year 1,224 volunteers were involved, of whom 67% were not in paid work. The average volunteer's time commitment was 6.7 hours per week. A total of 11,230 people benefited directly from services provided by volunteers, and in addition, information and advice activities received 2,655 contacts. The Small Grants Scheme received 30 applications for funding, of which eight were funded. Grants awarded totalled £25,000. Two supplementary grants amounted to £2,500.

The Ethnic Minorities Grant Scheme funded six new projects in addition to 14 existing projects in their second and third years of development. Grants awarded totalled £443,000. Projects addressed racial inequality and discrimination in the fields of education, employment, housing and social care. A capacity building grants programme was promoted for take up in 2005/06, when up to 50 new projects will be funded.

The Valuing Volunteers small grants programme attracted 657 applications, of which 589 were funded, amounting to £224,500. In these projects, grants to improve and enhance the contribution of volunteers provided resources for recruiting, supporting and particularly training.

The day-to-day grant administration for 652 projects included regular monitoring, in proportion to the size of grants awarded, and evaluation to secure evidence of their impact. This is demonstrated in terms of greater numbers of people volunteering across Scotland, of increased vocational and social skills especially benefiting people from disadvantaged and marginalised communities, of improved job readiness, increased access to mainstream services and greater participation in community life.

Future Developments

During 2005/06, the Voluntary Action Fund will work with Scotland's voluntary sector to achieve ints strategic aims. It will establish two new three-year funding programmes, namely:

- Volunteering Scotland Grants Scheme – to resource voluntary organisations to develop projects which ensure that those previously excluded from or unaware of volunteering have the information, support, training and encouragement to participate as volunteers. The sum of £813,000, which includes the ongoing commitments to the Unemployed Voluntary Action Fund's existing projects is included in this funding. The amounts of £840,000 for 2006/07 and £867,000 for 2007/08 have been intimated, subject to Parliamentary approval.

- GO4Volunteering (Get Organised for Volunteering) – to increase the capacity of small grassroots voluntary and community organisations to develop sustainable volunteering. The sum of £125,000 in 2005/06 has been approved and £126,000 in 2006/07 and £127,000 in 2007/08, subject to Parliamentary approval.

Exclusions Schemes which cannot be considered include exhibitions, arts clubs and performances; business cooperatives; credit unions; food cooperatives; out-of-school care; housing and hostel welfare; formal educational or vocational courses and skills and training; clean-ups and one-off projects; holidays and camps; conservation schemes; building projects, including playgrounds; social clubs; sports centres and sports activities; campaigning and political activities.

Applications In writing to the correspondent. The trustees meet quarterly.

The Waterside Trust

Christian causes, welfare

£1.6 million (2004)

Beneficial area Unrestricted, but mainly UK.

56 Palmerston Place, Edinburgh EH12 5AY

Tel. 0131 225 6366 **Fax** 0131 220 1041

e-mail robert@mccp.co.uk

Correspondent Robert Clark

Trustees *Irvine Bay Trustee Company.*

Scottish Charity No. SC003232

Information available Accounts were provided by the trust.

General This trust is believed to be one expression of the philanthropy of the Brenninkmeyer family. Long-term fundraisers will remember organisations such as the Marble Arch Trust. The family always sought the minimum of publicity for their energetic and much admired work and it may be that the increasing calls in England for transparency for such bodies were one reason why those trusts were closed down and some of the work relocated to Scotland.

Though the family's Catholic interests were always apparent, the range of their philanthropic interests have been wide and enterprising over the years.

It had been expected that this trust would no longer be making grants on a scale previously seen over the past few years, with its reserves being spent and it subsequently relying on its income from donations to distribute as grants. In fact, donations to the charity have remained significant, with £1.7 million being received in 2004, most of which was distributed as grants.

It is the intention of the trust to distribute all of its annual income. Grants are now smaller and made to more organisations, with few now for work overseas.

There is no information about grantmaking policy or practice in the annual reports but the trust has said it gives grants 'to improve the lives of disadvantaged people' and has supplied the following further information on its policy:

'Grants are made to organisations which provide adult Christian formation and pastoral care, offer educational and recreational activities for disadvantaged young people and young offenders, provide care and support for the elderly and deprived families, and organisations engaged in community development. Ethics and Church management and finance are also areas of interest.'

In 2004 it made 152 grants (from 631 applications) totalling £1.6 million, with some organisations receiving multiple grants. With one notable exception, no single grant was for more than £50,000, and most were for £10,000 or less.

The main beneficiary during the year, as in previous years, was Derwent Charitable Consultancy, a connected organisation (Waterside trustee D J Burnstone is also a director of the consultancy) which aims to 'improve the management of charities and help charities in the most effective use of their resources', which received three grants totalling £225,000 – one of which was for £200,000.

Other beneficiaries receiving multiple grants during the year included: Scottish Marriage Care (£60,000 in total); Catholic Trust for England and Wales (£58,000 in total); Heythrop College (£45,000 in total); Catholic Children's Society (£42,000 in total); Catholic Caring Services Ltd – Lancaster (£30,000 in total); Maryvale Institute (£19,000 in total).

Single grants included those to the Passage – London (£50,000), Plater College (£40,000), Grubb Institute and Craighead Institute of Faith and Life (£30,000 each), Vision Charity (£27,000), Shrine of the Sacred Heart and Tyburn Martyrs (£25,000), Crew Trust (£15,000), Archdiocese of St Andrew & Edinburgh (£10,000), Action for Prisoners' Families and Disablement Income Group Scotland (£8,000 each), Teachers' Enterprise in Religious Education (£5,000), Westgate Whirlybirds (£4,000), Action on Elder Abuse (£3,000), University of Aberdeen (£2,500), Aberdeen Diocesan Youth Office (£2,000) and Aftermath (£1,000).

Exclusions No grants to:

- individuals
- environmental projects
- construction costs or purchase of buildings
- arts organisations
- conservation groups
- endowment appeals
- major research projects.

Applications In writing to the correspondent, for consideration on an ongoing basis.

John Watson's Trust

Children and young people

£130,000 to organisations and individuals
(2004)

Beneficial area Scotland, with a preference for Lothian.

Signet Library, Parliament Square, Edinburgh EH1 1RF

Tel. 0131 220 1640 **Fax** 0131 220 4016

e-mail johnwatsons@onetel.com

website www.johnwatsons.com

Correspondent Iola Wilson, Administrator

Trustees *Six representatives of the Society of Writers to Her Majesty's Signet: two from Lothian Regional Council – Cllr Chris Wigglesworth, Ian Glen: one from the Lothian Association of Youth Clubs – Alastair Campbell: co-opted trustees – Fraser D Falconer; Dr David C Drummond; Pippa Snell; John Kerr; R Shaun Pringle.*

Scottish Charity No. SC014004

Information available Information was provided by the trust.

General This trust makes grants to children and young people under 21 who are physically or mentally disabled or socially disadvantaged, for education and training, equipment, travel, recreational and cultural activities. Grants are given both to individuals and charitable organisations. There is a preference for Lothian residents. There is also provision for a limited number of boarding school grants, for residents in Scotland only.

In 2004 it had assets of £3.7 million and an income of £170,000. Grants totalled £130,000, distributed as follows:

Organisations

There were 61 grants to organisations, including mainstream schools serving people who are socially disadvantaged and disabled. Almost all the beneficiaries were based in the Lothians. The trust states that there was a wide range of specific grants. Grants ranged from £50 to £2,500, but most were for £500 or £1,000 for youth activities or equipment. The trust continued to support the setting up of after-school clubs and summer schemes for children who are disabled.

Beneficiaries of £1,000 or more included Woods Youth Centre for a youth exchange residential, Edinburgh Council for Single Homeless for equipment for a young person's flat, Dundee Young Women's Centre for volunteer costs, Heart and Minds for an arts workshop, Magdalene Youth Project for a youth programme residential trip and South Side and Old Town Sports Centre Association for sports equipment.

Individuals

123 individual grants for education and 'advancement in life'. Grants to individuals included equipment for people who are disabled, in–school special expenses, tutoring for children who are dyslexic, fees for special schools, post–school education for people who are

disadvantaged, apprentice tools and equipment and other grants to encourage educational, sporting, cultural and social opportunities. Grants ranged from £30 to £2,500.

Boarding education

Grants of between £600 to £6,000 were given to 14 young people.

Exclusions   No grants to people over 21, nor for overseas causes or medical purposes. Grants are not available for day school fees.

Applications   On a form, available from the correspondent, or downloadable from the trust's clear and informative website. Trustees meet five times a year (early February, late March, early June, middle of August and late October). The trust is happy to receive telephone enquiries.

The Whitaker Charitable Trust

Education, environment, music, personal development

£195,000 (2003/04)

Beneficial area UK, but mostly east Midlands and Scotland.

c/o Currey & Co., 21 Buckingham Gate, London SW1E 6LS

Correspondent   Edward Perks, Trustee

Trustees   *Edward Ronald Haslewood Perks; David W J Price; Lady Elizabeth Jane Ravenscroft Whitaker.*

Charity Commission no. 234491

Information available   Accounts were provided by the trust.

General   The trust has general charitable objects, although with stated preferences for music education, agricultural and silvicultural education, countryside conservation, scottish charities and prison-related charities.

Grants are made to UK-wide organisations and local organisations in Nottinghamshire and the east Midlands.

In 2003/04 the trust had assets of £5.4 million, which generated an income of £183,000. Grants to 30 organisations totalled £195,000.

A substantial grant of £60,000 was made to Atlantic College. The next largest grants were

£30,000 to Jasmine Trust, £25,000 to Opera North and £10,000 to Nottingham University. Remaining donations were mainly in the range of £500 to £8,000.

Beneficiaries of the smaller grants included Leith School of Art (£8,000), Opera North – Education and Royal Forestry Society (£5,000 each), Game Conservancy Scottish Research Trust (£3,000) and Bassetlaw Hospice and Soul of Europe (£2,000 each).

Exclusions   Support is given to registered charities only. No grants are given to individuals or for the repair or maintenance of individual churches.

Applications   In writing to the correspondent. Trustees meet half-yearly. Applications should include clear details of the need the intended project is designed to meet plus a copy of the latest accounts available and an outline budget. If an acknowledgement of the application, or notification in the event of the application not being accepted, is required, an sae should be enclosed.

J and J R Wilson Trust

Older people, animal welfare

£125,000 (2002/03)

Beneficial area Mainly Scotland, particularly Glasgow and the west coast of Scotland.

Tho and J W Barty, 61 High Street, Dunblane, Perthshire FK15 0EH

Tel. 01786 822296

Correspondent   Hugh Hopkins, Trustee

Trustees   *Hugh M K Hopkins; John G L Robinson.*

Scottish Charity No. SC007411

Information available   Information was provided by the trust.

General   The trust supports older people and also wild or domestic animals and birds. The trust only makes animal and bird related grants in Glasgow and the west coast of Scotland. Donations to charities related to elderly people are made across Scotland.

In 2002/03 the trust had assets of £2.3 million and an income of £120,000. Grants totalled £125,000. Of this £92,000 went to charities in support of older people, and £33,000 went to charities in support of animals and birds.

Large grants given to charities related to older people included Age Concern Scotland and Alzheimer's Scotland (£5,000 each) and Marie Curie Cancer Care and Church of Scotland Board of Social Responsibility (£3,000 each). There were 13 grants of £2,000 each, with beneficiaries including Accord Hospice – Paisley, Ardgowan Hospice – Greenock, Prince and Princess of Wales Hospice and Salvation Army. Another 27 grants of £1,000 each were made, with recipients including Balmanno House, British Diabetic Association, Enable – Glasgow Branch, Lintel Trust and Princess Louise Scottish Hospital. Other grants not exceeding £1,000 came to £14,000. The majority of grants were recurrent.

The largest grants given to animal and bird related organisations were £5,500 to PDSA, £5,000 to National Trust, Crarae in Crisis Appeal, £3,000 to BCTV Scotland and £2,000 to RSPB. Another 12 grants of £1,000 each were made, with beneficiaries including Borders Forest Trust, John Muir Trust, SSPCA, Scottish Wildlife Trust and Zoological Society of Glasgow & the West of Scotland.

Exclusions No grants to individuals.

Applications In writing to the correspondent. The trustees meet at least once a year.

The James Wood Bequest Fund

General

£47,000 (2003/04)

Beneficial area Glasgow and the 'central belt of Scotland'.

Mitchells Roberton Solicitors, George House, 36 North Hanover Street, Glasgow G1 2AD

Tel. 0141 552 3422 **Fax** 0141 552 2935

e-mail darb@mitchells-roberton.co.uk

Correspondent David A R Ballantine, Trustee

Trustees *Eric H Webster; David A R Ballantine; Alistair James Campbell.*

Scottish Charity No. SC000459

Information available Accounts were provided by the trust.

General The trust gives to home and foreign missions of the Church of Scotland and other charitable organisations in the beneficial area.

In 2003/04 it had assets of £1.4 million and an income of £77,500. There were 55 grants made totalling £47,000. Most grants were for either £500 or £1,000; the exceptions were those to Church of Scotland – Central Fabric Fund and Retired Missionaries Fund (£7,500 in total) and Royal Scottish National Orchestra (£3,000).

Recipients of £1,000 each included Society of Friends of Glasgow Cathedral, Scottish Brass Band Association, Shelter Scotland, Children 1st, Princess Royal Trust for Carers, Erskine Hospital and Scottish Spina Bifida Association.

Grants of £500 each included those to Glasgow and West of Scotland Society for the Blind, Mental Health Foundation, Aberlour Child Care Trust, RSPB Scotland, Hopscotch Theatre Company, Reality at Work in Scotland and Sense Scotland.

Exclusions Registered charities only. Grants cannot be made to individuals.

Applications In writing to the correspondent, including if possible a copy of the latest accounts, a budget for the project, sources of funding received and other relevant financial information. Trustees meet in January, April, July and October. Applications should be received by the preceding month.

The Konrad Zweig Trust

Ecology, environment and conservation

£10,000

Beneficial area UK, with a preference for Scotland.

House with Arches, Ormiston Hall, Tranent, East Lothian EH35 5NJ

Tel. 01875 340541

e-mail uel@ednet.co.uk

Correspondent Mrs Francesca Loening, Trustee

Trustees *U Loening; Mrs F Loening; Prof. A Manning; Ms A Marland; Ms M Ashmole; Ms A Rookwood.*

Scottish Charity No. SC004375

Information available Information was provided by the trust.

General The trust funds charities and individuals undertaking academic and/or practical projects based on environmental concerns or on economic or social concerns which have a strong environmental dimension.

The trustees are themselves engaged in ecological teaching and practical work and welcome discussion about potential projects. They like to be kept in touch with the developments of projects they have supported.

The trust has made the decision to change its funding policy. It no longer invites applications but uses its funds for specific projects identified by the trustees. The trust has joined with other trusts to form a consortium of with broadly similar objectives.

The trust is presently funding a major project on sustainable housing and the changes this would require of the planning regulations.

Exclusions Beneficiaries must be registered charities. The trust does not support students for higher degrees.

Applications In view of the above it would therefore not appear to be appropriate for unsolicited applications to be made to this trust.

Aberdeen & Perthshire

The Aberdeen Endowments Trust

Education, the arts

£574,000 to individuals and organisations (2004)

Beneficial area The former City and Royal Burgh of Aberdeen (pre-1975).

19 Albert Street, Aberdeen AB9 1QF

Tel. 01224 640194 **Fax** 01224 643918

Correspondent William Russell, Clerk

Trustees *Three persons elected by Aberdeen City Council; one by the Senatus Academicus of the University of Aberdeen; two by the governors of Robert Gordon's College, Aberdeen; two by the Church of Scotland Presbytery of Aberdeen; one by the churches of Aberdeen other than the Church of Scotland; one by the Society of Advocates in Aberdeen; one by the Convener Court of the Seven Incorporated Trades of Aberdeen; one by the trade unions having branches in Aberdeen; one by the Aberdeen Local Association of the Educational Institute of Scotland; plus not less than two and not more than four co-optees.*

Scottish Charity No. SC010507

Information available Guidance notes are available on request. The annual report is also available on payment of an administration fee.

General The main purpose of the trust is to give financial assistance to individuals for educational purposes. The beneficial area is the City and Royal Burgh of Aberdeen. A few grants are given in the former Grampian region under one category of support.

At the end of 2004 the trust had assets of £12.7 million. Its revenue is mainly derived from agricultural land and properties, supported with income from a modest investment portfolio. Costs of running the trust and the upkeep of the land and properties totalled £281,000 in 2004.

Grants were made during the year totalling £574,000.

The majority of financial assistance is given to pupils attending Robert Gordon's College, Aberdeen – £550,000 in 2004. Bursaries are also given to pupils at secondary schools in the former Grampian region (£7,000 in 2004).

Under the category 'Plan Expenditure' both individuals and organisations from Aberdeen can be supported and £14,000 was awarded during the year. Awards are given towards the costs of 'certain aspects of adult education' (£6,000), or for 'certain types of group activities and educational travel for children' (£6,000). The trust also supports activities in the fields of music, visual arts and drama (£2,500). Awards tend to average around £200.

Exclusions No grants to people or organisations from outside the former City and Royal Burgh of Aberdeen.

Applications Application forms are available from the correspondent. The Benefactions Committee of the trust, which makes financial awards, normally meets nine or ten times a year.

The Aberdeenshire Educational Trust Scheme

Education

£39,000 (2004/05)

Beneficial area The former county of Aberdeen.

Finance Section, Aberdeenshire Council, St Leonard's, Sandyhill Road, Banff, Aberdeenshire AB45 1BH

Tel. 01261 813334 **Fax** 01261 813332

e-mail tracy.bremner@aberdeenshire.gov.uk

Correspondent Mrs Tracy Bremner

Scottish Charity No. SC028382

Information available   Information was provided by the trust.

General   The trust makes educational grants to people resident in the former county of Aberdeen, including pupils or students whose parents are resident in the former county of Aberdeen. Educational grants include, for example, apprentices, postgraduate scholarships, bursaries, travel grants and for further education. (For more information about grants to individuals see The Educational Grants Directory.)

Grants are also made to Aberdeen County schools and further education centres, as well as to clubs and organisations benefiting people in the county.

In 2004/05 the trust had an income of £76,000, of which £39,000 was given in grants. The maximum grant is £200. Details of beneficiaries were not provided.

Grants can be given to:

- assist in providing and maintaining playing fields and other sports facilities including equipment as the Education Authority see fit
- schools and further education centres to assist in providing special equipment
- clubs, societies and organisations which include amongst their activities work of an educational nature
- schools and organisations to assist education in art, music and drama
- individuals and bodies to undertake educational experiments and research which will be for the benefit of people belonging to Aberdeen County. Help may also be given towards 'regional and national enterprises of an educational nature'.

All grants are seen as a minimal contribution towards the total cost of a project. Grants to individuals normally range between £10 and £200 depending upon need.

Applications   On a form available from Amanda Watson at the address above (tel: 01224 813335; email: amanda.watson@ aberdeenshire.gov.uk.

Full guidelines are also available upon request.

The Joseph Alexander Trust

Arts, general
About £6,000

Beneficial area Kirriemuir.

Thorntons Law LLP, 53 East High Street, Forfar, Angus DD8 2EL

Tel. 01307 466886 **Fax** 01307 464643

Correspondent   J M G Blair

Scottish Charity No. SC014277

Information available   Information was provided by the trust.

General   The trust gives grants in Kirriemuir: to musical societies; for the study of art and drama; and for prizes to school children and to voluntary groups promoting interest in literature, art and recreation. It also supports local charities in Kirriemuir. It has about £6,000 to give away each year. The maximum grant given is £5,000. Previous beneficiaries have included the local Boys' Brigade, Scout groups and local schools for art and drama purposes.

Exclusions   Only registered charities are supported. No grants to individuals.

Applications   In writing to the correspondent. Trustees meet twice a year in the spring and autumn.

Alvor Charitable Trust

Christian, humanitarian, 'social change'
£250,000 (2004)

Beneficial area UK, with a preference for Sussex, Norfolk and north east Scotland.

'Monks Wood', Tompsets Bank, Forest Row, East Sussex RH18 5LW

Correspondent   I Wilkins, Chair

Trustees   *Clive Wills; Mrs Wills; Mark Atherton; Mrs Atherton; I Wilkins; Mrs Wilkins.*

Charity Commission no. 1093890

Information available   Information was provided by the trust.

General Established in August 2002, this Christian and humanitarian charity predominately supports Christian social change projects in the UK and overseas. A proportion of its target funding goes to local projects around Sussex, Norfolk and north east Scotland where the trust has personal interests. The trust tends to support smaller projects where the grant will meet a specific need. It typically makes one large donation each year (£175,000 in 2003/04) and a number of smaller grants (around £25,000 to £50,000 in 2003/04).

In 2004 it had an income of £25,000; it funded a dozen projects with grants totalling £250,000. Assets stood at about £2 million.

Exclusions The trust does not look to support animal charities or medical charities outside of the geographic areas mentioned above.

Applications In writing to the correspondent.

Boyd Anderson Bequest

Improving amenities

About £1,000 (2004/05)

Beneficial area Lossiemouth.

Moray Council, High Street, Elgin, Moray IV30 1BX

Tel. 01343 543451 **Fax** 01343 563402

e-mail jeananne.goodbrand@moray.gov.uk

Correspondent Jean-Anne Goodbrand

Scottish Charity No. SC019068

Information available Information was provided by the trust.

General The trust operates in Lossiemouth, primarily funding improvements to local amenities. It was established in 1952. In 2004/05 the total amount distributed was around £1,000, a typical figure from year to year.

Applications In writing to the correspondent.

Angus Council Charitable Trusts

General

About £2,000

Beneficial area Angus area

Angus Council, St James's House, St James's Road, Forfar DD8 2ZE

Tel. 01307 473596 **Fax** 01307 464834

e-mail gourlays@angus.gov.uk

website www.angus.gov.uk

Correspondent Sarah Gourlay

Scottish Charity No. SC025065

Information available Information was provided by the trust.

General This is a collection of over 100 small trusts managed by the council and which give about £2,000 per year in total. Each trust has its own specific criteria and operates individually. Those trusts which consider unsolicited applications usually advertise locally when money is available. The remaining trusts tend to have councillors acting as trustees who decide how the funds should be distributed.

Applications The application process opens in October each year, with distributions occurring in early December.

The Arbroath Improvement Trust

Arts, education, young people

£5,000 (2004)

Beneficial area Arbroath and district.

7 Tarry Dykes, Arbroath, Angus DD11 1NF

Tel. 01241 878305

Correspondent A Derek Scott, Hon. Secretary & Treasurer

Trustees *Dr A W Fraser; Revd V Allen; A Smith; G M Dunlop; Dr R B Speirs; A D Massie; A Lauchlan; E F Gilbert; R C Matthew; T R R Wood; I Angus; R R Spink; Mrs S Welsh.*

Scottish Charity No. SC005622

Information available Information was provided by the trust.

General The objects of the trust as outlined in the trust's accounts are described as: 'the improvement and beautifying of the town; acquiring works of art for the art gallery; purchasing books for the benefit of local students in supplement to those provided out of the library funds; encouragement of promising pupils from the town schools in any way not provided for by the educational authorities; encouragement of youth movements; in fact, anything on these or similar lines that will make the town a better place to live in, and tend to give the inhabitants a greater pride and produce a greater interest in their native town'.

Grants usually range between £200 and £500 and in 2004 totalled £5,000 given to 28 local organisations. The trust tends to make recurrent grants. The assets of the trust stood at £143,000 and the income for the year was £7,500.

A total of £700 was distributed between seven Arbroath primary schools and £400 between two secondary schools. The other grants were all for £200. Recipients included a male voice choir, Boys' Brigade, horticultural society, swimming club and instrumental band.

Exclusions Churches and organisations with liquor licences are not considered.

Applications In writing to the correspondent providing full details of the organisation, the scheme requiring funding, costings and details of other funds sought/received. Trustees meet in March and September and applications should be received by the preceding month.

The Astor of Hever Trust

Youth, medical research, education

£35,000 (2003/04)

Beneficial area UK and worldwide, with a preference for Kent and the Grampian region of Scotland.

Frenchstreet House, Westerham, Kent TN16 1PW

Tel. 01959 565070 **Fax** 01959 561286

Correspondent Lord Astor of Hever, Trustee

Trustees *John Jacob, Third Baron Astor of Hever; Hon Camilla Astor; Hon. Philip D P Astor.*

Charity Commission no. 264134

Information available Accounts were on file at the Charity Commission.

General The trust gives grants UK-wide and internationally. It states that there is a preference for Kent and the Grampian region of Scotland, although the preference for Kent is much stronger.

When Gavin Astor, second Baron Astor of Hever, founded the trust in 1955, its main areas of support were arts, medicine, religion, education, conservation, youth and sport. Reflecting the settlor's wishes, the trust makes grants to local youth organisations, medical research and educational programmes. Most beneficiaries are UK-wide charities or a local branch.

In 2003/04 the trust had assets of £893,000 and an income of £34,000. Grants totalled £35,000 with beneficiaries including Game Conservancy Scottish Research Trust (£2,000), Airborne Initiative Scotland (£1,000), Lonach Highland & Friendly Society (£550), Alzheimer Research Trust Scotland (£250), Aberdeen International Youth Festival (£200), Grampian Society for the Blind and National Youth Orchestra of Scotland (£150 each), Haemophilia Society Scotland (£100) and Royal Scottish Agricultural Benevolent Association (£50).

Exclusions No grants to individuals.

Applications In writing to the correspondent. Unsuccessful applications are not acknowledged.

A G Bain's Trust

Older and young people, children who are disabled (in homes operated by Voluntary Services Aberdeen)

About £50,000 (2004/05)

Beneficial area Aberdeen.

2 Bon-Accord Crescent, Aberdeen AB1 2DH

Tel. 01224 587261

e-mail info@storiecs.co.uk

Correspondent J C Chisholm, Trustee

Trustees *W S Crosby; C A B Crosby; J C Chisholm.*

Scottish Charity No. SC003250

Information available Limited information was provided by the trust.

General The trust was set up in 1990 to work in the areas of the care, maintenance, welfare and education of people who are elderly or disabled in the Grampian region.

Since then, the trustees have paid the free income of the residue of the trust fund to Voluntary Service Aberdeen, with certain sums designated to particular areas of the organisation's work.

The amount donated to VSA each year is around £50,000. No other grants are made.

Exclusions No grants to organisations unconnected to Voluntary Services Aberdeen.

Applications Contact the correspondent.

Blair Charitable Trust

Historic buildings, general

£3,000 (2003/04)

Beneficial area Tayside.

Atholl Estates Office, Blair Atholl, Pitlochry, Perthshire PH18 5TH

Tel. 01796 481355 **Fax** 01796 481211

e-mail abw@atholl-estates.co.uk

Correspondent The Trustees

Trustees *Mrs S H Troughton; A Stewart; Dickinson Trust Ltd.*

Scottish Charity No. SC001433

Information available Brief information was supplied by the trust.

General The trust's main concern is 'the maintenance, repair and preservation for the public benefit of buildings of historic or architectural interest, land of scenic, historic or scientific interest, or objects of national, scientific, historic or artistic interest in its ownership'. In practice, this relates almost exclusively to Blair Castle, its grounds and estates. However, after expenditure on the castle, surplus funds can be given in grants to other charitable organisations whose purpose in general is similar to the Blair Charitable Trust, and/or are local.

In 2003/04 the total income was £373,000 with expenditure on property and relevant historic buildings totalling £205,000. Grants to other organisations during the year totalled £3,000.

Applications In writing to the correspondent.

Miss Margaret Cameron's Trust

Young people, general

About £20,000

Beneficial area Forres and the county of Moray.

Grigor & Young Solicitors, 1 North Street, Elgin, Moray IV30 1UA

Tel. 01343 544077

Correspondent Sheena Shaw

Trustees *Robert A Young; William Mennie; Grigor & Young Trustees Limited.*

Scottish Charity No. SC008910

Information available Information was provided by the trust.

General This trust operates solely in Forres and the county of Moray. It was originally established to assist young people's organisations. Whilst it now gives for a wider variety of causes, it still mainly supports organisations such as playgroups and young people's groups. It usually supports organisations rather than individuals.

Grants total around £20,000 each year, with the trust supporting a number of regular beneficiaries. These include Braille Books for Children, Samaritans, Riding for the Disabled, Sea Cadets and Noah's Ark. One-off grants are also made.

Applications In writing to the correspondent. Funds are distributed once a year.

Cash for Kids – Northsound Radio

Children

£143,000 (2004/05)

Beneficial area North east Scotland (Grampian region).

Northsound Radio, Abbotswell Road, West Tullos, Aberdeen AB12 3AJ

Tel. 01224 337000 **Fax** 01224 400003

e-mail ruth.morrison@northsound.co.uk

website www.northsound2.com

Correspondent Ruth Morrison, Coordinator

Trustees *David Johnston; James Knowles; George Ross; John Curran; Margaret Donald; Iain McKenna.*

Scottish Charity No. SCO25317

Information available Accounts were provided by the trust.

General This trust was established in 1999 by Northsound Radio to help local organisations working with young people aged 18 and under:

- with mental, physical or sensory disabilities
- with behavioural or psychological disorders
- living in poverty or situations of deprivation
- suffering through distress, abuse or neglect.

The following additional information was provided by the trust:

Cash for Kids is a local grant-making trust which last year [2004/05] raised more than £200,000. The fundraising continues and the sixth disbursements have now been awarded. There is no set limits for grant awards.

The trustees have local and voluntary sector knowledge. We may phone you or your referees to discuss your application or to ask you to send additional information.

We expect to receive many applications asking for money. You can help yourself and us by reading our information carefully and following the instructions.

Who can apply

We welcome applications from properly constituted, non-profit groups working with disadvantaged children and young people aged 18 and under throughout the Grampian area. Their work must be of clear benefit to these children and young people. They may be:

- self-help groups
- voluntary organisations
- registered charities.

We give low priority to applications from statutory services and local authorities.
Applications from schools, hospitals, social and probation services, etc. must explain why the project of work applied for should not be funded from departmental budgets.

We do give grants for individual children, but only through organisations which apply on their behalf and can vouch for the financial and other circumstances of the family.

We regret that we cannot accept applications from private individuals or parents, nor from social workers or other welfare professionals on behalf of their clients.

In 2004/05 the trust had an income of £215,000 and made grants totalling £143,000. Beneficiaries

during the year included 55th Aberdeen Boys' Brigade, Aberdeen and North-East Deaf Society, Aberdeenshire Disability Sport, Ashgrove Children's Centre, Boddam Playgroup, Cornhill After School Project, Friends of Hazlewood, Home Start in Aberdeen, Marchburn Infant School, Printfield Community Project, St Machar Parent Support Group, Special Needs Youth Club, Take a Break Respite Care, Victoria Road School Toy Library and Woodside After School Playgroup.

Exclusions Grants will not be given for:

- trips and projects abroad
- medical treatment or medical research
- unspecified expenditure
- deficit funding or repayment of loans
- distribution to other organisations
- retrospective funding of projects which will take place before applications can be processed
- projects which are unable to start within 12 months
- the relief of statutory responsibilities.

Applications On an application form available from the correspondent. Guidelines on completing the form are also available. Applications must be received by 31 March.

Mrs Edith Beattie Dundas Trust

Community
About £7,000 a year

Beneficial area Arbroath.

c/o Connelly & Yeoman, 78 High Street, Arbroath, Angus DD11 1HL

Tel. 01241 434200 **Fax** 01241 434100

Correspondent D J Mackintosh

Scottish Charity No. SC015213

Information available Information was provided by the trust.

General The trust states it will give grants in Arbroath for improving amenities and the social and cultural activities of the town. Grants are available for the benefit of individuals and organisations within the town. About £7,000 is available each year to be given in grants, although the trust may accumulate funds and therefore spend more in the following years.

Applications In writing to the correspondent. Applications must arrive by 1 August each year.

The Ellis Campbell Foundation

Youth, education, conservation

£62,000 (2003/04)

Beneficial area Hampshire, Perth and Kinross/ Tayside.

Shalden Park Steading, Shalden, Alton, Hampshire GU34 4DS

Tel. 01256 381821 **Fax** 01256 381921

e-mail mdccc@elliscampbell.co.uk

Correspondent Michael Campbell, Trustee

Trustees *Michael Campbell, Chair; Mrs Linda Campbell; Mrs Doris Campbell; Jamie Campbell; Mrs Alexandra Andrew; Laura Campbell; Trevor Aldridge.*

Charity Commission no. 802717

Information available Information was provided by the trust.

General Trustees normally stipulate that recipients must be based in Hampshire, Perth and Kinross or Tayside. One-off and recurrent grants are considered. The trust aims to support organisations concerned with the education of disadvantaged people under 25, encouragement of rural community-based projects and preservation of historic buildings.

In 2004 the trust had assets of £1 million and an income of £60,000. Grants were made totalling £62,000.

In 2003 grants ranged from £25 to £10,000, with typical grants being from £500 to £1,000. In total the trust received 164 applications of which 70 were successful. Grants were broken down as in the table below.

Grants included: £20,000 to The Scottish Community Foundation who vet Perthshire/ Tayside applications and make grants on the trust's behalf; £10,000 to the Jubilee Sailing Trust; £5,000 each to Treloar Trust and Game Conservancy Trust; £3,000 to Community Foundation for Hampshire; £2,000 to Mary Rose Trust and Fairbridge; £1,500 to Canine Partners; and £1,000 each to Surrey Scouts, Hampshire and Isle of Wight Youth Options, Alzheimer's Society, The CP Centre, Hampledon PCC Roof Appeal and North Hampshire Medical Fund.

A number of grants the trust makes are committed on an annual basis.

Exclusions No grants to individuals. Other than the grants made annually over a period, no grants will be made more regularly than every other year. No funding for annual running costs.

Applications In writing to the correspondent. Trustees meet in April and November. Applications should be submitted before the preceding month and will only be acknowledged if they fall strictly within the trust's eligibility guidelines.

David Gordon Memorial Trust

Arts, youth work, Christian, community centres

£12,000 a year

Beneficial area Former Grampian region only.

89 Beaconsfield Place, Aberdeen AB15 4AD

Correspondent Ms B L MacFarlane

Scottish Charity No. SC002664

THE ELLIS CAMPBELL FOUNDATION
Grants 2003

	Education		Heritage		Other		Youth		Community	
	No.	Total	No.	Total	No.	Total	No.	Total	No.	Total
Hampshire	6	£8,000	2	£2,000	17	£9,000	7	£8,900	nil	
Other areas	nil		1	£100	25	£5,550	5	£3,300	nil	
Perthshire and Scotland	1	£1,000	2	£80	2	£750	1	£50	nil	
Scottish Community Foundation	nil		nil		nil		nil		1	£20,000
Total	7	£9,000	5	£3,000	44	£15,300	13	£12,250	1	£20,000

Information available Information was provided by the trust.

General The trust supports the following:

- music, drama and the arts
- Christian ecumenical church services
- community centres for social welfare
- youth work.

It has about £12,000 to give in grants. Further information was unavailable.

Applications In writing to the correspondent. The trustees meet in November, which is when most of the grants are dispersed. The finance committee meets an additional two or three times a year, when emergency grants can be considered.

The Neil Gow Charitable Trust

Poverty, homelessness, community

£1,200 (2003/04)

Beneficial area Perth and Kinross.

Messrs Miller Hendry, 10 Blackfriars Street, Perth PH1 5NS

Tel. 01738 637311 **Fax** 01738 638685

Correspondent A G Dorward

Trustees *Robert William Young; Harry Robertson; Alastair Gilmour Doward.*

Information available Accounts were provided by the trust.

General The trust makes grants to local organisations for the relief of poverty and gives annuities to individuals living in Perth and Kinross for relief-in-need purposes.

In 2003/04 the trust had assets of £207,000 and an income of £12,000. Charitable expenditure totalled £9,400, including £8,300 in annuities and £1,200 in donations to organisations. Grants were £500 to Perth Indigent Old Men's Society, £350 to Perth and Kinross Council – The Go Project and £300 to Association for Improving the Condition of the Poor in Perth.

Applications In writing to the correspondent.

Grampian Police Diced Cap Charitable Fund

Charitable and needy causes

£35,000 a year

Beneficial area Within the Grampian police force area only.

Queen Street, Aberdeen AB10 1ZA

Correspondent The Secretary

Scottish Charity No. SC017901

Information available Limited information was available on this trust.

General The total given in grants varies year on year, but have totalled around £35,000.

Donations are made to needy causes who apply for funds to be used within the force area.

Exclusions National charities and those outside the beneficial area cannot be supported.

Applications In writing to the correspondent.

The Guildry Incorporation of Perth

Education, local community

£29,000 to organisations (2004/05)

Beneficial area Perth.

42 George Street, Perth, Perthshire PH1 5JL

Tel. 01738 623195

Correspondent Lorna Peacock, Secretary

Trustees *Dean and eight comittee members.*

Scottish Charity No. SC008072

Information available Information was provided by the trust.

General The main purpose of the trust is to provide support for its members and their families by way of educational bursaries and pensions.

In 2004/05 it had an income of £172,000 and distributed £79,000 in donations, pensions and bursaries. These were broken down as follows:

Charitable donations	£29,000
Weekly pensions	£18,000
Bursaries	£15,000
Quarterly pensions	£8,500
Coal allowances	£5,000
School prizes	£4,500

Applications In writing to the correspondent. The trust meets to consider grants on the last Tuesday of every month.

The Mary Jamieson Hall and John F Hall Trust

Social welfare

See below

Beneficial area Aberdeen and surrounding area.

Messrs Gray & Kellas, 12 Bon Accord Crescent, Aberdeen AB11 6XG

Tel. 01224 586301 **Fax** 01224 571705

Trustees *P G R Saxon; J H Gray; J Birnie; J P Grant.*

Scottish Charity No. SC007754

Information available Information was provided by the trust.

General This trust continues to make twice yearly grants to ex-employees of Hall and Tawse Scotland Ltd in Aberdeen, or their families. More recently, however, it has decided to allocate funds to certain educational establishments and as such has not been making annual awards to local charities.

As a consequence, the trust believes 'It would therefore be misleading to suggest that the trust has available funds to disperse to applicants and indeed our preference would be to have no entry in your guide and thus avoid receiving requests which will ultimately be unsuccessful'.

Applications See above.

The Patrick Mitchell Hunter Fund

General

About £10,000 a year

Beneficial area Aberdeen only.

Wilsone & Duffus, PO Box 81, 7 Golden Square, Aberdeen AB10 1EP

Tel. 01224 651700 **Fax** 01224 647329

e-mail info@wilsoneduffus.co.uk

Correspondent The Administrator

Trustees *W Howie; B Lindsey; Mary Fettes.*

Scottish Charity No. SC017380

Information available Limited information was provided by the trust.

General This trust supports charities in Aberdeen. Grants range from £250 to £1,000, and total about £10,000 each year.

Exclusions Grants are not given to individuals or organisations which are not based in Aberdeen.

Applications In writing to the correspondent.

The Kincardineshire Educational Trust Scheme

Education

£4,000 to organisations and individuals (2004/05)

Beneficial area The former county of Kincardineshire.

Finance Section, Aberdeenshire Council, St Leonard's, Sandyhill Road, Banff, Aberdeenshire AB45 1BH

Tel. 01261 813334 **Fax** 01261 813332

e-mail tracy.bremner@aberdeenshire.gov.uk

Correspondent Mrs Tracy Bremner

Scottish Charity No. SC028381

Information available Information was provided by the trust.

General The trust makes educational grants to people resident in the former county of

Kincardineshire, including pupils or students whose parents are resident in the former county. (Educational grants include, for example, apprentices, postgraduate scholarships, bursaries, travel grants and for further education – for more information about grants to individuals, see the *Educational Grants Directory*, also published by the Directory of Social Change.)

Grants are also made to Kincardineshire schools and further education centres, as well as to clubs and organisations benefiting people in the area.

In 2004/05 the trust had an income of £4,200, almost all or which was given in grants during the year. Information on beneficiaries was not available.

Grants can be given:

- to assist in providing and maintaining playing fields and other sporting facilities including equipment
- to schools and further education centres to assist in providing special equipment
- to clubs, societies and organisations which include amongst their activities work of an educational nature
- to schools and organisations to assist education in art, music and drama
- to individuals and organisations to undertake education experiments and research which will be for the benefit of the people of the former county of Kincardineshire. Help may also be given towards 'regional and national enterprises of an educational nature'.

The trust sees all the grants it awards as a minimal contribution to the total cost of a project.

Applications On a form available from Amanda Watson at the address above (tel: 01224 813335; email: amanda.watson@ aberdeenshire.gov.uk.

Full guidelines are also available upon request.

Leng Charitable Trust

General

£180,000 (2004)

Beneficial area Tayside, but primarily Dundee and to major national Scottish charities.

Thorntons Law LLP, 50 Castle Street, Dundee DD1 3RU

Tel. 01382 229111 **Fax** 01382 202288

e-mail afmcdonald@thorntons-law.co.uk

Correspondent A F McDonald, Trustee

Trustees *A F McDonald; J S Fair; Dr J Wood; Thorntons Trustees Ltd.*

Scottish Charity No. SC009285

Information available Information was provided by the trust.

General This trust supports organisations working in Tayside, primarily Dundee. It will also support 'significant national Scottish causes' with a Tayside involvement. It gives to a wide range of causes including the arts, education, health, social welfare and the environment. In 2004 it had assets of £5.6 million and an income of £200,000. Grants totalled £180,000. Information on beneficiaries was not available.

Exclusions Grants are not given to individuals, overseas projects, political or religious appeals or for sports or recreation.

Applications In writing to the correspondent. Trustees meet to consider grants in January, May and September.

The Mathew Trust

General

£137,000 to organisations (2003/04)

Beneficial area City of Dundee, Angus, Perth & Kinross and Fife.

Henderson Loggie, Chartered Accountants, Royal Exchange, Panmure Street, Dundee DD1 1DZ

Tel. 01382 201234 **Fax** 01382 221240

e-mail fbullions@hendersonloggie.co.uk

Correspondent Fiona Bullions

Trustees *D B Grant, Chair; G S Lowden; A F McDonald; Prof. P Howie; The Lord Provost of the City of Dundee.*

Scottish Charity No. SC016284

Information available Accounts were provided by the trust.

General The trust makes grants and loans for:

- the advancement of the education of adults in the following local government areas: City of Dundee, Angus, Perth and Kinross, and Fife
- the advancement of the vocational and professional training of such people
- the relief of poverty by providing assistance in the recruitment of such people who are

unemployed, or who are likely to become unemployed in the near future.

In 2003/04 the trust had assets of £5.4 million and an income of £188,000. Grants to organisations totalled £137,000, an increase on the £26,000 distributed in the previous year, although grant totals have reached around £450,000 in previous years.

Grants were made to 14 organisations during the year. Beneficiaries were Institute of Cardiovascular Research (£50,000), Dundee University Association (£36,000), Wellcome Trust Biocentre (£25,000), Helm Training Limited and Dundee Science Centre (£5,000 each), Sir James Caird's Travelling Scholarships Trust (£4,000), Macmillan Cancer Relief, Fairbridge in Scotland and Perth Six Circle Project (£2,500 each), University of Dundee Botanical Gardens & Grounds (£2,000), Dundee Blind & Partially Sighted Society (£1,500) and Boys' and Girls' Clubs of Scotland, Dundee International Women's Centre and HOPE (£1,000 each).

Applications   In writing to the correspondent.

Mrs Williamina McLaren's Trust Fund

People who are poor, disabled, infirm or in need

About £9,000 a year

Beneficial area Angus.

Thorntons Law LLP, 53 East High Street, Forfar, Angus DD8 2EL

Tel. 01307 466886 **Fax** 01307 464643

Correspondent   J M G Blair

Scottish Charity No. SC003233

Information available   Limited information was provided by the trust.

General   The trust gives only to organisations recognised as charities which assist people in need in Angus. Grants total about £9,000 each year. No further information was available.

Exclusions   No grants to individuals. Only recognised Scottish charities are supported.

Applications   On a form available from the correspondent.

The Mollison Fund

Social welfare

About £9,000

Beneficial area City of Aberdeen.

Craigens Solicitors, 13 Bon-Accord Crescent, Aberdeen AB11 6NN

Tel. 01224 588295 **Fax** 01224 575400

Correspondent   D J Crombie

Trustees   *Douglas Watson; Mrs Doris Meston; Laurence Reid.*

Scottish Charity No. SC002300

Information available   Information was provided by the trust.

General   The trust's deed stipulates it must fund Belmedie Eventide Home and Endowment Fund for Cornhill Hospital. The remaining income is given to social welfare charities in Aberdeen. About £9,000 is given in total each year in grants.

Exclusions   The trust's deed states that applicants must not receive any central or local authority funding. Applicants are required to certify this in their application.

Applications   In writing to the correspondent. The trustees meet in June/July each year; applications should be submitted by the end of May.

Moray Council Charitable Trusts

Education

About £35,000 (2004/05)

Beneficial area Morayshire, Nairnshire and Banffshire.

Educational Services, Moray Council, High Street, Elgin, Moray IV30 1BX

Tel. 01343 563151 **Fax** 01343 563402

e-mail jeananne.goodbrand@moray.gov.uk

Correspondent   Jean-Anne Goodbrand

Information available   Information taken from the council's website.

General   The council administers a number of small trusts, mainly for the benefit of individuals.

Two trusts, however, can also consider applications from local organisations which seek to run educational projects for local children and young people, such as schools, after-school clubs and playgroups:

Banffshire Educational Trust

Grants can be given for the purchase of specialist school equipment, sports equipment and facilities and the promotion of education in drama, music and visual arts.

Moray & Nairn Educational Trust

Grants can be given to organisations for the purchase of specialist equipment and sports facilities.

Applications On a form available from the correspondent.

Miss Gertrude Pattullo Advancement Award Scheme

Young people aged 16 to 25 who are physically disabled

£2,700 to organisations and individuals
(2003/04)

Beneficial area Dundee and Angus.

Help Unit, Blackadders Solicitors, 30 & 34 Reform Street, Dundee DD1 1RJ

Tel. 01382 229222 **Fax** 01382 342220

e-mail beth.anderson@blackadders.co.uk

Correspondent Beth Anderson

Trustees *C F S Williamson; D N Gordon; D Sneddon.*

Scottish Charity No. SC000811

Information available Information was provided by the trust.

General This trust operates in Dundee and Angus for the benefit of 16 to 25 year olds who are physically disabled. It operates by:

- awarding grants for the advancement in life of physically handicapped children and young persons including the payment of fees for special training and the purchase of books and equipment

- providing grants to enable physically handicapped young persons to establish themselves in a trade or profession for which they appear to be particularly suited
- paying subsistence grants to physically handicapped children and young people during their period of training for any trade or profession
- contributing to any scheme, trust, organisation or other body, other than those controlled or administered by a public or local authority, whose aims are similar to the purposes of the trust.

In 2003/04 the trust had assets of £105,000 and an income of £4,300 and a total expenditure of £2,400. Grants were made to organisations and individuals totalling £2,700.

Beneficiaries included Prince's Scottish Youth Business Trust (£500) and Sense Scotland (£250).

Applications On a form available from the correspondent at any time.

Miss Gertrude Pattullo Trust For Handicapped Boys

Boys aged 18 or under who are physically disabled

£4,200 to organisations and individuals
(2003/04)

Beneficial area Dundee and Angus.

Help Unit, Blackadders Solicitors, 30 & 34 Reform Street, Dundee DD1 1RJ

Tel. 01382 229222 **Fax** 01382 342220

e-mail beth.anderson@blackadders.co.uk

Correspondent Beth Anderson

Trustees *C F S Williamson; D N Gordon; D Sneddon.*

Scottish Charity No. SC015505

Information available Information was provided by the trust.

General This trust supports boys aged 18 or under in Dundee and Angus who are physically disabled by providing grants ranging from £100 to £1,000 each. It achieves this by:

- making financial provision for such medical service appliances and comforts as may be required by physically handicapped boys and are not obtainable under the National Health Service facilities available at the time

- making financial provision whereby physically handicapped boys may enjoy a holiday in suitable surroundings with such nursing or other attention as their condition may require
- making grants to physically handicapped boys for the purposes of obtaining clothes and other necessaries
- contributing to any scheme, trust, organisation or other body, other than those controlled or administered by a public or local authority, whose aims are similar to the purpose of the trust.

In 2003/04 it had assets of £105,000 and an income of £4,700. Grants were made to individuals and organisations totalling £4,200. Beneficiaries included Angus Special Playscheme (£500) and Disability Aid Fund (£400).

Applications On a form available from the correspondent.

Miss Gertrude Pattullo Trust For Handicapped Girls

Girls aged under 18 who are physically disabled

£3,600 to organisations and individuals (2003/04)

Beneficial area Dundee and Angus.

Help Unit, Blackadders Solicitors, 30 & 34 Reform Street, Dundee DD1 1RJ

Tel. 01382 229222 **Fax** 01382 342220

e-mail beth.anderson@blackadders.co.uk

Correspondent Beth Anderson

Trustees *C F S Williamson; D N Gordon; D Sneddon.*

Scottish Charity No. SC011829

Information available Information was provided by the trust.

General This trust operates in Dundee and Angus benefiting girls aged 18 or under who are physically disabled by giving grants generally ranging from £100 to £1,000 each. It achieves its aims by:

- making financial provision for such medical services, appliances and comforts as may be required by

physically handicapped girls and are not obtainable under the National Health Service facilities available at the time

- making financial provision whereby physically handicapped girls may enjoy a holiday in suitable surroundings with such nursing or other attention as their condition may require
- making grants to physically handicapped girls for the purpose of obtaining clothing and other necessaries
- contributing to any scheme, trust, organisation or other body, other than those controlled or administered by a public or local authority, whose aims are similar to the purposes of this trust.

In 2003/04 the trust had assets of £141,500 and an income of £6,000. Grants were made to individuals and organisations totalling £3,600. Beneficiaries included Barnardo's and Dundee Congregational Church (£250 each) and Ward Road Gym (£200).

Applications On a form available from the correspondent, at any time.

Perth & Kinross District Council Charitable Trusts

General
See below

Beneficial area Perth & Kinross district.

Perth & Kinross Grants Direct, 2 High Street, Perth PH1 5PH

Tel. 08456 052000

e-mail enquiries@pkgrantsdirect.com

website www.pkgrantsdirect.com

Trustees *Perth & Kinross Charitable Trusts*

Scottish Charity No. SC019658

Information available Information was provided by the council.

General In October 2005 we were informed by the council that its charitable trusts have been inactive during the past couple of years for several reasons. However, it appears that various issues have now been resolved, and the council is preparing to resume distributing charitable funds to organisations, although how much and for what purposes was still uncertain. The advice from the council was that potential applicants should call Perth & Kinross Grants Direct for up-to-date information on available funds.

Visitors to Perth & Kinross Grants Direct's website can also access information on other sources of funding from the council, including downloading the information sheet, *Financial Assistance to the Voluntary Sector – A Guide.*

Applications Contact Perth & Kinross Grants Direct for further information.

The Thomas Primrose Trust

General

£8,000 (2004/05)

Beneficial area The City of Aberdeen.

100 Union Street, Aberdeen AB10 1QR

Tel. 01224 428000 **Fax** 01224 644479

Correspondent Alan J Innes, Trustee

Trustees *A J Innes; Miss B L McFarlane.*

Scottish Charity No. SC004048

Information available Information was provided by the trust.

General The trust awards grants to organisations of a 'philanthropic, benevolent, charitable or educational character and objects connected with the City of Aberdeen'. Organisations must be non-sectarian and non-political in their constitution and management.

In 2004/05 the trust gave grants totalling £8,000. Grants ranged from £100 to £1,500. Beneficiaries included Aberdeen Care and Repair Group, Alzheimer's Scotland – Action on Dementia, North East of Scotland Music School, Voluntary Service Aberdeen to the crisis fund and the fuel fund. A few grants were recurrent.

Exclusions Organisations must not be supported by rates, taxes or from public funds or sources. Grants are not given to individuals.

Applications In writing to the correspondent. Trustees meet in once a year, in November.

Sight And Hearing New Experiences Fund

Education and welfare of sensory impaired children and young people

Not known

Beneficial area Dundee and surrounding areas.

8 Jedburgh Road, Dundee DD2 1BP

Correspondent The Chair

Scottish Charity No. SC026326

Information available Limited information was provided by the trust.

General The fund works with children and young people who have sensory impairment. It assists with improving education and general welfare, and will make grants to other organisations working in the same field.

Applications In writing to the correspondent.

Miss Margaret J Stephen's Charitable Trust

General

About £6,000

Beneficial area Mainly Dundee.

Maclay Murray & Spens, 151 St Vincent Street, Glasgow G2 5NJ

Tel. 0141 248 5011 **Fax** 0141 248 5019

Correspondent The Trustees

Trustees *P J R Miller; G R G Graham.*

Scottish Charity No. SC017487

Information available Information was provided by the trust.

General The trust will support a wide range of organisations with a strong preference for Dundee. There also appears to be a preference for health and welfare causes. It gives about £6,000 in grants each year, ranging from £500 to £1,000 each. Recent beneficiaries have included Chest, Heart & Stroke Association, Crossroads Care

Attendants Scheme and Girl Guides Association, all in Dundee.

Past beneficiaries have included Dundee School Exchange for Muscular Dystrophy, The Good Shepherd Sisters, Scottish Council on Alcohol and Tayside Mountain Rescue Association.

Individuals can also be supported, but it is not the policy of the current trustees to do so.

Applications In writing to the correspondent. Trustees meet once a year in March to consider grants.

The Verden Sykes Trust

See below

£14,000 (2004/05)

Beneficial area Aberdeen.

20 Forvie Circle, Bridge of Don, Aberdeen AB22 8TA

Tel. 01224 704907

e-mail merrilees.forvie@btinternet.com

Correspondent Mrs Irene Merrilees, Administrator

Trustees *R Ellis; Dr James Merrilees; Mrs I Merrilees; Mrs A McCallum; Miss Anne Watt; A McRobb; Mrs Margaret Petrie.*

Scottish Charity No. SC007281

Information available Accounts were provided by the trust.

General The trust has a wide brief, but primarily supports:

- churches and Christian missions, especially Kirk of St Nicholas' in Aberdeen
- religious education and music
- pensions to retired ministers.

It can also support:

- education for children and adults
- work with young people
- the welfare of elderly and infirm people
- scientific research into disease and physical and mental disability
- the relief of poverty and the effects of natural disasters in any part of the world.

The trust supports projects mainly in Scotland, especially in Aberdeen. It can also give in the UK and supports UK-based organisations which work overseas. However, please note that applications are only invited from Aberdeen. The trust gives one-off grants for specific projects and not for capital costs. A few individuals are supported, however only if they are working with a registered charity.

In 2004/05 the trust had assets of £349,000 and an income of £17,000. It gave 27 grants totalling £14,000, ranging from £100 to £1,500. There were five donations of £1,000 or more. Beneficiaries were Northern Area Council – Orkney trip (£1,500), Aberdeen Cyrenians (£1,250) and Partnership, Pillar Aberdeen and Nairn URC – organ replacement (£1,000 each).

Smaller grants were made in the range of £100 to £750. Beneficiaries included Help Society, Kaleidoscope, Marie Curie Cancer Care, Oldmachar Academy Ceilidh Band, Penumbra, Salvation Army Music School, SPLORE and Wheelchair Loan Service.

Exclusions Applications from the Aberdeen area only. Normally only registered charities are supported.

Applications An application form is available from the correspondent. The trust is looking for the following details:

- objectives of the organisation
- structure and management
- method for meeting goals
- funding and budgeting.

Where additional information is included this should be restricted to one side of A4. Audited accounts should be included when available. Trustees meet three times a year in February, June and November. Applications should be submitted by the second week of the preceding month.

The Arthur & Margaret Thompson Charitable Trust

General

£142,000 (2004/05)

Beneficial area The towns or burghs of Kinross and Milnathort.

Miller Hendry, 10 Blackfriars Street, Perth PH1 5NS

Tel. 01738 637311 **Fax** 01738 638685

e-mail info@miller-hendry.co.uk

Correspondent   Alastair Dorward

Trustees   *Dr D P Anderson;
Revd Dr J P L Munro; J Greig; D L Sands;
A G Dorward; I D Donaldson.*

Scottish Charity No. SC012103

Information available   Accounts were provided by the trust.

General   The trust supports 'charitable institutions, societies and/or indigent persons connected with the Town or Burgh of Kinross and its immediate neighbourhood at the discretion of the trustees'.

In 2004/05 it had assets of £2.9 million and an income of £130,000. Grants made during the year totalled £142,000.

No information was available on beneficiaries during the year.

Applications   The trustees meet to consider applications about every four months.

D C Thomson Charitable Trust

General

Around £20,000 (2005)

Beneficial area Dundee and Tayside.

William Thomson & Sons, 22 Meadowside, Dundee DD1 1LN

Tel. 01382 201534 **Fax** 01382 227654

e-mail idouglas@wtandsons.co.uk

Correspondent   Irene Douglas

Trustees   *D C Thomson & Co. Ltd; W D C & F Thomson Ltd.*

Scottish Charity No. SC018413

Information available   Accounts are available from the trust for £10.

General   This trust is connected to the Northwood Charitable Trust and was founded by D C Thomson & Company.

The trust has previously stated that grants total around £20,000 each year and donations range from £100 to £6,000. Recurrent grants are made mainly to local organisations working in social welfare, the arts, youth and disability.

Beneficiaries receiving regular support include British Blind Sport, Operation Shipshape – RRS

Discovery Appeal, Scottish Commonwealth Games Youth Trust, Scottish Fisheries Museum Trust and Talking Newspaper Association.

Exclusions   No grants to individuals.

Applications   The trust states that no applications will be considered or acknowledged.

The A F Wallace Charity Trust

General, older people

£34,000 to individuals and organisations (2003/04)

Beneficial area UK, with a preference for north east Scotland.

NCL Investments Ltd, Bartlett House, 9–12 Basinghall Street, London EC2V 5NS

Tel. 020 7600 2801

Correspondent   S J Thornton

Trustees   *Falconer Alexander Wallace; Alistair James Wishart Falconer Wallace.*

Charity Commission no. 207110

Information available   Information was provided by the trust.

General   This trust has general charitable purposes, particularly supporting older people in the Upper Donside area of west Aberdeenshire. The Wallace family originated in Aberdeenshire and the trustees try to reflect this in their grantmaking.

In 2003/04 the trust had assets of £928,000 and an income of £52,000. Grants were made totalling £34,000. The grants were £19,000 to senior citizens in the Upper Donside area of west Aberdeenshire, £10,000 to former employees of Bombay Burmah Trading Corporation and £5,000 towards other charitable purposes.

Applications   In writing to the correspondent.

Central Scotland

The Appletree Trust

Disability, sickness, poverty

About £30,000 (2005)

Beneficial area UK and overseas, with a preference for Scotland and the north east Fife district.

Royal Bank of Scotland plc, Trust & Estate Services, 2 Festival Square, Edinburgh EH3 9SU

Tel. 0131 523 2648 **Fax** 0131 228 9889

Trustees *The Royal Bank of Scotland plc; Revd W McKane; Revd Dr J D Martin; Revd L R Brown.*

Scottish Charity No. SC004851

Information available Accounts are available from the trust for the prohibitive cost of almost £30.

General This trust was established in the will of the late William Brown Moncour in 1982 to relieve disability, sickness and poverty. The settlor recommended that Action Research for the Crippled Child, British Heart Foundation and National Society for Cancer Relief should receive funding from his trust, particularly for their work in the north east Fife district.

In previous years the trust's annual grant total has been around £30,000. Unfortunately we were unable to view the latest accounts for this trust as the administrators required a £30 'administration fee'.

Previous beneficiaries include Home-Start, British Heart Foundation, Children's Hospice Association, Marie Curie Cancer Care, Rymonth Housing Association, Arthritis Care – Scotland, Prince's Trust and British Wireless for the Blind.

Exclusions No grants to individuals.

Applications In writing to the correspondent. Trustees meet to consider grants in April.

The Bruce Charitable Trust

Community work

£8,500 (2004/05)

Beneficial area Cupar, Fife.

James Murray & Co., Chartered Accountants, 58 Bonnygate, Cupar, Fife KY15 4LD

Tel. 01334 654044 **Fax** 01334 654873

e-mail info@jamesmurray.co.uk

Correspondent Gordon Lindsay, Trustee

Trustees *P W Hutchison; G Lindsay; Ms Elizabeth L Calderwood; Ms Loretta Mordi.*

Scottish Charity No. SC014927

Information available Accounts were provided by the trust.

General The trust's purposes (confined to the borough of Cupar) are to support:

1. Poor, aged, infirm or distressed people and charities or organisations providing assistance to, or facilities for, such people.

2. The creation or maintenance of youth organisations which provide cultural or recreational facilities for young people and creation and maintenance of other organisations which exist for the welfare of young people.

3. Holidays or convalescing facilities at home or abroad for people who are suffering from or recovering from illness or disability and whose circumstances are such that they are unable to meet the cost of holidays or periods of convalescence.

4. Cultural, educational and recreational facilities and any project which the trustees may consider for the benefit of the community.

In 2004/05 the trust had an income of £54,000 and made 26 grants totalling £8,500. All grants, except one, were for £500 or less. The beneficiary of this larger grant was Fife Council Social Work Department (£1,000).

Other beneficiaries included Cupar and District Scouts, Cupar Youth Cafe, Diamonds Cheerleading Squad, Fieldfare Trust, Haemophilia Society, Howe of Fife Rugby Club, Marie Curie Cancer Care, Scottish Adoption Association, Sir Douglas Bader Garden for the Disabled and Scottish Blind Golf Society.

Applications In writing to the correspondent at any time.

The Carnegie Dunfermline Trust

Social, recreational or cultural facilities

£103,000 (2004)

Beneficial area Dunfermline and Rosyth.

Abbey Park House, Abbey Park Place, Dunfermline KY12 7PB

Tel. 01383 723638 **Fax** 01383 721862

e-mail admin@carnegietrust.com

Correspondent The Chief Executive

Trustees *Dr D M Fraser, Chair; A M Hogg Vice-Chair; plus 13 other life trustees, 4 trustees appointed by Fife Council and 2 honorary trustees.*

Scottish Charity No. SC015710

Information available The trust publishes a very comprehensive annual report and guidance notes for applicants.

General 'The trust was founded in August 1903. In Mr Carnegie's original instructions to the Gentlemen of the Commission, he said the endowment was 'all to be used in attempts to bring into the monotonous lives of the toiling masses of Dunfermline more of sweetness and light ... some elevating conditions of life ... that the child of my native town, looking back in after years, however far from home it may have roamed, will feel simply by virtue of being such life has been made happier and better. If this be the fruit of your labours you will have succeeded; if not, you will have failed ... I have said your work is experimental ... If you can prove that good can be done you open new fields to the rich which I am certain they are to be more and more anxious to find for their surplus wealth ... Remember you are pioneers, and do not be afraid of making mistakes; those who never make

mistakes never make anything. Try many things freely, but discard just as freely ... As conditions of life change rapidly, you will not be restricted as to your plans or the scope of your activities'.

The trust states: 'Grants can usually be given to any non-profit making organisation which is properly constituted. They can also be given as pump-priming or start-up grants.

'Your club, organisation or school must be based in Dunfermline or Rosyth. Outwith these areas help is restricted to Cairneyhill, Crossford and Limekilns Primary Schools and Inverkeithing High School.

'Support is given, for example, to projects in arts, music, entertainment, education, play, sport, recreation, local history, local research, heritage, tourism, welfare etc.

'New or innovative projects are especially welcome as are schemes to help young people and those disadvantaged.'

In 2004 the trust had assets of £9.7 million, which generated an income of £310,000. Grants were made totalling £103,000, broken down as follows:

Band concerts/competitions	£5,000
Clubs and organisations (other than sporting)	£4,000
Community projects	£23,000
Museum: Andrew Carnegie birthplace	£20,000
Music in homes and hospitals	£2,000
Sport	£12,000
Theatre/music/dance	£3,000
Youth: outings	£2,000
Youth: Guides/Scouts/Boys' Brigade	£2,000
Youth: high schools	£4,500
Youth: primary schools	£25,500

Projects receiving support included: Peace in the Park – Dunfermline, which received funding to enable the broadcast of a visit by the Dalai Lama, who participated in a range of events, to surrounding crowds (£10,000); Head in the Clouds, which received support for a number of school workshops aimed at inspiring an interest in science and technology (£7,000); City First, which received support for an ice skating rink at Christmas in Pittencrieff Park (£5,000); Gig in the Glen, which received funding for an event during Dunfermline Civic Week at which local young bands performed (£3,500); Dunfermline Fencing Club, which received a grant to replace protective equipment for youngsters (£700).

Exclusions No grants for:
- individuals
- closed clubs (i.e. groups not open to the general

public to join – this does not exclude minority groups catering for specialised interests)

- political organisations or causes, commercial enterprises, religious or sectarian bodies, or military or warlike pursuits
- organisations which simply want help with maintenance and running costs; the trustees think these should be met out of subscription income. Exceptions might be made in special cases or for new bodies
- projects which have already been started
- overseas projects
- health and medical organisations.

Applications By letter at any time, an sae is not required. Initial telephone calls are welcome. Application forms and guidelines available.

Falkirk Temperance Trust

Alcohol, drug and sustance abuse related projects

About £1,000 to £5,000

Beneficial area The former burgh of Falkirk.

Falkirk Council, Municipal Buildings, Falkirk FK1 5RS

Tel. 01324 506070 **Fax** 01324 506363

Correspondent A Jannetta, Director of Finance

Trustees *Three elected members are appointed to the trust.*

Scottish Charity No. SC001904

Information available Information was provided by the trust.

General The trust gives grants to address alcohol, drug and other substance abuse related projects. Organisations and individuals are supported in the former burgh of Falkirk. The grant total is about £1,000 to £5,000 each year. Grants usually range from £1,000 to £2,000 each. Most grants are given to organisations.

Applications In writing to the correspondent. Apply at any time.

Fife Council/Common Good Funds and Trusts (East)

Individuals in need, community groups

£72,000 (2004/05)

Beneficial area East Fife.

Fife Council, County Buildings, St Catherine Street, Cupar, Fife KY15 4TA

Tel. 01334 412914 **Fax** 01334 412940

Correspondent Mike J Melville, Team Leader (Administration)

Scottish Charity No. SC019393

Information available Information was provided by the council.

General The Common Good Funds and Trusts (East) administered by Fife Council is a collection of about 100 small trusts. Both individuals in need and local community groups can be supported, for example community councils, sports clubs and so on. The following types of causes will be considered:

- arts
- buildings
- conservation/environment
- disability
- education/training
- heritage
- hospitals/hospices
- social welfare, people of all ages
- sports/recreation.

Most towns and large villages in East Fife feature in the beneficial area of this collection of trusts, details of which can be obtained from the correspondent.

In 2004/05 the combined funds and trusts had assets of £435,000 and an income of £190,000. Grants were made totalling £72,000. The size of the grant depends on the individual trusts.

Exclusions The following causes are not supported:

- animal welfare
- medical/health and medical research
- overseas projects
- political appeals
- religious appeals.

Applications Contact the correspondent for further details. An application form and guidelines are available for the Common Good Funds but not for the trusts. Applications can be made at any time.

The George McLean Trust

Disability

£33,500 to organisations and individuals (2004/05)

Beneficial area Tayside and Fife.

Help Unit, Blackadders Solicitors, 30 & 34 Reform Street, Dundee DD1 1RJ

Tel. 01382 229222 **Fax** 01382 342220

e-mail beth.anderson@blackadders.co.uk

Correspondent Beth Anderson

Trustees *C F S Williamson; D N Gordon; D Sneddon.*

Scottish Charity No. SC020963

Information available Information was provided by the trust.

General Grants of between £100 and £1,000 are given to local disability organisations. In 2004/05 it had assets of £786,000 and an income of £29,000. Grants were made to organisations and individuals totalling £33,500.

Beneficiaries included Tayside Association for the Deaf, Perth and Kinross Council and Forfar Group – Driving for the Disabled.

Applications On a form available from the correspondent.

The Annie Ramsay McLean Trust for the Elderly

Health, older people

About £12,000 to organisations

Beneficial area Tayside and Fife.

Help Unit, Blackadders Solicitors, 30 & 34 Reform Street, Dundee DD1 1RJ

Tel. 01382 229222 **Fax** 01382 342220

e-mail beth.anderson@blackadders.co.uk

Correspondent Beth Anderson

Trustees *C F S Williamson; D N Gordon; D Sneddon.*

Scottish Charity No. SC014238

Information available Information was provided by the trust.

General The trust provides core funding towards health projects such as palliative care units, hospices and music in hospitals as well as services for older people and carers. Grants range from £100 to £1,000 each.

Grants to organisations total around £10,000 to £15,000, with about half that amount again given to individuals.

Recent beneficiaries include Bullionfield Recreation, Disabled Carers' Centre, Dundee Visually Impaired and Kick-Start.

Applications In writing to the correspondent. Applications are considered monthly.

New St Andrews Japan Golf Trust

Sport, recreation

£2,500 to organisations (2003/04)

Beneficial area The county of Fife.

Chestney House, 149 Market Street, St Andrews, Fife KY16 9PF

Tel. 01334 472255 **Fax** 01334 475792

Correspondent David S D Robertson, Secretary

Trustees *Sir Michael Bonallack; John Philp; Michael L Joy; David S D Robertson.*

Scottish Charity No. SC005668

Information available Information was provided by the trust.

General The trust aims to organise, provide or assist in the organisation and provision of facilities which will enable and encourage both individuals and groups associated with younger people to play golf or other sports, games or recreational activities. It mainly makes one-off grants within the county of Fife, with donations ranging from £200 to £1,500.

In 2003/04 the trust had assets of £80,000 and an income of £8,000. Grants were made to organisations totalling £2,500, with a further £5,500 being given to individuals.

Applications   In writing to the correspondent.

Paul Charitable Trust

Community work

£30,000 (2003/04)

Beneficial area Balfron and Killearn and the surrounding area.

Bishops, 2 Blythswood Square, Glasgow G2 4AD

Tel. 0141 248 4672 **Fax** 0141 221 9270

e-mail jamie.millar@bishopslaw.biz

Correspondent   James Millar

Trustees   *W G Davidson; G A Murray; J N P Ford; J F Bisset.*

Scottish Charity No. SC023880

Information available   Information was provided by the trust.

General   The trust makes grants for the provision of sports and recreation facilites, adult education and drama and music or other recreational activities. It gives grants to people in need and also to voluntary organisations or clubs with similar objects. The trust's work is for the benefit of people in the Balfron and Kilearn area.

In 2003/04 it had assets of £633,000, an income of £32,000 and gave grants totalling £30,000.

Beneficiaries included Accord Hospice, Children's Hospice Association Scotland, Macmillan Cancer Relief and Strathcarron Hospice (£5,000 each), Emergency Resuscitation Equipment Fund (£3,000) and Neurosciences Foundation, Crossroads (West Stirlingshire) Care Attendant Scheme and Nepal Trust (£2,000 each).

Applications   In writing to the correspondent. The trustees meet quarterly.

The St Andrews Welfare Trust

Young and older people

£4,000 a year to organisations

Beneficial area Within approximately 6 miles of St Andrews.

Pagan Osborne, 106 South Street, St Andrews, Fife KY16 9QD

Tel. 01334 475001 **Fax** 01334 476332

e-mail enquiries@pagan.co.uk

Correspondent   Miss Calderwood

Scottish Charity No. SC008660

Information available   Information was provided by the trust.

General   Grants of up to £300 each are given to organisations working with young or older people, such as playgroups, childcare facilities, family welfare, trips, outings, sheltered accommodation or Christmas teas. It tends to give around £4,000 a year to organisations and £10,000 to individuals.

Applications   In writing to the correspondent, at any time.

Stirling Council Charitable Trusts

General

Not known

Beneficial area Stirling.

Stirling Council, Viewforth, Stirling FK8 2ET

Tel. 01786 443293 **Fax** 01786 443394

website www.stirling.gov.uk

Correspondent   Bob Jack, Director of Corporate Services

Scottish Charity No. SC025090

Information available   Limited information was available.

General   A number of local trusts are administered by the council. Grants are made to a range of organisations in Stirling. Contact the council directly for further information.

Applications   In writing to the correspondent.

Edinburgh, the Lothians & the Borders

The Benfield Motors Charitable Trust

Poverty, sickness, older people, general

£29,000 (2003/04)

Beneficial area Worldwide with preferences for north east England, Leeds and Edinburgh.

c/o Benfield Motor Group, Asama Court, Newcastle Business Park, Newcastle upon Tyne NE4 7YD

Tel. 0191 226 1700

Correspondent Mrs Lynn Squires, Hon. Secretary

Trustees *John Squires, Chair; Malcolm Squires; Stephen Squires.*

Charity Commission no. 328149

Information available Full accounts were on file at the Charity Commission.

General This trust is financed by annual donations of £50,000 from Addison Motors and has general charitable purposes, with a preference for the north east of England.

In 2003/04 the trust had assets of £36,000, an income of £50,000 and made grants totalling £29,000.

The largest grants were £6,000 to Benfield Motors towards St Oswalds Hospice Raffle Car and Newcastle Royal Grammar School; £3,000 each to Christian Aid and Newcastle Society for Blind People and £1,000 each to Northern Sinfonia Trust and Theatre Royal.

Other grants included Cancer Bridge, Help the Aged and Ryton Music Festival (£100 each) and Ethiopiaid (£50).

Exclusions Expeditions, scholarships and animal charities are not funded.

Applications In writing to the correspondent. The trustees meet twice a year; this is usually in May and November with applications needing to be received by the beginning of April or October respectively.

The Courant Fund for Children

Children in need

£7,000 (2003/04)

Beneficial area Edinburgh and the Lothians.

41 Buckstone Loan, Edinburgh EH10 6UJ

Correspondent David A G Taylor, Honorary Secretary

Trustees *Mrs M Hammond, Chair; W Stevenson; Mrs J Brown; Ms A Black; B Kelly; D Taylor; Miss M Allan; Mrs S Ogilvie.*

Scottish Charity No. SC017462

Information available Information was provided by the trust.

General The trust supports children under 18 years of age, resident in the Lothians, who are in need. Grants are awarded to organisations working with children to cover the costs of holidays, outings and equipment. Priority is given to individuals.

In 2003/04 the trust made grants totalling £7,000. With the exception of a grant for £1,500 to City of Edinburgh Council, all grants were for £600 or less, with some beneficiaries receiving more than one grant during the year. Beneficiaries included Aberlour Childcare Trust, Bethany Christian Trust, City Life, Edinburgh Family Service Unit,

Edinburgh Young Carers, Forth Primary School Fund, Lothian Primary Care Trust, Multicultural Family Base, Princess Royal Trust, Royal Hospital for Sick Children, Scripture Union Scotland, Special Needs Information Point, Visual Impairment Services and YWCA.

Exclusions   No grants are made for computers.

Applications   Applications in writing only to the correspondent from an organisation or professional (health visitor, G.P., social worker, hospital worker and so on). Grants are not paid directly to or negotiated with recipients of the fund.

Grants to organisations or individuals are considered by the trustees in February and September. Applications should therefore be received by January and August respectively. Grants to individuals may be considered between meetings.

East Lothian Educational Trust

Education, recreation

£33,000 (2003/04)

Beneficial area East Lothian council area, excluding Wallyford, Whitecraig and Musselburgh.

John Muir House, Council Buildings, Haddington, East Lothian EH41 3HA

Tel. 01620 827436

Correspondent   Kim Brand, Clerk

Scottish Charity No. SC010587

Information available   Information was provided by the trust.

General   The trust supports education, sports and recreation and the arts. It supports schools and individuals.

In 2003/04 the trust had assets of £1 million and an income of £51,000. Grants totalled £33,000. Grants are not usually more than £700. It supported university undergraduate and postgraduate students, schools, athletics and visits abroad by young people.

Applications   On a form available from the correspondent. Trustees meet to consider grants in August and November. Applications should be sent by 10 August and 10 November.

City of Edinburgh Charitable Trusts

General

£453,000 to organisations and individuals (2004/05)

Beneficial area Edinburgh.

Investment and Treasury Division, City of Edinburgh Council, 12 St Giles Street, Edinburgh EH1 1PT

Tel. 0131 469 3518 **Fax** 0131 225 6356

e-mail marlyn.McConaghie@edinburgh.gov.uk

Correspondent   Marlyn McConaghie

Scottish Charity No. SC006504

Information available   No recent information was available from the council.

General   The City of Edinburgh Charitable Trusts is a collection of about 130 trusts administered by Edinburgh City Council. Each trust has specific objectives, most having been gifted into the council to provide funding for particular schools and to assist the very poor of Edinburgh.

Support is given to individuals and organisations in Edinburgh, especially in connection with the following causes:

• arts
• children and young people
• education/training
• hospitals/hospices
• older people
• religious appeals
• social welfare
• sports/recreation.

However, it should be noted that the vast majority of beneficiaries have funds already committed to them. Only occasionally will outside organisations be considered. Grants can be one-off or recurrent and usually range from £10 to £100. Grants to individuals are made in the form of pensions.

In 2004/05 the combined assets of the trusts totalled £16 million. Grants were made totalling £453,000. No details of beneficiaries were provided.

Exclusions   The trusts do not support:

• animal welfare
• buildings

- disability
- environment/conservation
- heritage
- medical/health, including medical research
- overseas projects
- political appeals.

Applications The application procedure varies with each individual trust. Contact the correspondent for further details.

Edinburgh Children's Holiday Fund

Organisations providing holidays for children or helping with children's welfare

£61,000 (2003/04)

Beneficial area Edinburgh and the Lothians.

Bryce, Wilson & Co. Chartered Accountants, 26a Walker Street, Edinburgh EH3 7HR

Tel. 0131 225 5111 **Fax** 0131 220 0283

Correspondent The Secretaries

Trustees *W G Waterson, Chair; Lady Clerk; Mrs P Balfour.*

Scottish Charity No. SC010312

Information available Information was provided by the trust.

General 'The objectives of the fund are to make grants for the benefit of children who may be considered to be in need of financial assistance principally to enable them to have holidays, and to charitable bodies concerned with the welfare and provision of holidays for children.'

In 2003/04 it had assets of £1.4 million and an income of £62,000. Grants totalled £61,000 and ranged from £150 to £8,000. Beneficiaries included Children First (£8,000), Hopscotch (£4,500), Roses Charitable Trust (£4,000), St Catherine's Primary School and St John Vianney Primary School (£2,000 each) and Mother's Union Holiday Scheme (£1,000).

Exclusions No grants directly to individuals.

Applications On a form available from the correspondent. Trustees meet to consider grants in January and May. Applications should be sent in mid-December and mid-April respectively.

Edinburgh Merchant Company Charitable Trust

Schools

Not known

Beneficial area City of Edinburgh and county of Midlothian.

Edinburgh Merchant Company, 22 Hanover Street, Edinburgh EH2 2EP

Correspondent Mrs Margaret Allan, Secretary

Scottish Charity No. SC022283

Information available Brief information was supplied by the trust.

General The trustees for this trust administer a number of other trusts, which are concerned with education provision at Edinburgh Merchant Company schools and in the care of older people.

No financial information was available.

Applications In writing to the correspondent.

Edinburgh Voluntary Organisations' Trust Funds

Social welfare, local community

£110,000 (2003/04)

Beneficial area Edinburgh and the Lothians.

14 Ashley Place, Edinburgh EH6 5PX

Tel. 0131 555 9109 **Fax** 0131 555 9101

e-mail janettescappaticco@evoc.org.uk

Correspondent Janette Scappaticcio, Trust Fund Administrator

Trustees *Penny Richardson; Helen Berry; Graeme Thom; Geoffrey Lord; Monica Langa.*

Scottish Charity No. SC031561

Information available Information was provided by the trust.

General At present the Edinburgh Voluntary Organisations Council is the administrative structure for the following trusts: Miss A Beveridge's Trust, William Thyne Trust and

Edinburgh Voluntary Organisations' Trust. It now administers these together and there is one application form for organisations. The trustees then decide which fund is most appropriate.

In addition the trust also administer grants via Children in Need and Ponton House.

In broad terms the trusts operate in the area of social welfare and assist voluntary organisations in their work. The purposes of the trusts are to:

- relieve poverty principally within Edinburgh and the Lothians
- give financial assistance to individuals who by reason of health, physical or mental disability or otherwise, are in necessitous circumstances
- assist financially or otherwise other charitable organisations whose purposes are similar to above.

Grants to individuals are made on the basis of referrals from the City of Edinburgh Council Social Work Department to families in need.

The current policy of the trustees is to support smaller organisations with a turnover of under £250,000, with grants towards core costs.

Priority is given to:

- local organisations – national organisations must indicate need in Edinburgh and the Lothians and have an independent local committee and accounts so the responsibility is with the local initiative (financial restrictions above will apply only to the local unit)
- organisations that are not eligible for large sums of statutory or Community Fund funding
- organisations providing social service activities that assist people most in need
- organisations involving appropriate participation of volunteers.

Examples of activities that will be considered include: support groups for carers, older people, single parents, homeless young people, young people's clubs and work with, and by, people who are disabled. Arts or environmental tasks will only be considered when a social service or therapeutic service is the main aim.

In 2003/04 the trust had assets of £3 million and an income of £153,000. Grants were made totalling £110,000. Beneficiaries included CCLASP and Midlothian Befriending Society (£3,000 each), Dosti Muslim Group and Lothian Shop Mobility (£2,000 each), Home Start and Dads to Work (£1,500 each) and LIBRA and Rights Office (£1,000 each).

Exclusions No grants are given to or for:

- non-registered charities
- general appeals
- statutory agencies or to replace statutory funding
- commercial organisations or purposes
- private schools and colleges
- distribution by other agencies
- repairs, extensions and alterations for property or for new buildings (grants can be given for essential equipment as part of a project).

Applications On a form available from the correspondent. Applications must be submitted to Edinburgh Voluntary Organisations' Trust (EVOT) and not to the individual trusts. (If an applicant wishes to prepare an application by computer, the headings and respective information should be entered in the order and style of the application form.) A copy of the latest annual report and audited accounts must be included otherwise the application will not be considered (if not available a copy of the most recent unaudited accounts with an explanation). Only one application for a particular project will be considered in a twelve-month period, whether successful or not.

Deadlines for applications are the end of February, May, August or November. Guidelines and application forms are available in large print and on tape.

The Edinvar Trust

Community welfare, housing research

About £25,000

Beneficial area Edinburgh, the Lothians and areas in which Edinvar works.

Wellgate House, 200 Cowgate, Edinburgh EH1 1NQ

Tel. 0131 225 2299 **Fax** 0131 225 4400

e-mail helenforsyth@edinvar.co.uk

Correspondent Helen Forsyth, Trustee

Trustees *Norma Jones; Derek Munn; Helen Forsyth; Angela Yih; Simon Shearer.*

Scottish Charity No. SC011638

Information available No recent information was available.

General The trust was founded by Edinvar Housing Association to benefit its charitable activities.

The objects of the trust are:

- the provision of housing and associated amenities for people who are old, infirm and otherwise in need
- research into housing and related matters.

The trust normally considers grants for housing, supported living and community activities which will assist the charitable work of Edinvar Housing Association, its subsidiaries, associated bodies and the communities in which they work.

No recent information was available from the correspondent. Previous research indicates that grants are made totalling around £25,000 each year. Previous beneficiaries include Dedridge Community Council, Edinburgh Volunteer Tutors' Organisation, Positive Action in Housing, Scottish Housing and Support Conference, Edinburgh & Lothian Council on Alcohol and Wester Hailes Children's Play Project.

Exclusions Grants are not normally made to grant-giving trusts, for revenue funding beyond one year, or to individuals.

Applications On a form available from the correspondent. Trustees meet twice a year in response to applications.

R S Hayward Trust

Education and training, community, older people, ex-services, health

Not known

Beneficial area Mainly Galashiels.

c/o Pike & Chapman, Solicitors, Bank Street, Galashiels, Selkirkshire TD1 1ER

Tel. 01896 752379 **Fax** 01896 754439

Correspondent Mr Hunt

Scottish Charity No. SC015427

Information available Limited information was available on this trust.

General The trust supports the following causes in Galashiels:

- educational organisations or clubs concerned with arts and crafts or culture
- the improvement of amenities in the burgh

- general welfare and accommodation of retired people
- the training in a trade or profession of anyone who has been incapacitated while in the armed forces
- Scottish organisations concerned with the care of people who are elderly, sick or blind.

No financial information was available.

Applications In writing to the correspondent.

Jewel Miners' Welfare Charitable Society

Recreation, leisure

Not known

Beneficial area Jewel area of Edinburgh.

56 Duddingston Park South, Edinburgh EH15 3LJ

Tel. 0131 669 5955

Correspondent The Secretary

Scottish Charity No. SC015240

Information available Limited information was available on this trust.

General The society makes grants to organisations working to improve the Jewel area of Edinburgh generally and the living conditions of the community. No further information was available.

Applications In writing to the correspondent.

Melville Trust for Care and Cure of Cancer

Medical research

£164,000 (2004)

Beneficial area Lothian, Borders or Fife only.

Tods Murray LLP, Edinburgh Quay, 133 Fountainbridge, Edinburgh EH3 9AG

Tel. 0131 656 2000 **Fax** 0131 656 2020

e-mail melvilletrust@todsmurray.com

Trustees *Melville Estate Trustees.*

Scottish Charity No. SC032409

Information available Information was provided by the trust.

General   The trust funds scientific or clinical investigations on cancer. It will give grants for fellowships, research assistantships and equipment. In 2004 the trust had assets of £2.7 million and an income of £132,000. Grants were made totalling £164,000.

Exclusions   Grants are not given for other causes.

Applications   Application forms are available from the correspondent. They must be submitted no later than 31 March each year.

The J P Morgan Foundations

Education

£628,000 (2004)

Beneficial area UK, with a special interest in Islington, Havering, east London, Bournemouth, Edinburgh and Glasgow.

10 Aldermanbury, London EC2V 7RF

Tel. 020 7325 1308 **Fax** 020 7325 8195

e-mail duncan.grant@jpmorgan.com

Correspondent   Duncan Grant, Director

Trustees   Mark Gavin, Chair; Duncan Grant; Ed Banks; Stephanie Emery; Richard Gildea; Richard Kaye; Carol Lake; Paul Murphy; Michael Ridley; Jonathan White; Dorcas Williams.

Charity Commission no. 291617

Information available   Annual report and accounts were provided by the trusts.

General   This entry covers both J P Morgan Educational Trust and J P Morgan Foundation, which now operate simply as J P Morgan Foundations.

In 2004 the educational trust, currently the larger of the two, made grants totalling £406,000 to 54 organisations. The foundation awarded £222,000 to 35 projects.

Grantmaking policy 2005

Grantmaking policy will focus on three strategic areas of giving, and within those areas concentrate on the following local needs:

Community asset development
- education and homelessness
- workforce development
- economic development.

Youth education
- primary and secondary education
- special needs education
- financial literacy
- school, parent and community partnerships.

Community life
- visual and performing arts
- community-based arts
- civil enhancement
- diversity in society.

J P Morgan seeks to strengthen the communities it works in and for this reason new grants will be concentrated in the local community areas where there is a J P Morgan presence. They are:

- London
- Bournemouth
- Glasgow
- Edinburgh.

Level of support provided

J P Morgan wishes to develop good partnerships with the local communities and this will be reflected in fewer projects but with larger awards over a longer period of time.

Most new grants will be in the range of £1,000 to £5,000 per annum over a period of one to three years.

Grants in 2004

In 2004 we awarded £628,000 to 89 organisations, including schools, charities and not-for-profit groups. The total administration charge was £69,000 (10%).

The trustee committee understands that it is not always easy for charities and not-for-profit organisations to fund the basic maintenance costs of keeping an organisation working. Of the total awards, 34% (£214,000) supported day-to-day running costs including maintenance and salary expenses. The remaining 66% (£414,000) of awards directly funded educational projects.

Communities where funds were directed:

- London (£276,000 – 43%)
- Bournemouth (£176,000 – 28%)
- Havering (£89,000 – 14%)
- Edinburgh (£37,500 – 6%)
- Glasgow (£10,000 – 2%)

Organisations in London and Bournemouth received over 71% of the grants, reflecting the fact that over 90% of UK J P Morgan employees work in these two locations.

Five projects in Scotland received grants during 2004. They were:

- Harmeny School – Edinburgh (£15,000): 'the school is a grant-aided special school for primary aged pupils with pronounced social, emotional and behavioural difficulties. The £15,000 award (part of a £30,000 award over two years) has supported the Harmeny Outdoor Project, which aims to increase specific personal traits such as self-esteem, trust and communication, through outdoor activities including climbing, camping, canoeing and after school activity clubs.'
- Blackford Brae School – Edinburgh (£10,000): 'the school, founded in 1990, is situated in Edinburgh. It has funding from Barnardo's and the City of Edinburgh and East Lothian Councils to provide day education for pupils of primary school age. All pupils [have] social, emotional and behavioural difficulties. In addition, all [have] learning difficulties arising from discontinuity in their education.' The grant from the foundations was to purchase a minibus for the school.
- Duke of Edinburgh's Award – Educational Participatory Youth Programmes in Edinburgh and Glasgow (£10,000 each).
- Kaimes Special School – Edinburgh (£1,800): the grant was towards the school's Residential Experience Programme.
- Scottish European Educational Trust – Edinburgh (£500): towards the annual Euroquiz for Primary Schools.

Exclusions   Projects not usually supported include:
- open appeals from national charities
- building appeals
- charity gala nights and similar events
- appeals by individuals for study grants, travel scholarships or charity sponsorships.

Applications   To apply for funding please write a brief letter (not more than two sides of A4) to Duncan Grant, the director. Please avoid bulky items such as cassettes in the original request.

Please set out your reasons for applying along with an indication of the level of funding required. There is no application form or specific closing dates for initial inquiries. Applications are always acknowledged, and will be reviewed within

eight weeks. We will contact you within this time if we can take your applications forward.

Final approval for funding must come from trustees who meet four times a year, in January, March, July and October.

If your application is unsuccessful we suggest you wait at least a year before re-applying.

Kenneth Paul Trust

General
About £4,000 each year
Beneficial area West Linton.

23 Bogsbank Road, West Linton, Peeblesshire EH46 7EN

Correspondent   G L H Barlee

Scottish Charity No. SC019967

Information available   Information was provided by the trust.

General   The trust supports St Andrew's Church and various local groups in West Linton. Grants total about £4,000 and range from £25 to £3,000.

Applications   In writing to the correspondent at any time.

The Pleasance Trust

Disadvantaged young people
£17,500 (2002/03)
Beneficial area Edinburgh.

22 Charlotte Square, Edinburgh EH2 4DF

Tel. 0131 225 8484 **Fax** 0131 220 2357

Correspondent   Liz Smillie, Secretary

Trustees   *Niall Campbell; Barry McCorkell; Revd Liz Henderson; William Ivory.*

Scottish Charity No. SC000309

Information available   Information was provided by the trust.

General   The trust gives grants to voluntary organisations such as youth clubs working with disadvantaged young people in Edinburgh and also to schools. In 2002/03 it had an income of £22,000 and gave grants totalling £17,500. Grants usually range from £100 to £1,000. Of the 36 grants made, 2 were for £1,000. These were to

Stepping Stones and the Magdalene Youth Strategy Project.

Smaller grants went to youth groups, schools and a variety of other young people's organisations and projects.

Exclusions   No grants to individuals or to national organisations (except occasionally for specific local projects).

Applications   In writing to the correspondent. Trustees distribute grants quarterly in January, April, July and October.

The Ponton House Trust

Young people, disadvantaged groups

£25,000 to organisations (2003/04)

Beneficial area The Lothians.

Lindsays Solicitors, 11 Atholl Crescent, Edinburgh EH3 8HE

Tel. 0131 477 8708 **Fax** 0131 477 8703

e-mail dsr@lindsays.co.uk

Correspondent   David S Reith, Secretary

Trustees   *Hon. Lord Grieve; Mrs J Gilliat; Revd J Munro; Mrs F Meikle; A Dobson; Shulah Allen.*

Scottish Charity No. SC021716

Information available   Accounts were provided by the trust.

General   Grants are mainly given to charities working with people aged 16 to 25, particularly to disadvantaged groups as well as those providing training. The trustees are also keen to help charities where help would make all the difference to their financial viability. Grants usually range between £300 and £2,000.

In 2004 the trust had assets of £1 million and an income of £56,000. Grants were made to 37 organisations totalling £25,000.

The largest grants were made to Venture Scotland (£3,000), Family Holiday Association (£2,500), Home Link (£2,000) and Fairbridge in Scotland and Bethany Christian Trust (£1,000 each).

Smaller grants included those to West Lothian Cyrenians, Hopscotch Holidays Ltd, Enlighten, Inclusion Alliance, Kaimes Special School

Association, Edinburgh & Lothian Council on Alcohol, Rock Trust, Partners in Advocacy, Acorn Centre Youth Project and Pilmeny Youth Centre.

Exclusions   No grants to individuals or non-charitable organisations.

Applications   In writing to the correspondent, there are no specific application forms. Trustees usually meet in January, April, July and October. Applications should include a full explanation of the project for which funding is sought plus annual reports and accounts.

The Red House Home Trust

Education and training, young people

£4,700 to organisations (2003/04)

Beneficial area East Lothian.

Scott-Moncrieff, Chartered Accountants, 17 Melville Street, Edinburgh EH3 7PH

Tel. 0131 473 3500 **Fax** 0131 473 3500

e-mail janicecooper@scott-moncrieff.com

Correspondent   Janice Cooper, Secretary

Trustees   *Dr R E J George, Chair; Revd R H Brown; M Mavor; Mrs M McBride; Revd A Keulemans; Ms M S McIntosh; A Knowles; C Weatherley.*

Scottish Charity No. SC015748

Information available   Information was provided by the trust.

General   The trust promotes the education and training of disadvantaged young people under the age of 22, to help them into independent living.

In 2003/04 the trust's assets totalled £440,000, it had an income of £15,000 and it gave grants totalling £7,400, including £4,700 to organisations and £2,700 to individuals.

Grants ranged from £300 to £1,000. The largest grants were £1,000 to Whitecraig Community Centre and £800 to Red School Youth Centre. Other beneficiaries include Longniddry After School Club (£540), Wallyford Playgroup (£500), Musselburgh Grammar School and Cockenzie and Port Seton Community Council (£400 each), Pinkie St Peter's Out of School Club (£370), Pinkie St Peter's Primary – Support Base (£360) and Preston Lodge High School (£300).

Applications   On a form available from the correspondent.

Lord Rosebery Charitable Settlement

General

About £5,000

Beneficial area Mainly Edinburgh and the Lothians.

PricewaterhouseCoopers, Erskine House, 68 Queen Street, Edinburgh EH2 4NH

Tel. 0131 226 4488

Correspondent   Grant Middleton

Trustees   *Rt Hon. Seventh Earl of Rosebery; Countess of Rosebery; D M Henderson.*

Scottish Charity No. SC008740

Information available   Information was provided by the trust.

General   The trust supports general charitable purposes mainly in Edinburgh and the Lothians. It has a preference for children's organisations and organisations working with disadvantaged people. It has about £5,000 to give away in grants. The maximum grant is normally £1,000. Examples of beneficiaries were not available.

Exclusions   No grants to individuals.

Applications   In writing to the correspondent. Trustees meet in February to consider grants.

The Russell Bequest

Sport

£8,000 (2005)

Beneficial area North Berwick.

Lyle Crawford & Co., 15 Glenorchy Road, North Berwick EH39 4PE

Tel. 01620 892090 **Fax** 01620 892091

e-mail lyle.crawford@btinternet.com

Correspondent   Lyle Crawford

Trustees   *J B Macnair; Cllr P O'Brien; Cllr Diana Kinnear.*

Scottish Charity No. SC001207

Information available   Limited information was provided by the trust.

General   The trust gives grants to sports organisations in North Berwick. Schools, Scouts and Highland games can be supported. In 2005 grants were made totalling £8,000.

Exclusions   Grants are only awarded for sports in North Berwick and are not available for private clubs.

Applications   In writing to the correspondent. Apply at any time.

W J Underwood's Testamentary Trust

Medical research

£4,000 (2004/05)

Beneficial area Edinburgh.

Lindsays' Solicitors, 11 Atholl Crescent, Edinburgh EH3 8HE

Tel. 0131 229 1212

e-mail csk@lindsays.co.uk

Correspondent   Callum S Kennedy, Trustee

Trustees   *C S Kennedy; Mrs Helen Geddes; J F M Murray.*

Scottish Charity No. SC001625

Information available   Information was confirmed by the trust.

General   The trust supports medical research projects in Edinburgh. In 2004/05 it made grants totalling £4,000.

Applications   In writing to the correspondent.

West Lothian Educational Trust

Education

£10,000 to individuals and organisations (2004)

Beneficial area West Lothian.

Scott-Moncrieff, Chartered Accountants, 17 Melville Street, Edinburgh EH3 7PH

Tel. 0131 473 3500 **Fax** 0131 473 3535

e-mail janicecooper@scott-moncrieff.com

Correspondent   Janice Cooper, Secretary

Trustees *A J Pirie, Chair; W D Stewart; W Scoular; F James; A McLachlam; Mrs J Taylor; Mrs N A Watson; Cllr D McGrouther; Cllr W Russell; Cllr A Miller; Cllr T Smith; Cllr J McGinty; Miss A Neate; J W Johnston.*

Scottish Charity No. SC015454

Information available Accounts were provided by the trust.

General The trust mainly makes grants for educational purposes to schools, organisations and individuals, particularly those who cannot obtain grants from the Scottish Education Department. Recipients of grants must be from, or live in, West Lothian. The largest grants given are of £500, and grants are usually one-off. Interests supported by the trust include graduate and postgraduate studies, the provision of sports and other equipment for schools and colleges, clubs with activities of an educational nature, adult education and promoting education in the visual arts/drama/music field.

In 2003/04 it had assets of £183,000 and an income of £15,000. The trust made grants totalling £10,000 which were distributed as follows:

Prize money – £1,700
John Newland bursaries – £1,000
Anderson bursary – £1,200
Educational awards – £5,900

Exclusions Applications from outside the beneficial area will not be considered.

Applications Application forms are available from the correspondent. Applications must be received by 1 February, 1 May and 1 September each year.

The John K Young Endowment Fund

Research, medical research, health, young people

About £20,000 a year

Beneficial area Edinburgh.

Skene Edwards WS, 5 Albyn Place, Edinburgh EH2 4NJ

Tel. 0131 225 6665 **Fax** 0131 220 1015

Correspondent Alistair Ferguson, Trustee

Trustees *T C Foggo; A J R Ferguson; R J S Morton; R I F Macdonald.*

Scottish Charity No. SC002264

Information available Information was provided by the trust.

General The trust supports medical and surgical research and also research into chemistry to aid UK industry. It also supports young people in Edinburgh and health organisations in Scotland.

In June 2005 the trust informed us that grants total around £20,000 each year. Grants are usually one-off and range from £500 to £2,000. Previous beneficiaries have included Barnardo's, Edinburgh and Leith Age Concern, Marie Curie Cancer Care, Shelter and Waverley Care.

Exclusions No grants to individuals or non-registered charities.

Applications In writing to the correspondent. Trustees meet to consider grants in the autumn.

Glasgow & the West of Scotland

Argyll and Bute Trust

Young people

About £5,000

Beneficial area Argyll and Bute area.

c/o Bank of Scotland Buildings, Oban, Argyll PA34 4LN

Tel. 01546 602524

Correspondent James Kirk, Hon. Secretary

Scottish Charity No. SC010534

Information available Information was provided by the trust.

General The trust aims to encourage young people up to the age of 25 to work together to provide charitable help for people of all ages in the community. It will support the work of young people in small, charitable projects. Both individuals and voluntary groups are supported, with emphasis on funds being used to put something back into the community. About £5,000 is available for distribution each year. Grants usually range from £100 to £250. The amount given to groups varies according to the applications received.

It also administers funds, generated from a landfill tax, for the purpose of cleaning the shores/roadside blackspots. The funds are given to voluntary groups (of any age group) which are paid per mile or blackspot which they work on. About £12,000 is currently available for these grants.

Applications In writing to the correspondent, at 'Duntiblae', Wilson Road, Lochgilphead, Argyll TR31 8RT. Apply at any time.

Charitable Trusts of North Ayrshire Council

Local community

About £20,000

Beneficial area North Ayrshire district.

North Ayrshire Council, Cunninghame House, Irvine KA12 8EE

Tel. 01294 324100

Correspondent The Chief Executive's Department

Scottish Charity No. SC008443

Information available Information was provided by the trust.

General The trusts support community projects which benefit people in the North Ayrshire district. It gives about £20,000 each year in total. Further information was not available.

Applications In writing to the correspondent.

Charitable Trusts of East Ayrshire Council

General

See below

Beneficial area East Ayrshire.

East Ayrshire Council, Council Headquarters, London Road, Kilmarnock KA3 7BU

Tel. 01563 576000 **Fax** 01563 576500

e-mail gillian.hamilton@east-ayrshire.gov.uk

Correspondent Gillian Hamilton

Scottish Charity No. SC025073

Information available   Information was provided by the council.

General   The council is the administrative body for a number of trusts which serve different aspects of the community. The trusts and their objects are listed below. Some of these trusts and guidelines suggest preferences for individuals, however they appear to be flexible in their approach to grantmaking. It is likely that support may be given to organisations helping such individuals.

The Bessie C Roxburgh Bequest

Established to benefit the former burgh of Darvel, this trust meets annually in August to consider applications from clubs and organisations. Preference is given to proposals or projects which wholly or mainly benefit residents of Darvel. The trust is particularly keen that its funds encourage 'self-help' where appropriate, for example, by raising matching funding or providing voluntary labour. The trust prefers proposals which benefit large numbers of people, either directly or indirectly. Applications should be for single payments and not for continuing support beyond any one financial year.

Miss Annie Smith Mair Bequest

This trust was established to provide assistance to needy individuals, especially spinsters and orphans, who are natives of, or residents in, the former burgh of Newmilns and Greenholm. The trustees meet three times a year in February, June and November, although applications can be considered between meetings.

The John Fulton Soup Kitchen Trust

This was established to provide a soup kitchen for the poor of Kilmarnock, the food from which must be sold at no more than half the cost of the price of the ingredients. While the trust does not provide a soup kitchen, it has provided financial assistance to similar organisations such as Salvation Army. The trustees meet on an ad-hoc basis when required.

Ayrshire Educational Trust

There are six sections of this trust currently in use. These are:

Section 28 – first scheduled payments paid to three churches in November of each year. The churches involved are Beith, Girvan and Kilbirmie.

Section 36 – travel grants are made to inhabitants of Ayrshire to enable them to travel either in the UK or abroad for any purpose of an educational nature.

Section 38 – special equipment grants are available for the purchase of special equipment, in supplement of that which is provided by a local authority, to improve the efficiency of education for schoolchildren with mental disabilities. Equipment for pilot projects or of an experimental nature will be considered.

Section 41 – support to clubs. Grants to assist in the formation, maintenance and encouragement of clubs, societies and organisations for the educational benefit of children and young people in Ayrshire. Equipment which is classed as 'personal' e.g. uniforms, musical instruments etc. are not considered under this section.

Section 43 – grants are awarded to defray or assist in defraying the expenses of organised school excursions for the benefit of children or young persons attending schools in Aryshire. The excursion must be outside the boundaries of the former county of Ayr and include an overnight stay.

Section 45 – grants are awarded towards the cost of expenses incurred in organised parties, approved by the governing body, for visits abroad which are of an educational nature.

Applications   Further details and application forms are available from the administration manager at the council offices.

Charitable Trusts of South Ayrshire Council

General

£147,000 (2004/05)

Beneficial area South Ayrshire.

Development, Safety and Regulation, South Ayrshire Council, Newton House, 30 Green Street Lane, Ayr, South Ayrshire KA8 0BH

Tel. 01292 612966 **Fax** 01292 613062

e-mail down.kilday@south-ayrshire.gov.uk

website www.south-ayrshire.gov.uk/community/grants.htm

Correspondent   The Grants Officer

Scottish Charity No. SC025088

Information available   Information was provided by the council.

General The following is taken from the detailed guidance notes for voluntary and community organisations available to potential applicants:

South Ayrshire Council will consider applications from community and voluntary organisations which are consistent with the information given below. Applicants should note that no guarantee of funding should be assumed by any organisation.

Who can apply?

Financial support may be available to national or local voluntary organisations and locally based community groups which are properly constituted and can assure the council that they operate for the benefit of the wider community.

Organisations may apply more than once in any financial year but it should be noted that as demand increases careful consideration will be given to individual applications and no guarantees can be given that any specific application will be approved.

In considering applications the council will take into account the extent to which groups are prepared and able to make a financial contribution towards their project/activities.

What can groups/organisations apply for?

Financial support may be available to support voluntary organisations and community groups which provide and promote social, cultural, economic, environmental and recreational facilities, or support projects which are in the interest of people living in South Ayrshire.

In all cases no financial support will be provided retrospectively and all applications must be in advance of any project/activity being started.

In 2004/05 grants to organisations totalled £147,000. Grants were distributed as follows:

• Awards £5,000 and over – Grants totalling £90,000 to 11 organisations.

The largest grant was £15,000 to Volunteer Centre South Ayrshire. Other beneficiaries included LEAD Scotland (£11,000), Council for Voluntary Organisations (£8,000), South Ayrshire Sports Council (£7,000), Girvan Bowling Club, Crosshill Bowling Club and Carrick Community Transport Group (£6,000 each) and One Plus: One Parent Families (£5,500).

• Awards less than £5,000 – Grants totalling £109,000 were made to 125 organisations and 17 individuals.

The largest grants were £4,500 each to Workers Educational Association – Capacity Building

Programme and Deafblind Scotland; a further £4,000 to Deafblind Scotland and £4,000 each to Sensory Impaired Support Group – Ayrshire, Girvan Traditional Folk Festival and Family Meditation West. Other recipients of £1,000 or more included Dalmellington Band (£3,500), Ayrshire Cancer Support (£3,000), Ayr PHAB Club (£2,500), Ayr Choral Union (£2,000), Scottish Marriage Care – Ayrshire (£1,500) and Victim Support Scotland (£1,000).

Smaller grants to organisations include £350 to Troon Blind Club, £250 to Prestwick Arts Guild, £200 to Scottish Amateur Flute Band Association, £100 to North Ayr Community Events Committee and £50 to Cragie Over 60s Club. Individuals received grants of £150 each.

Applications On a form available from the correspondent or from the council's website. The following guidelines on applying are provided by the council:

How to apply

All sections [of the application form] must be completed and all additional information e.g. constitution, financial details, included. Incomplete applications will not be considered by the council.

Wherever possible please detail costs of any equipment requested and, in the case of refurbishment or building projects attach copy plans or drawings.

Your application will be acknowledged and a member of staff from an appropriate council department will contact your organisation/group if required to discuss your application and compile an assessment report for the council.

You should note that it is the responsibility of all organisations to arrange appropriate insurance cover for any equipment purchased with financial support provided by the council.

The general criteria for financial assistance states:

The following general criteria are applied by the council for funding voluntary bodies. These criteria are independent of conditions applied in existing standard contracts or service agreements.

1. Voluntary bodies applying for council support either in kind or financial should be able to clearly demonstrate their contribution towards the council's overall objectives and specific objectives.

2. Voluntary bodies should demonstrate that they consult on an ongoing basis and have the support of the local communities and/or the groups intended to benefit from the service provided.

3. Voluntary bodies should seek to provide a service or activity that is based upon best practice and which makes the most effective and efficient use of available resources.

4. Voluntary bodies funded by the council are expected to demonstrate that they will incorporate equal opportunities principles and legislation into their policy and practices.

5. Voluntary bodies are required to set out expectations for the use of the award or resource and to specify clear outcomes with timescales, methods of monitoring and evaluation, and clarify the appropriate reporting requirements.

6. The council will state clearly its criteria for making the award or resource available and its financial relationship with that organisation.

7. The council will confirm the role, responsibilities and obligations of its officers' and/or members' representatives on the management committee or board of initiative (as appropriate).

8. The council will provide the voluntary board with a copy of the Standard Conditions for Grant Assistance, and will attach any additional conditions required, relevant to the specific grant, loan or service requirement.

The Balmore Trust

Developing world, social welfare, young people, women's projects

£36,000 (2004)

Beneficial area Developing countries and UK, with a preference for Strathclyde.

Viewfield, Balmore, Torrance, Glasgow G64 4AE

Tel. 01360 620742 **Fax** 01360 620742

e-mail mail@balmoretrust.org.uk

website www.balmoretrust.org.uk

Correspondent The Secretary

Trustees J Riches; G Burns; J Eldridge; B Holman; Ms R Jarvis; Ms R Riches.

Scottish Charity No. SC008930

Information available The trust produces a newsletter available free in its shop, The Coach House charity craft shop in Balmore, or by sending an sae to the company secretary at the above address.

General The trust's objects are the relief of poverty, the promotion of health and education throughout the world, and any charitable purposes for the benefit of the community in the Strathclyde region of Scotland.

Its income is derived from the profits of the Coach House charity craft shop, which the trust owns. The shop is also a coffee and tea room, run almost entirely by volunteers, which carries a range of fairly traded and organic foods, fairly traded crafts, jewellery, accessories, toys, stationery and books.

In 2004 it had an income of £36,000, all of which was given in grants.

Over 70% of the trust's grant total was awarded to projects overseas, with the remainder given in the UK. Grants ranged from £50 to £7,000.

Grantmaking in the UK is concentrated mainly in the Glasgow area and favours families, teenagers, and women's aid groups. Major grants to UK projects in 2005 were to Family Action in Rogerfield and Easterhouse, Church House, Bridgeton and East Dunbartonshire Women's Aid.

The trust has close connections overseas with community development programmes in India (Kolkata, Rajasthan and Kerala), Burma and Africa (Kenya, South Africa, Swaziland, Lesotho and Namibia). Major grants to overseas projects in 2005 were to the Daynes Education Fund, South Africa; High Lands Development Association, Kerala, India; and the Sohpia Mission Institute, Burma.

The trust's policy in grantmaking is increasingly to build on partnerships already established.

Exclusions No grants to individuals.

Applications The trust is run entirely voluntarily and the trust states that it is unlikely that money will be available for new applicants, unless they have a personal link with the trust or its shop, The Coach House charity craft shop.

Applications should be made in writing to the correspondent at the above address at the very beginning of the year (main disbursement is made annually in February or March). The following information should be provided:

- details of the project for which funding is sought
- the amount requested
- details of past and current funders
- an outline of the background and experience of key staff

- a copy of the organisation's recent accounts
- references
- details of other funders the organisation is approaching
- any other relevant information.
Applications are acknowledged only if an sae is enclosed or an e-mail address provided.

The Bellahouston Bequest Fund

Religion, social welfare, health, education, restoration

£101,000 (2003/04)

Beneficial area Glasgow and district, but not more than five miles beyond the Glasgow city boundary.

Mitchells Roberton Solicitors, George House, 36 North Hanover Street, Glasgow G1 2AD

Tel. 0141 552 3422 **Fax** 0141 552 2935

e-mail jamc@mitchells-roberton.co.uk

Correspondent John A M Cuthbert, Administrator

Trustees *Bonar G Hardie; David H Galbraith; J Forbes MacPherson; Eric H Webster; Peter C Paisley; Peter L Fairley.*

Scottish Charity No. SC011781

Information available Accounts were provided by the trust.

General The trust supports a wide variety of causes. Its main priority is to help build, expand and repair Protestant evangelical churches or places of religious worship, as well as supporting the clergy of these churches. It further states that it is set up to give grants to charities for the relief of poverty or disease and to organisations concerned with promotion of the Protestant religion, education, and conservation of places of historical and artistic significance. It will consider social welfare causes generally and also animal welfare and sport and recreation. All organisations should be within the parliamentary boundaries of the city of Glasgow or within a five mile radius of this area.

In 2003/04 it had assets of £3.5 million and an income of £160,000. It gave grants totalling £101,000. Grants ranged between £250 and £5,000.

The largest grants were made to House for an Art Lover and Kelvingrove Refurbishment Appeal (£5,000 each) and Church of Scotland (£4,000). Beneficiaries receiving £2,000 each included Girlguiding Scotland, Maryhill Parish Church, Williamwood Parish Church, Prince & Princess of Wales Hospice, Ballieston Community Care, Govanhill Youth Project and St Paul's Parish Council.

Grants of £1,000 each included those to University of Strathclyde, Citizens' Theatre, Dalmarnock After School Care, Crosshill Evangelical Church, Erskine Hospital, William McCunn's Trust, Airborne Initiative, Bellahouston Academy, Northwest Women's Centre, Trinity Possil & Henry Drummond Church and Glasgow School of Art.

Smaller grants included those to 119th Glasgow Boys Brigade, Shawlands United Reformed Church, Strathclyde Youth Club Association, Glasgow YMCA, Glasgow Old People's Welfare Association, Colquhoun Trust, Calvay Social Action Group and Pearce Institute.

Exclusions No grants to organisations or churches whose work does not fall within the geographical remit of the fund. Overseas projects and political appeals are not supported.

Applications On a form available from the trust for church applications only. Other charitable organisations can apply in writing to the correspondent. The trustees meet to consider grants in March, July, October and December.

The Geoff Brown Charitable Trust

General

About £1,500 to individuals and organisations (2003/04)

Beneficial area Cumbria and south west Scotland.

Albert Cottage, Harker, Carlisle CA6 4HW

Tel. 01228 537149 **Fax** 01228 544913

Correspondent Geoff Brown

Charity Commission no. 1044019

Information available Accounts are on file at the Charity Commission.

General   Geoff Brown's fundraising began in 1989 when he staged a dance in Burgh-By-Sands which raised £110 that was donated to a local person in need. His fundraising efforts continued and in 1997 was registered with the Charity Commission. It raises its funds by sponsorships from local businesses as well as conducting its own fundraising in Cumbria and south west Scotland, donating the income back to the local community.

Small grants are mostly given to individuals to create a memorable moment for people who are experiencing a particular hardship, although grants are also available to organisations, with beneficiaries including older people's homes and special needs schools. In 2003/04 the trust's income had fallen below £1,000, with its total expenditure being just £1,500. It may be the case that the trust is winding down its activities.

Applications   In writing to the correspondent.

The W A Cargill Fund

General
About £140,000

Beneficial area Glasgow and the west of Scotland.

Miller Beckett & Jackson Solicitors, 190 St Vincent Street, Glasgow G2 5SP

Tel. 0141 204 2833 **Fax** 0141 248 7185

e-mail mail@millerbj.co.uk

Correspondent   Norman A Fyfe, Trustee

Trustees   *A C Fyfe; W G Peacock; N A Fyfe; Mirren Elizabeth Graham.*

Scottish Charity No. SC008456

Information available   Limited information was provided by the trust.

General   This trust has the same address and trustees as two other trusts, DWT Cargill Fund and WA Cargill Charitable Trust, although they all operate independently.

It supports a wide remit of causes in the west of Scotland, particularly in Glasgow. It gives a large number of grants generally ranging from £1,000 to £3,000, although a few larger grants are given. Grants are made totalling around £140,000 each year. No further information was available.

Grants have previously been broken down into the following categories:

- medical research
- medical care
- care of children
- care of the elderly
- youth organisations
- heritage
- arts
- educational
- religious organisations
- ex-servicemen, sailors, police, fire services etc.

Exclusions   Individuals are not supported.

Applications   In writing to the correspondent, including a copy of the charity's latest accounts or details of its financial position.

The D W T Cargill Fund

General
See below

Beneficial area UK, with a preference for the west of Scotland.

Miller Beckett & Jackson Solicitors, 190 St Vincent Street, Glasgow G2 5SP

Tel. 0141 204 2833 **Fax** 0141 248 7185

e-mail mail@millerbj.co.uk

Correspondent   Norman A Fyfe, Trustee

Trustees   *A C Fyfe; W G Peacock; N A Fyfe; Mirren Elizabeth Graham.*

Scottish Charity No. SC012703

Information available   Limited information was provided by the trust.

General   This trust has the same address and trustees as two other trusts, W A Cargill Charitable Trust and W A Cargill Fund, although they all operate independently.

It supports 'any hospitals, institutions, societies or others whose work in the opinion of the trustees is likely to be beneficial to the community'.

Grants have previously totalled around £200,000. No further information was available.

Previous beneficiaries include Greenock Medical Aid Society, City of Glasgow Society of Social Service, Glasgow and West of Scotland Society for the Blind, Scottish Maritime Museum – Irvine, Scottish Episcopal Church, Colquhoun Bequest Fund for Incurables, Glasgow City Mission, Scottish Motor Neurone Disease Association, Lead Scotland, Three Towns Blind Bowling/Social

Club, North Glasgow Community Forum and Crathie Opportunity Holidays.

Exclusions No grants are made to individuals.

Applications In writing to the correspondent, supported by up-to-date accounts. Trustees meet quarterly.

Castlemilk Environment Trust

Conservation, environmental work/events

Around £10,000 a year

Beneficial area Castlemilk (Glasgow G45).

Glenwood Business Centre, 21 Glenwood Place, Castlemilk, Glasgow G45 9UH

Tel. 0141 630 1919 **Fax** 0141 630 2422

e-mail matthewfinkle@btconnect.com

website www.castlemilkenvironmenttrust.org.uk

Correspondent Matthew J Finkle, Project Officer

Trustees *Lewis MacSween; Janet Hayes; Jim Paterson.*

Scottish Charity No. SC024420

Information available Information was provided by the trust.

General The trust works in the Castlemilk area of Glasgow to improve the environment; conserve local woodlands, train and employ local people, and fund groups involved in improving the environment. Grants are only given in support of projects which are of benefit to the Castlemilk area. Participation by local people is encouraged in projects, which will themselves be for public benefit. The trust runs a group of volunteers and a young people's group.

It has received over £2 million in grant aid since 1996.

Exclusions No grants to profit-making organisations.

Applications In writing to the correspondent.

Clyde Cruising Club Seamanship and Pilotage Trust

Young people, disabled

About £3,000 a year

Beneficial area Glasgow.

Suite 101, The Pentagon Centre, 36 Washington Street, Glasgow G3 8AZ

Tel. 0141 221 2774 **Fax** 0141 221 2775

Correspondent J Baird

Scottish Charity No. SC009099

Information available Limited information was available on this trust.

General This trust provides courses for people who are disabled and assists in the preservation of craft. It also aims to: educate the public in the knowledge and practice of seamanship; provide recreational sailing facilities for young people, especially from deprived areas; and to generally improve safety at sea. About £3,000 is available each year in grants. No further information was available on beneficiaries.

Applications On a form available from the correspondent.

Cumberland Building Society Charitable Foundation

General

£45,000 (2004/05)

Beneficial area Cumbria, Dumfries and Galloway, Lancashire (Preston area) and Northumberland (Haltwhistle area).

Cumberland House, Castle Street, Carlisle CA3 8RX

Tel. 01228 541341 **Fax** 01228 403111

e-mail executives@cumberland.co.uk

Correspondent Judi Thomson

Trustees *J G Gaddes; Mrs H Irving; M J Shannon; J Stewart; W R Wilkinson.*

Charity Commission no. 1072435

Information available   Information was provided by the trust.

General   This trust has general charitable purposes in Cumbria, Dumfries and Galloway, Lancashire and Northumberland, giving grants of up to £1,000.

In 2004/05 grants totalled £45,000. Beneficiaries included Currock House Association, Hospice at Home, St John Ambulance, The Genesis Appeal, DEBRA, Children's Heart Federation and The Food Train.

Exclusions   No grants to non-registered charities and those working outside the operating area.

Applications   In writing to the correspondent, including a description of your organisation, what it does, what the grant will be used for and the size of grant requested. Trustees meet every quarter in March, June, September and December.

Dalrymple Donaldson Fund

Building conservation
See below

Beneficial area Scotland.

Banklug Farm, Neilston, East Renfrewshire G78 3AY

Trustees   *John Malden; Roland Golightly; Dr Ian Campbell; Dr Richard Fawcett; Prof. David Walker; Mrs Irene Hughson.*

Scottish Charity No. SC014803

Information available   Limited information was available on this trust.

General   The fund gives grants towards the repair and restoration of historically significant buildings, usually in cases where local initiative has deserved encouragement and often where money is forthcoming from other sources as well.

The trustees stated that they aim to help as many projects as are eligible throughout Scotland, but that this is dependent upon the level of income generated by investments. Grants usually range between £1,000 and £5,000.

No further information was available.

Exclusions   No grants towards new building work, e.g. for the provision of disabled access.

Work on the interiors of buildings such as re-decorating and re-wiring is not eligible.

Refurbishment projects that would damage or destroy original features of the building would also not be eligible.

Applications   In writing to the correspondent. (Applicants are asked to complete an information summary form in advance of the trustees' meeting, so that up-to-date information on the progress of fundraising can be taken into account.) Trustees meet in December each year to consider projects starting within the following twelve months, together with details of any funding already in place. Grants cannot be given retrospectively.

Darroch Charitable Trust

General
About £25,000 each year

Beneficial area UK, with a preference for the West of Scotland.   *Harper*

Bird Semple Solicitors, 21 Blythswood Square, Glasgow G2 4BL   *Macleod*

Tel. 0141 304 3434

Correspondent   Thomas W Monteith

Scottish Charity No. SC018378

Information available   Information was provided by the trust.

General   The trust has general charitable purposes, with a preference for the West of Scotland. It gives about £25,000 a year to organisations. Grants ranged from £200 to £3,000. Beneficiaries have included Ayrshire Dementia Support Association, Ayrshire Hospice, East Kilbride Befriending Project, Oxfam, Visual Impairment Services Scotland and West Kilbride Out of School Care Group.

Exclusions   No support to individuals.

Applications   In writing to the correspondent. Trustees meet once a year in October.

Applications are considered throughout the year.

Dumfries and Galloway Council Charitable Trusts

General

£48,000 to organisations and individuals (2003/04)

Beneficial area Dumfries and Galloway.

Dumfries and Galloway Council, Carruthers House, English Street, Dumfries DG1 2HP

Tel. 01387 260000 **Fax** 01387 260034

website www.dumgal.gov.uk

Correspondent The Director of Finance

Trustees *The Members of the Council.*

Scottish Charity No. SC025071

Information available Information was provided by the council.

General The educational trusts administered by the council are used to provide educational grants, school equipment and prizes. The welfare trusts are used for the well-being of residents of children's homes and the users of adult resource centres and family centres.

In 2003/04 the trusts had an income of £70,000 from assets totalling £1 million. Grants totalling £48,000 were disbursed in support of education, social welfare, and general charitable causes, according to the purposes of the individual trusts. Most expenditure related to grants to individuals and local organisations.

A list of recent beneficiaries was not available. Previous beneficiaries include Lockerbie Academy students, Dalbeattie Day Centre and Sanquhar Academy.

Exclusions No support for arts, religious appeals, health/medical appeals, animal welfare or environment/heritage.

Applications In writing to the correspondent.

The Dumfriesshire Educational Trust

Education

About £22,000 to organisations and individuals a year

Beneficial area The former county of Dumfriesshire.

Dumfries and Galloway Council, Municipal Chambers, Buccleuch Street, Dumfries DG1 2AD

Tel. 01387 245960 **Fax** 01387 245961

Correspondent Robert Thom

Scottish Charity No. SC003411

Information available Information was supplied by the trust.

General The trust gives educational grants to individuals and organisations. It will support arts, training, sports and recreation, overseas projects and school excursions. Grants are one-off and usually range from £60 to about £300. Beneficiaries include schools, students (including mature students), local clubs and societies and adult education. The trust gives about £22,000 a year in grants.

Exclusions No grants to organisations or individuals based outside Dumfriesshire.

Applications On a form available from the correspondent. The trustees meet to consider grants in March, June, September and December. Applications should be sent by February, May, August and November.

Endrick Trust

General

About £9,000 a year £13 2K

Beneficial area UK.

c/o T C Young Solicitors, 30 George Square, Glasgow G2 1LH

Tel. 0141 221 5562 **Fax** 0141 221 5024

Correspondent A O Robertson

Scottish Charity No. SC012043

Information available Limited information was available on this trust.

max £2m income

General   The trust makes grants to a range of national causes in the UK and local causes in the west of Scotland. No details of the beneficiaries were provided, although research shows that grants have previously included those to Weipers Centre for Equine Welfare and Emmaus Glasgow.

Applications   In writing to the correspondent.

The Ferguson Bequest Fund

Churches

£144,000 (2004)

Beneficial area South west Scotland.

182 Bath Street, Glasgow G2 4HG

Tel. 0141 332 0476 **Fax** 0141 331 0874

Correspondent   Ronald D Oakes, Secretary

Trustees   *R B Copleton, Chair; W S Carswell; S Bell; Revd R W M Johnston; I F Mackay; J Boyle; T G Fielding; D Macrae; Revd D Kay; Revd J D Fulton.*

Scottish Charity No. SC009305

Information available   Information was provided by the trust.

General   'The principle objective of the fund, established by an Act of Parliament in 1869, is the provision of grants for the maintenance and repair of church buildings although it may also grant aid other activities of the churches, especially in the field of education. Under the Act of Parliament, the fund can assist only certain Scottish churches. As a rule, the operations are limited to the south west of Scotland.'

In 2004 it had assets of £3.5 million and an income of £166,000. Grants were made during the year totalling £144,000, and were broken down as follows:

Church of Scotland:
Church repairs – £76,000
Other grants – £16,000

Free Church:
Other grants – £1,500

Reformed Presbyterian:
Ministers' Stipend – £9,500
Church repairs – £2,000

United Reformed Church:
Church repairs – £8,000
Other grants – £1,500

United Free Church:
Church repairs – £8,000
Other grants – £1,500

Other:
Church repairs – £13,000
Other grants – £7,500

Applications   Written requests for application forms should be sent to the correspondent. Applications can be considered at any time.

The Gemmell Bequest Fund

General

About £9,000 each year

Beneficial area Glasgow and the parish of Sorn, Ayrshire.

Bishops Solicitors, 2 Blythswood Square, Glasgow G2 4AD

Tel. 0141 248 4672 **Fax** 0141 221 9270

Correspondent   Helen E Stirling, Trustee

Trustees   *Helen E Stirling; I L Dunsmore.*

Scottish Charity No. SC001344

Information available   Information was provided by the trust.

General   From the end of 2005, following several years of inactivity, the fund will again be making grants to the value of about £9,000 each year.

Most grants will be awarded on an annual recurrent basis, but one-off grants ranging between £50 and £100 can be made.

Exclusions   No grants to individuals nor to charities outside the stated beneficial area.

Applications   In writing to the correspondent.

The City of Glasgow Society of Social Service

General

£5,000 to organisations (2003/04)

Beneficial area Glasgow.

30 George Square, Glasgow G2 1EG

Tel. 0141 248 3535

e-mail cgsss@btconnect.com

website www.glasgowsociety.org

Correspondent Mrs Joy Stevenson, Secretary

Trustees *Dr Sarah Orr; Daniel J Brewster; Ronald G Fulton, Chair; A C Fyfe; John Keith; Mrs Joyce Stevenson; Graeme Whyte; Mrs Ann Peet; Mrs Philomena Strachan; Mrs Margaret Robertson; William Scoullex.*

Scottish Charity No. SC000906

Information available Full accounts were provided by the trust.

General This trust is an amalgamation of 20 smaller funds, all of which give grants in Glasgow. Most of the funds are given to individuals for a variety of reasons (for further information on its grants to individuals, please see *A Guide to Grants for Individuals in Need*, also published by DSC).

In 2003/04 it had assets of £2.6 million and an income of £226,000. Grants were made totalling £148,000, most of which went to individuals but which included £5,000 in grants to organisations. This consisted of £4,000 to Glasgow Children's Holiday Scheme and £1,000 to Shakespeare Street Youth Club.

Applications In writing to the correspondent.

The Glendoune Charitable Trust

Armed forces' charities

Not known

Beneficial area Ayrshire.

Messrs Morrisons, 105 West George Street, Glasgow G2 1QA

Tel. 0141 204 4225 **Fax** 0141 204 4511

Correspondent J A Aitkenhead

Scottish Charity No. SC016249

Information available Information was provided by the trust.

General The trust supports armed forces' charities and similar causes, e.g. ex-service charities. The majority of the grants are recurrent. Recent beneficiaries have included Erskine Hospital, Gurkha Welfare Trust and South Ayrshire Forces' Association. Unfortunately financial information was not available but the trust stated that donations are usually for £500 or more each.

Exclusions No grants to individuals and not generally to non-registered charities.

Applications In writing to the correspondent. Applications should be received in December or January.

The Dora Hay Charitable Trust

General

£3,000 (2004)

Beneficial area Moffat.

Bannerman Johnstone Maclay Accountants, Tara House, 46 Bath Street, Glasgow G2 1HG

Tel. 0141 332 2999 **Fax** 0141 333 0171

e-mail solutions@bjm-ca.co.uk

Correspondent G J Johnstone, Trustee

Trustees *T P C Taylor; G J Johnstone.*

Scottish Charity No. SC008886

Information available Information was provided by the trust.

General In 2004 the trust had net assets totalling £84,000, generating an income of £4,500. Grants totalled £3,000. Organisations based in Moffat are given preference. No further information was available.

Applications Contact the correspondent for further details.

M V Hillhouse Trust

General

About £50,000

Beneficial area Ayrshire and Gloucestershire.

Mitchells Roberton Solicitors, George House, 36 North Hanover Street, Glasgow G1 2AD

Tel. 0141 552 3422 **Fax** 0141 552 2935

Trustees *G E M Vernon; H R M Vernon.*

Scottish Charity No. SC012904

Information available Limited information was provided by the trust.

General The trust supports only local organisations that are known personally to the trustees. It gives grants local to Hillhouse Estate in Ayrshire and in Gloucestershire. The grant total, of about £50,000 each year, is divided equally between England and Scotland.

Applications The trust states that unsolicited applications are not welcome and cannot be responded to. All available funds are allocated each year to organisations previously supported.

The Holywood Trust

Disadvantaged young people between 15 and 25 years

£348,000 to individuals and organisations (2003/04)

Beneficial area Dumfries and Galloway.

Mount St Michael, Craigs Road, Dumfries DG1 4UT

Tel. 01387 269176 **Fax** 01387 269175

e-mail funds@holywood-trust.org.uk

website www.holywood-trust.org.uk

Correspondent Peter O Robertson, Director

Trustees *Mrs E A Nelson, Chair; C A Jencks; J J G Brown; A M McLeod; B J K Weatherall; Ms L L Fox.*

Scottish Charity No. SC009942

Information available Information was provided by the trust.

General The trust supports young people, aged 15 to 25 who live in Dumfries and Galloway, particularly those experiencing mental, physical or social disadvantage. It does this through grant awards to young people and by actively seeking opportunities to support others working directly with or for young people, by means of secondment of staff, management, clerical or administration support and fundraising activity.

It is involved with projects or organisations concerned with:

- homeless young people (Nithsdale Trust)
- youth work (YMCA, Youth Clubs Scotland)
- personal development of young people
- detached youth work
- drop in centres for young people
- counselling support of young people involved with drug and solvent abuse (Lochbank Trust)
- other trusts supporting young people (BBC Children in Need, Rank Foundation).

Grants generally range between £50 to £500 for individuals and up to £3,000 for organisations but sometimes the trust makes a major investment in developing a response to the needs of young people. Grants are given to self-help groups and organisations involving the wider community. A wide range of groups are supported, for example groups concerned with arts, buildings, environment, education/training, disability, health, overseas projects, social welfare or sport. Individuals are also supported.

In 2003/04 the trust had assets of £15 million and an income of £945,000. Grants were made totalling £348,000. The largest grant was made to Maggie Jencks Cancer Caring Trust (£50,000). Other larger grants included those to YMCA (£19,000), Arrest Referral Scheme (£18,000), Nithsdale Trust (£15,000) and Moffat Youth Theatre (£7,500).

Exclusions Grants are not given to political parties, as a substitute for statutory funding, for retrospective applications and rarely for landlord's deposits.

Applications On a form available from the correspondent. Applications are considered by the trustees at least four times a year.

The Hoover Foundation

Education, health, welfare

£14,000 (2003/04)

Beneficial area UK, but with a special interest in South Wales, Glasgow and Bolton.

Pentrebach, Merthyr Tydfil, Mid Glamorgan CF48 1TU

Tel. 01685 721222 **Fax** 01685 382946

Correspondent Mrs Marion Heaffey

Trustees *D J Lunt; A Bertali; C Jones.*

Charity Commission no. 200274

Information available Information was supplied by the trust.

General The objectives of the trust are primarily to support educational, environmental and charitable work in and around the areas of Hoover Limited locations throughout the UK namely South Wales, Glasgow and Bolton.

In 2003/04 the trust had assets of £2.4 million and an income of £38,000. Grants were made totalling £14,000 with the beneficiaries including National Asthma Campaign 'Point of Diagnosis Project' (£10,000) and Bolton Borough Band (£2,000). All other grants totalled £2,500 and were for less than £1,000 each.

Exclusions The trustees do not make grants to individuals, including students.

Applications In writing to the correspondent.

The George Hunter Trust

General – see below

£3,000 (2004/05)

Beneficial area Lochmaben.

Dumfries & Galloway Council, Council Offices, High Street, Annan, Dumfries & Galloway DG12 6AQ

Tel. 01461 203311 **Fax** 01461 207040

Correspondent Julie Douglas, Clerk to the Trust

Trustees *Revd J Brown; Michael Dickie; Marjorie McQueen; Anne Simpson.*

Scottish Charity No. SC004898

Information available Information was provided by the trust.

General The trust supports organisations in Lochmaben in Dumfries and Galloway. It supports community groups and voluntary organisations promoting the well-being of the local community of Lochmaben. It will consider the following types of causes: arts, children and young people, disability, education/training, environment/conservation, heritage, older people, social welfare and sports/recreation.

In 2004/05 the trust had an income of £3,000. Grants are one-off and range from £50 to £400. Beneficiaries have included Lochmaben Sunday School, Annan Sailing Club, Lochmaben Pipe Band, Lochmaben Primary School and Dumfries and Galloway ME Network.

Applications On a form available from the correspondent.

The Inverclyde Bequest Fund

Sailors' charities

£50,000 (2004)

Beneficial area UK and USA, with a preference for Glasgow and the west of Scotland.

Merchants' House of Glasgow, 7 West George Street, Glasgow G2 1BA

Tel. 0141 221 8272

Correspondent Jimmy Dykes, Assistant Collector

Trustees *The Directors of the Merchants' House of Glasgow.*

Information available Information was provided by the trust.

General The trust supports seamen's missions. Forty per cent of the fund's income is distributed in Glasgow and the west of Scotland. Due to the decline in the shipping industry there are fewer missions and the trust states that most grants are recurrent. It prefers to support long-established missions. Grants total around £60,000 each year and range from £500 to £15,000.

Exclusions No grants to individuals.

Applications In writing to the correspondent, including your annual report and audited accounts.

The Kennyhill Bequest Fund

People who are disadvantaged

About £10,000 (2004/05)

Beneficial area Glasgow only.

Mitchells Roberton Solicitors, George House, 36 North Hanover Street, Glasgow G1 2AD

Tel. 0141 552 3422 **Fax** 0141 552 2935

e-mail jamc@mitchells-roberton.co.uk

Correspondent John A M Cuthbert, Trustee

Trustees *P C Paisley; Mrs Carolyn Normand; John A M Cuthbert; Peter Forrester.*

Scottish Charity No. SC000122

Information available Limited information was provided by the trust.

General The trust supports charitable organisations in Glasgow working for people who are disadvantaged.

No recent financial information was provided by the trust. In previous years grants of £500 and £800 have been awarded amounting to around £10,000 each year.

Previous beneficiaries included ACET Scotland, Centre for Project Ability, Fairbridge in Strathclyde, Glasgow Council on Alcohol, Glasgow Veteran Seafarers' Society and SYCA.

Exclusions No grants to organisations outside the stated beneficial area.

Applications In writing to the correspondent at the above address. The trustees meet annually in December.

Lamb, Middleton and MacGregor Bequest Funds

Relief of poverty and suffering

About £10,000

Beneficial area Glasgow.

Glasgow City Council, City Chambers, 285 George Street, Glasgow G2 1DU

Tel. 0141 287 5925 **Fax** 0141 287 3911

Correspondent The Director of Finance

Trustees *Glasgow District Council Finance Committee.*

Scottish Charity No. SC019200

Information available No recent financial information was available from the council.

General The trust is an amalgamation of three funds, now administered together. It gives grants to charities in Glasgow for the relief of poverty and suffering. Local branches of national organisations will be supported. Grants are made totalling around £10,000 each year and range from £300 to £500. No further information was available. Recent beneficiaries include the Big Issue, Barnardo's, Glasgow Council on Alcohol and Shelter.

Exclusions No grants to individuals.

Applications In writing to the correspondent. Trustees meet once a year in December to consider grants.

The Landale Charitable Trust

Churches, hospitals, the arts

£10,000 (2003/04)

Beneficial area South west Scotland.

Chiene & Tait, Cairn House, 61 Dublin Street, Edinburgh EH3 6NL

Tel. 0131 558 5800 **Fax** 0131 558 5899

Correspondent J Younger

Trustees *Sir David Landale; William Landale; James Landale; Lady Landale; Peter Landale.*

Charity Commission no. 274722

Information available Accounts were on file at the Charity Commission.

General Grants are mainly given in Scotland, to churches, hospitals and the arts. In 2003/04 the trust had an income of £10,000 and a total expenditure of £12,000. Grants are made for about £10,000 in total each year.

Exclusions No grants to individuals.

Applications The trustees stated: 'Funds are effectively committed to the extent that cold applications from people who pick up the name from [this] directory are in every case refused.'

Duncan Campbell Leggat's Charitable Trust

General

About £20,000

Beneficial area The west of Scotland.

Miller Beckett & Jackson Solicitors, 190 St Vincent Street, Glasgow G2 5SP

Tel. 0141 204 2833 **Fax** 0141 248 7185

e-mail mail@millerbj.co.uk

Correspondent G A Maguire, Trustee

Trustees *G A Maguire; N A Fyfe; H C Leggat.*

Scottish Charity No. SC011512

Information available Limited information was provided by the trust.

General This trust gives for general purposes in the west of Scotland. Grants are made totalling around £20,000 and are usually for £500 each, although they can be for up to £2,000.

Previous beneficiaries include Moral Re-Armament, Alzheimer's Scotland, Barcaple Christian Outdoor Centre, Glasgow Zoo, Howwood Playgroup, Princess Louise Scottish Hospital, Shelter Scotland and Tak Tent.

Applications In writing to the correspondent.

Lethbridge – Abell Charitable Bequest

Welfare

Not known

Beneficial area Glasgow.

Glasgow City Council, City Chambers, 285 George Street, Glasgow G2 1DU

Tel. 0141 287 4002

Correspondent The Private Secretary to the Lord Provost

Scottish Charity No. SC019203

Information available Limited information was available on this trust.

General The fund assists poor people in Glasgow. Most grants are given to people in need, however, small, local community groups can also be supported. Grants to both individuals and community groups can be for up to £300 each.

No further information was available.

Applications In writing to the correspondent.

The Andrew & Mary Elizabeth Little Charitable Trust

Disadvantaged people

About £70,000 (2005)

Beneficial area Mainly Glasgow and the surrounding area.

Low Beaton Richmond, Solicitors, Sterling House, 20 Renfield Street, Glasgow G2 5AP

Tel. 0141 221 8931 **Fax** 0141 248 4411

Correspondent R Munton

Scottish Charity No. SC011185

Information available Limited information was provided by the trust.

General The trust mainly supports organisations based in Scotland such as infirmaries, hospitals, homes for the aged, orphanages and other such institutions, which provide direct or indirect help to disadvantaged people. There is a preference for the Glasgow area.

No recent financial information was provided by the trust, however grants have previously totalled around £70,000 a year. Previous beneficiaries have included Ayrshire Hospice, Glasgow City Mission, Glasgow Marriage Guidance Council, Glasgow Old People's Welfare Committee, St Margaret's of Scotland Adoption Society and Strathclyde Youth Club Association.

Applications In writing to the correspondent. Trustees meet to consider grants once a month. Individuals should provide financial details of income support.

Loaningdale School Company

Children and young people

£5,000 to organisations (2003/04)

Beneficial area Lanarkshire.

Scott-Moncrieff, Chartered Accountants, 17 Melville Street, Edinburgh EH3 7PH

Tel. 0131 473 3500 **Fax** 0131 473 3535

e-mail graemethom@scott-moncrieff.com

Correspondent R Graeme Thom

Trustees E H Gordon, Chair; J H Harvie; A Knox; G W Littlejohn; I A Murray; T Penman.

Scottish Charity No. SC001065

Information available Information was provided by the trust.

General The trust was established to benefit children and young people in need and, where appropriate, gives preference to those living within the Clydesdale local area of South Lanarkshire. Both individuals and organisations are supported. In practice, grants are given towards creative and outdoor pursuits for young people, to support young people who are unemployed or in post-school education and training of young people.

Priority is given to:

- young people aged 12 to 20 years inclusive
- creative and outdoor pursuits for young people
- young unemployed people
- post-school education and training of young people.

In 2003/04 the trust had assets of £237,000 and an income of £9,500. Grants totalled £6,000 of which £5,000 went to organisations and £1,000 to individuals.

Beneficiaries included Biggar Museum Trust and Stablestone Primary School (£300 each), KODA (£250), Stanmore Adventure Holiday Group, Carluke Development Trust and J-Team Youth Group (£200 each), Kirkfieldbank Primary School (£150) and Rigside Primary School (£100).

Applications On a form available from the correspondent, including a copy of the constitution and latest audited accounts. Trustees meet in March, June, September and December, applications should be received by the preceding month.

Lockerbie Trust

General

£35,000 (2004/05)

Beneficial area Lockerbie.

Dumfries and Galloway Council, Council Offices, English Street, Dumfries DG1 2DD

Tel. 01387 260022 **Fax** 01387 260034

e-mail carolhe2@dumgal.gov.uk

Correspondent Alex Haswell, Clerk

Trustees Local MP; Chair of Lockerbie and District Community Council; two Lockerbie councillors.

Scottish Charity No. SC019796

Information available Information was provided by the trust.

General The trust supports projects for the community in Lockerbie. It will consider the following causes: arts, children/young people, conservation, disability, education/training, heritage, social welfare and sports/recreation. It makes grants of up to 50% of the cost and for pump-priming only.

In 2004/05 grants were made totalling £35,000. Information was not available on recent beneficiaries.

Previous recipients of smaller grants have included Lockerbie Jazz Festival, Lockerbie Scout Group and South of Scotland Ice Rink Club.

Applications On a form available from the correspondent. Trustees meet to consider grants in February, July and December. Applications should be sent in the month prior to the meetings.

Lord Provost's Charities Fund

Welfare

Not known

Beneficial area Glasgow.

Glasgow City Council, City Chambers, 285 George Street, Glasgow G2 1DU

Tel. 0141 287 4003

Correspondent The Private Secretary to the Lord Provost

Scottish Charity No. SC019204

Information available Limited information was available from the trust.

General The fund assists poor people in Glasgow. Most grants are given to people in need, however, small, local community groups can also be supported. Grants to both individuals and community groups can be for up to £300 each.

No further information was available.

Applications In writing to the correspondent.

The Lord Margadale Charitable Trust

Health and welfare, general

£3,600 (2003/04)

Beneficial area Wiltshire and the Scottish Island of Islay.

The Old Rectory, Fonthill Bishop, Salisbury, Wiltshire SP3 5SF

Tel. 01747 820231

Correspondent Mrs V Meeker, Secretary

Trustees *Lord A J Margadale; Hon. Mary A Morrison.*

Charity Commission no. 276410

Information available Information was provided by the trust.

General In 2003/04 the trust had an income of around £3,500 all of which was given in donations. Grants were made to 22 organisations in the range of £50 to £450. Those supported were health and welfare related charities.

Larger grants included £450 to Fonthill Bishop PCC, £400 each to Islay and Jura Community Trust and Leonard Cheshire Care at Home. Other grants were made to Kilarrow PCC (£200), Museum of Islay Life (£150) and Islay and Jura Guides Association and RNLI Islay Branch (£100 each).

Exclusions Only applications for Wiltshire and Island of Islay are considered. No applications from individuals considered.

Applications In writing to the correspondent. Applications are considered at trustees' meetings twice a year.

Dr J N Marshall (Island of Bute) Memorial Trust

General

About £8,000

Beneficial area Preference for Isle of Bute.

Mitchells Roberton Solicitors, George House, 36 North Hanover Street, Glasgow G1 2AD

Tel. 0141 552 3422 **Fax** 0141 552 2935

e-mail dbr@mitchells-roberton.co.uk

Correspondent Donald B Reid, Trustee

Trustees *I Maclagan; A Thomson; R Alexander; H MacLeod; Donald B Reid.*

Scottish Charity No. SC008765

Information available Information was provided by the trust.

General This trust has general charitable purposes, favouring appeals from the Isle of Bute. Grants are usually for 'a few hundred' pounds each. No further information was available.

Applications Application forms are available from the correspondent. Applications should be received by 1 March or 1 October.

The trust stated that it will not respond to 'scatter gun' enquiries.

The McCallum Bequest Fund

Relief of poverty and illness

About £10,000

Beneficial area Greater Glasgow.

MacDonalds Solicitors, 279 Bath Street, Glasgow G2 4JL

Tel. 0141 303 7100

Correspondent T McNeil

Trustees *G G Morris; Mrs G E Morris.*

Scottish Charity No. SC007713

Information available Information was provided by the trust.

General The trust supports the relief of poverty and illness, preferring to give grants to established organisations and for specific projects. Where grants are not for specific projects, the money must be used to benefit the people of Glasgow.

Grants have previously totalled about £10,000. No further information was available. Previous beneficiaries include Alzheimer's Scotland, Glasgow City Mission, Maxie Foundation, York Hill Children's Foundation, Big Issue Foundation in Scotland, East Park Home, Elutheria Company and Sounds of Progress.

Exclusions Grants are not normally given to individuals, or to organisations of a purely religious, educational or sporting nature.

Applications In writing to the correspondent. It is helpful if the application is backed up by a copy of accounts. Applications should received by October. Trustees distribute grants in December/January.

The McCrone Charitable Trust

Relief of poverty, education, religion, general

About £16,000

Beneficial area Glasgow and the west of Scotland.

Donn Sheldon Accountants, 1 Silk Street, Paisley PA1 1HG

Tel. 0141 849 1721 **Fax** 0141 848 6231

e-mail mm@donnsheldon.co.uk

Correspondent Mary McTaggart ✓

Trustees *G A Maguire; Charles Jackson; Mrs E K F Hudson; Dr H E M McCrone.*

Scottish Charity No. SC015385

Information available Limited information was provided by the trust.

General The trust was established in 1977 by the McCrone family. It will support the relief of poverty, education and religion as well as general charitable purposes. Grants are mostly recurrent but new applications will be considered. Grants range between £50 and £1,000.

No recent financial information was available from the correspondent, although previous research indicates that grants total around £16,000 each year. Previous beneficiaries include Glasgow High School, Help the Aged and Red Cross – Glasgow.

Applications In writing to the correspondent. Applications should be received before August each year.

The Merchants' House of Glasgow

General

£24,000 to organisations (2004)

Beneficial area Glasgow and the west of Scotland.

7 West George Street, Glasgow G2 1BA

Tel. 0141 221 8272 **Fax** 0141 226 2275

e-mail theoffice@merchantshouse.org.uk

Correspondent   Jimmy Dykes, Assistant Collector

Scottish Charity No. SC008900

Information available   Accounts were provided by the trust.

General   The trust will normally consider applications from the following:

- organisations providing care and assistance to people with disabilities, older people, people who are terminally ill and people who have been socially deprived
- organisations providing for the care, advancement and rehabilitation of youth
- universities, colleges of further education and schools
- organisations connected with the arts, including music, theatre and the visual arts
- institutions that are connected with and represented by the Merchants' House.

In 2004 it had assets of £5.3 million and an income of £793,000. Grants were made to organisations totalling £24,000.

The largest grants were made to Erskine Hospital (£3,000), Scottish International Piano Competition 2004 (£2,500), National Youth Orchestra of Scotland and Citizens' Theatre Limited (£1,500 each) and Boys' Brigade Glasgow Battalion, Girl Guiding Scotland, Meningitis Research Foundation, Merchants' City Townscape Heritage Initiative, Partners in Advocacy and Mark Scott Foundation (£1,000 each).

Grants of less than £1,000 totalled £9,000. Recipients included Abercorn School, Barnardo's, Childline Scotland, Community Central Hall, Glasgow Sea Cadet Unit, Paintings in Hospitals Scotland, Westbourne Music and Yorkhill Family Bereavement Service.

Exclusions   The trust will not, unless in exceptional circumstances, make grants to:

- individuals
- churches other than Glasgow Cathedral
- organisations that have received support in the two years preceding an application.

Applications   In writing to the correspondent at any time, supported by copy of accounts and information about the organisation's principal activities.

James and John Napier's Trust

Disabled young people, elderly people, maritime, medical research

£7,000 (2003/04)

Beneficial area Glasgow and the west of Scotland.

Headrick Inglis Glen & Co, Tara House, 46 Bath Street, Glasgow G2 1HL

Tel. 0141 332 3341 **Fax** 0141 331 2517

e-mail law@hig.sol.co.uk

Correspondent   Neil M Headrick, Trustee

Trustees   *N M Headrick; I Bruce; E Williamson.*

Scottish Charity No. SC002113

Information available   Information was provided by the trust.

General   The trust states that grants are awarded to small local organisations and charities in Glasgow and the west of Scotland, ranging between £500 and £1,000.

In 2003/04 it had assets of £172,000 and an income of £10,000. Grants were made totalling £7,000.

Beneficiaries included Whizz Kids, Hopscotch, RNLI, Momentum and Scottish Society for Autism.

Applications   In writing to the correspondent. Trustees meet in November, applications should be received by October.

New Templar Halls Trust

Temperance

About £10,000

Beneficial area Paisley.

48 Causeyside Street, Paisley PA1 1YJ

Tel. 0141 889 7531 **Fax** 0141 887 3380

e-mail mail@reidlaw.co.uk

Correspondent   W M Reid, Secretary/Treasurer

Trustees   *Earl Nicoll, Chair.*

Scottish Charity No. SC000615

Information available Information was provided by the trust.

General The trust gives to temperance organisations operating in Paisley. The trust will also give to individuals working in this field. Grants total about £10,000 a year.

Applications In writing to the correspondent.

Pastoral Care Trust

Welfare

£60,000 (2003/04)

Beneficial area Scotland, but mainly Glasgow.

196 Clyde Street, Glasgow G1 4JY

Tel. 0141 226 5898 **Fax** 0141 225 2600

e-mail pct@rcag.org.uk

website www.rcag.org.uk

Correspondent Elizabeth M McQuade, Development Officer

Trustees *Right Revd Monsignor Desmond Maguire; Mrs Kathleen McConville; Mr Frank McCormick; Miss Agnes Malone; Most Revd Mario Joseph Conti, Archbishop of Glasgow; Mr John McHugh; Mr John Geggan; Mr Michael Fitzpatrick; Mrs Sadie Fitzpatrick.*

Scottish Charity No. SC029832

Information available Information was provided by the trust.

General 'The Pastoral Care Trust was set up in 1992 to mark the 500th anniversary of the Archdiocese of Glasgow. It was founded to establish in a modern context the traditions of five centuries of Christian life and action here in Scotland. In particular it was established to offer small grants to groups, agencies and projects working for the common good of all Glasgow's people.'

The trust also provided the following information:

The trust exists to provide help in Christ's name to those most at need in our society regardless of their race, colour or creed. The trust encourages shared social action, so empowering local communities to combat identified social need. The trust gives preference to groups and organisations which operate on a self-help basis; where there is considerable involvement of local people as volunteers; and where funds are limited.

The trustees have decided that for the present the focus of their giving will be groups and organisations working in the areas where the greatest levels of deprivation are shown to be found. On reviewing the Scottish Index for Multiple Deprivation 2004, the greatest level was found within the Province of Glasgow. The Province of Glasgow represents that area covered by the City of Glasgow and the Districts of East and West Dunbartonshire, North and South Lanarkshire, Renfrewshire, East Renfrewshire and Inverclyde and the Western part of Argyll and Bute District around Helensburgh and the Gareloch.

Full guidance notes are available from the trust; a summary of the notes is as follows:

Who is the scheme aimed at?

Grants will be provided to organisations and community groups providing direct benefit to communities, particularly in the following priority areas:

- children and young people
- older people
- people with disabilities
- those suffering from the effects of poverty or unemployment
- those suffering as a result of alcoholism and/or drug abuse
- individuals or groups in the community suffering from the effects of discrimination
- those who have been, or are experiencing mental illness.

Preference will be given to groups:

- where there is considerable involvement of local people as volunteers
- which operate on a self-help basis
- where funds are limited
- where matched funding would be applicable
- who operate in an area where poverty and deprivation are daily realities.

In 2003/04, the trust had assets of £203,000 and an income of £100,000. Grants totalling £60,000 were made to 29 organisations.

The largest grant of £6,500 was made to St Joan of Arc School. All other grants were for £5,000 or less. Beneficiaries included: 3D Drumchapel, Pollok Village, Gallowgate and Calton Children's Project and The Safety Zone (£5,000 each), Young Heart Disabled Club and Positive Help (£3,000 each), Autism Aware, Leven West 60+ Group and The Wynd Centre (£2,500 each), Braendam Family House (£2,000) and Maryhill Community Health Project and Milton Bosco Community Holiday Group (£1,500 each).

Exclusions   Grants will not be made:

- to individuals
- towards salaries
- towards budget shortfalls
- for building work where it is solely to meet changes in legislation
- for political campaigning.

Applications   On a form available from the correspondent; full guidelines are also available. Closing dates for applications are the second Monday in February, May, August and November, for the trustees' meetings in March, June, September and December respectively.

The John Primrose Trust

Young people and older people

About £10,000 (2005)

Beneficial area Dumfries.

Primrose & Gordon, 92 Irish Street, Dumfries, Dumfries & Galloway DG1 2PF

Tel. 01387 267316 **Fax** 01387 269747

e-mail enquiries@primroseandgordon.co.uk

Correspondent   The Trustees

Scottish Charity No. SC009173

Information available   Information was provided by the trust.

General   This trust gives grants to young people 'to give them a start in life', supporting organisations and individuals. Some grants are also given to older people. About £10,000 is given in total each year.

Applications   On a form available by writing to the correspondent. The trustees meet in May/June and December.

Mrs Elizabeth Scott's Charitable Trust

General

£8,500 (2004/05)

Beneficial area Unrestricted, but with a preference for the west of Scotland.

c/o Neill Clerk & Murray, Solicitors, 3 Ardgowan Square, Greenock PA16 8NW

Tel. 01475 724522 **Fax** 01475 784339

Correspondent   D I Banner, Trustee

Trustees   *Miss J K Edgar; D I Banner; A M Urquhart.*

Scottish Charity No. SC015420

Information available   Information was provided by the trust.

General   In 2004/05 the trust's assets totalled £94,000 and it had an income of £4,500. General grants to charities totalled £8,500 and consisted mainly of £500 donations. The exception was £1,000 to Erskine Hospital.

Other beneficiaries included CHAS, Glasgow Humane Society, Maggie's Centre, Royal British Legion Scotland, RNLI, Glasgow Simon Community, Barnardo's 16+, Guide Dogs for the Blind and The Ark.

Applications   In writing to the correspondent. Distributions are normally made in June and December of each year.

South Lanarkshire Council Charitable Trusts

General

Not known

Beneficial area South Lanarkshire.

Council Offices, Almada Street, Hamilton ML3 0AA

Tel. 01698 454530 **Fax** 01698 454682

Correspondent   Archie Strang, Executive Director of Finance and IT Resources

Scottish Charity No. SC025089

Information available   Information was provided by the council.

General   117 trust funds are administered by the council. Grants are made to a range of organisations in South Lanarkshire. Many of the funds primarily support individuals. Further information was not available.

Applications   The council has previously told us that it does not donate grants and instead distributes bequests and other funds to pre-decided causes.

Strathclyde Police Benevolent Fund

Police, general

About £130,000 a year

Beneficial area Strathclyde.

Strathclyde Police Federation, 151 Merrylee Road, Glasgow G44 3DL

Tel. 0141 633 2020 **Fax** 0141 633 0276

Correspondent Linda McCartney, Trustee

Trustees *G Carmichael, Chair; A Gillies; Linda McCartney; J Foster; R Watterson.*

Scottish Charity No. SC009899

Information available Information was provided by the trust.

General Funds are mainly available for members of Strathclyde police, retired members, and widows or other dependants who may be in need. The trust may also donate to other registered charities for general charitable purposes.

Grants are made totalling around £130,000 each year. No details of beneficiaries were provided.

Applications In writing to the correspondent. Applications to be received by the end of March for consideration in the annual meeting held in April.

The Talbot-Crosbie Bequest

General

Around £16,000 a year

Beneficial area Bearsden.

Community Support, East Dunbartonshire Council, 36 Roman Road, Bearsden G61 2SQ

Tel. 0141 587 7521 **Fax** 0141 563 9800

e-mail communitygrants@eastdunbarton.gov.uk

Correspondent Alastair Ewen

Scottish Charity No. SC018494

Information available Limited information was available on this trust.

General The Talbot-Crosbie Bequest is distributed through the East Dunbartonshire

Community Grant Scheme. Applicants must be from constituted not-for-profit organisations and must benefit people resident in Bearsden.

Applications There are four opportunities to apply spread out across the year. Contact the correspondent for a grant pack. Applications are made via the East Dunbartonshire Community Grant Scheme.

The Templeton Goodwill Trust

General

£105,000 (2004/05)

Beneficial area Glasgow and the West of Scotland (the Glasgow postal area).

12 Doon Street, Motherwell ML1 2BN

Tel. 01698 262202

Correspondent W T P Barnstaple, Trustee and Administrator

Trustees *J H Millar; B Bannerman; W T P Barnstaple; C Barrowman*

Scottish Charity No. SC004177

Information available Information was provided by the trust.

General The trust supports a wide range of charities in Glasgow and the West of Scotland. It is interested in supporting organisations which help others. Types of beneficiaries include: youth organisations, medical research charities, churches, ex-services' organisations and other organisations concerned with social work and providing caring services for all age groups.

In 2004/05 the trust had assets of £2.1 million and an income of £293,000. Grants were made totalling £105,000 and were distributed to 62 different groups.

Beneficiaries included Girl Guides' Association (£4,500), YWCA (£4,000), City of Glasgow Society of Social Services (£3,500), The Boys' Brigade, Glasgow Retirement Council, Quarriers Homes, Salvation Army and Scout Association (£3,000 each), Scottish Furniture Trades' Benevolent Association (£2,500) and Cancer Research Campaign, Marie Curie Memorial Foundation and Macmillan Nursing (£2,000 each).

Exclusions   Support is given to Scottish registered charities only. Individuals are not supported and grants are generally not given to arts or cultural organisations.

Applications   In writing to the correspondent, preferably including a copy of accounts. Applications should be received by April as the trustees meet once a year, at the end of April or in May. Initial telephone calls are welcome. An sae is required from applicants to receive a reply.

Donald Thomson Memorial Educational Trust

Gaelic education

About £1,000 a year

Beneficial area Particular interest in Argyll.

Sannox, Crannaig-A-Mhinister, Oban PA34 4LU

Tel. 01631 563 977

Correspondent   R Macintyre

Scottish Charity No. SC013598

Information available   Information was provided by the trust.

General   The trust makes grants towards the advancement of Gaelic education in Argyll. Grants total about £1,000 a year.

Exclusions   No grants to individuals.

Applications   In writing to the correspondent.

The Trades House of Glasgow

Social welfare, general

£172,000 (2003/04)

Beneficial area Glasgow.

Administration Centre, North Gallery – Trades Hall, 85 Glassford Street, Glasgow G1 1UH

Tel. 0141 553 1605 **Fax** 0141 553 1233

website www.tradeshouse.org.uk

Correspondent   The Clerk

Scottish Charity No. SC012507

Information available   Full accounts were provided by the trust.

General   Grants are made to a range of charitable causes varying from a few hundred pounds up to £28,000, but more typically for £2,000 to £3,000. Awards are also made to individuals in the range of a few pounds to £3,000. All grants are one-off and the vast majority of funds are donated within Glasgow.

The Trades House of Glasgow was first established in 1605. It manages a number of trust funds, each bound to their separate trust deeds. Fourteen of these are very old and the Scottish equivalent of the craft guilds and livery companies which developed in European cities in the middle ages. They include the Hammermen, Barbers and Masons whose members now cover such diverse professions as electronic engineering, surgery, surveying and civil engineering. Most of the trusts are tied to specific causes and locations. The majority are concerned with various aspects of social welfare and individual need, particularly in Glasgow. Only one of the funds, the Commonweal Fund, is able to respond to applications from organisations. All the others can only support those organisations named in their trust deeds.

The Commonweal Fund makes grants to projects totalling about £100,000 each year. Grants are made to a range of charitable causes and can be for up to 'a few thousand pounds'. All grants are one-off and the vast majority of funds are donated within Glasgow.

The Trades House states:

The assistance of needy pensioners, the encouragement of youth and the fostering of industrial initiative are now its chief objects. It concerns itself not just with the maintenance of tradition but the disbursement of substantial funds for numerous good causes; helping those in need, encouraging promising youngsters at college or in industry, and many other worthwhile projects. In addition when particular causes are put forward the Trades House seeks to respond by raising new funds to support them.

The Trades House has always been concerned with the welfare of its least well-off members. It has provided hospitals for the sick, pensions for the elderly, succour for the needy. Over the years it has been concerned with the support of almshouses, schools, hospitals, asylums and even the raising of a battalion to fight in the Napoleonic Wars.

In addition to administering its own funds the Trades House is responsible for a number of other funds

189

some of which are of considerable size. This responsibility is discharged by committees with the assistance of a small staff including two qualified social workers who ensure the fair and efficient utilisation of funds.

The Trades House operates under the chairmanship of the Deacon Convener who is elected annually by its members, the representatives of the fourteen crafts and he plays a prominent role in the affairs of the city, including having an ex officio seat on the District Council.

The note above, that the charity seeks to raise new funds when needed for particular causes, is most welcome, and a precedent that might well be followed by other 'ancient' welfare charities which tend to limit their response to modern needs to the funds that have been handed down from the past.

In 2003/04 the charity had assets of £11.5 million and an income of £562,000, including £54,000 from fundraising activities. Grants were made to 163 organisations totalling £172,000, of which 108 were under £1,000. A further £93,000 was given in total to 262 individuals.

By far the largest grants was £28,000 to Columba 1400. Other grants included £15,000 to Trades Hall of Glasgow, £5,000 to Visual Statement, £4,000 each to Children's Classic Concerts and SYCA, £3,500 to Glasgow Bute Benevolent Society, £3,000 to University of Glasgow, £2,500 each to Association of Deacons and Grand Antiquity Society, and £2,000 each to Aberlour Child Care Trust, Erskine Hospital, Quarries, Church House, Fablevision, Fairbridge, Arches Circus Summer School and Tron St Mary's.

Exclusions The funds are held primarily for the benefit of Glasgow and its citizens, and if you fall outside those parameters you should not submit an application. Political, municipal, and ecclesiastical appeals cannot be entertained. Charities duplicating rather than complementing existing services and those with national purposes and/or large running surpluses normally cannot be helped.

Applicants receiving help one year will normally be refused the next.

Applications Application forms are available for organisations seeking help from the Trades House office. A summary should be written extending to not more than a single A4 sheet, backed as necessary by schedules and accompanied by the organisation's latest accounts and/or business plan. Evidence of need must be produced, as should evidence that client groups participate in decision making and that their quality of life and choice is enhanced. Where possible, costs and financial needs should be broken down, evidence of the difference which a grant would make be produced, and details given, with results, of other grants applied for. Applications should include evidence of charitable status, current funding and an explanation as to what this is being used for. Projects should be demonstrated to be practical and business-like. It is a condition of any grant that a report be made as to how the funds have been used. Grants not used for the purposes stated must be returned.

Tullochan Trust

Young people
About £25,000 a year

Beneficial area Dunbartonshire, Bearsden, Milngavie and Helensburgh.

Tullochan, Gartocharn G83 8ND

Tel. 01389 830205 **Fax** 01389 830653

Correspondent Mrs Fiona Stuart, Chair

Scottish Charity No. SC025309

Information available Information was provided by the trust.

General We were advised by the trust that it 'now concentrates its resources on establishing projects aimed at young people' and that the grants programme itself was no longer in operation.

Each year, only a few, local, discretionary grants are made, although this aspect of its work is not actively advertised.

Exclusions Applications from organisations unknown to the trustees are unlikely to be successful.

Applications In writing to the correspondent, but note above comments.

Walton Ian [handwritten]

Isidore & David Walton's Charitable Trust

Medical, education, general
About £130,000

Beneficial area West of Scotland. *MALO* [handwritten]

~~Deloitte & Touche, Lomond House, 9 George Square, Glasgow G2 1QQ~~

Tel. 0141 204 2800 **Fax** 0141 314 5893

Correspondent Margaret Glover

Trustees D Walton; Mrs C Walton; E Glen; M Walton; J R Walton. *E Walton* [handwritten]

Scottish Charity No. SC004005

Information available No recent information was available.

General The trust will support a wide variety of organisations, with a particular emphasis on education and medical causes, and Jewish organisations. Grants can range from £100 to £25,000 and are usually recurrent.

Previous research indicates that grants are made totalling around £120,000 to £150,000 each year. No recent financial information was available from the correspondent.

Previous beneficiaries include Jewish Care Scotland, which has received a large grant in the past. Other more typical grants have been given to organisations including British Council of SZMC, Lubavitch Foundation, Glasgow Jewish Education Trust, Jewish National Fund, Queens Park Hebrew Congregation, Glasgow Maccabi, Glasgow Jewish Representative Council, Scottish Jewish Archives and Glasgow Hebrew Burial Society.

Exclusions No grants to individuals. No grants for political causes.

Applications In writing to the correspondent. Trustees meet to consider grants in June; applications should be received by March.

The James Weir Foundation

Welfare, education, general
£181,000 (2004)

Beneficial area UK, with a preference for Ayrshire and Glasgow.

84 Cicada Road, London SW18 2NZ

Tel. 020 8870 6233 **Fax** 020 8870 6233

Correspondent Louisa Lawson, Secretary

Trustees Simon Bonham; William J Ducas; Elizabeth Bonham.

Charity Commission no. 251764

Information available Information was provided by the trust.

General The foundation has general charitable purposes, giving priority to schools and educational institutions; Scottish organisations, especially local charities in Ayrshire and Glasgow; and charities with which either James Weir or the trustees are particularly associated. These preferences, however, do not appear to be at the expense of other causes, UK-wide charities or local organisations outside of Scotland. The following six charities are listed in the trust deed as potential beneficiaries:

- Royal Society
- British Association for Advancement of Science
- RAF Benevolent Fund
- Royal College of Surgeons
- Royal College of Physicians
- University of Strathclyde.

In 2004 the trust had an income of £217,000, a total expenditure of £191,000 and assets of £5.9 million. Grants totalled £181,000.

The largest grants were for £3,000 each, given to the six organisations listed in the trust deed. Grants of £2,000 each went to 75 organisations, including Anthony Nolan Bone Marrow Trust, Changing Faces, Glasgow Old People's Welfare Association, Western Spirit, Toynbee Hall and Roy Castle Lung Cancer Foundation.

Exclusions Grants are given to recognised charities only. No grants to individuals.

Applications In writing to the correspondent. Distributions are made twice-yearly in June and November when the trustees meet. Applications should be received by May or October.

Western Recreation Trust

Recreation

Between £20,000 and £25,000

Beneficial area West of Scotland.

Scott-Moncrieff, 25 Bothwell Street, Glasgow G2 6NL

Tel. 0141 567 4500

Correspondent Ian Paterson

Scottish Charity No. SC002534

Information available Information was provided by the trust.

General The trust supports organisations in the west of Scotland working to improve recreational facilities for young people, older people and those who are unemployed. Grants are given towards the costs of equipment and are mostly of £200, although they can be up to £1,000 in exceptional cases. Between £20,000 and £25,000 is given in grants each year.

Exclusions Grants are not normally given to individuals.

Applications In writing to the correspondent at any time.

James Thomas Yuillie's Trust

General

About £4,000 a year

Beneficial area The burgh of Rothesay.

34 Castle Street, Rothesay PA20 9HD

Tel. 01700 503157

Correspondent Ian Maclagan, Trustee

Trustees Ian Maclagan; Mrs W C C Mackay; Revd R R Samuel; Mrs Marjorie J Bulloch.

Scottish Charity No. SC015388

Information available Information was provided by the trust.

General The trust donates to charitable organisations that operate within Rothesay. Grants total about £4,000 a year.

Applications On an application form available from the correspondent. Applications should be submitted by mid-June each year.

Zurich Community Trust (UK) Limited

Helping disadvantaged people move from dependence to independence

£2.7 million (2003)

Beneficial area UK and overseas, with a preference for Wiltshire, Hampshire, Birmingham, Cardiff, Leeds, London, Newcastle, Sutton, southern India, Belfast and Glasgow.

PO Box 1288, Swindon, Wiltshire SN1 1FL

Tel. 01793 511227 **Fax** 01793 506982

e-mail communityaffairs@uk.zurich.com

website www.zurich.org.uk

Correspondent Pam Webb, Community Affairs Manager

Trustees Chris Gillies; Eileen Hopkins; Ian Lovett; Andy Moore; David Sims; Chris Staples; Ian Stuart.

Charity Commission no. 266983

Information available Information was provided by the trust.

General There are two strands to Zurich's Community Trust:

1. Community Trust Programmes
Supports issues where the trust believes it is able to make a huge impact and bring about transformational change. Charity partners are selected whose projects are innovative, sustainable and could be replicated elsewhere. Often the issues are less popular ones and funding partnerships are normally for 3–5 years.

The programme is not open to ad hoc applications. Potential partners are identified, researched and selected by the community affairs team.

Current programmes include:

• Breaking the Cycle – £1 million over four years with Addaction to break the generational cycle of drug abuse

- Older People – £1.5 million over five years with six partners to support the most vulnerable older people
- Inclusion – £1 million over five years with four partners to tackle social exclusion issues
- Southern India – an ongoing programme which celebrated it's tenth year in 2004. Combines long term funding with personal development opportunities through skill transfer for senior managers.

2. Employee Involvement Programmes

Employees are encouraged to support charitable causes through contributions of time, money and skills through an internal fund called Zurich Cares. Zurich Cares works with 17 voluntary organisations, most of which are local partners around the sites of the associated company. Local fundraising and staff contributions fund these programmes. Grants in these areas are typically of £100 to £100,000 each. This programme has a preference for applications from around its main office locations in Gloucestershire, Wiltshire and Hampshire. There are also small funds available from their office locations in Belfast, Birmingham, Cardiff, Glasgow, Leeds, London, Newcastle and Sutton.

In addition the Openwork Foundation provides capital grants to organisations supporting disadvantaged children and young people under 18 through the Cares4Kids programme. This fund only accepts applications that have been nominated by financial advisers and staff and funds across the whole of the UK and overseas.

Examples of beneficiaries in 2004:

The largest grants were £50,000 to Age Concern Scotland to support older people and carers who are vulnerable to abuse and £50,000 of £275,000 over five years to The Calvert Trust for bursaries to enable 850 people with disabilities to benefit from adventure-style outdoor courses.

Other grants include £20,000 to Marie Curie Cancer Care to fund a nine-hour nursing shift every week in Swindon, London, Nottingham and Glasgow, £20,000 of £60,000 over three years to TWIGS in Swindon to fund an outreach worker and £10,000 of £30,000 over three years to Cheltenham Community Projects to fund a project worker.

Smaller grants were made to Wiltshire Young Stroke Group to expand their hand therapy service (£5,000), LEAVES in Swindon towards a low cost gardening service for people who are elderly or disabled (£2,100), Credence Charitable Trust in The Gambia to provide toilet and fresh water facilities, a perimeter fence and two uniforms for each of the 139 pupils (£1,400), St Mary's Hospice in Birmingham towards refurbishment of a day room (£1,100), Interact Reading Service in Birmingham to support people recovering from a stroke (£1,000) and Lodge Hill Trust, Sussex to fund two wheelchair-access picnic tables for people who are disabled (£700).

Exclusions   No grants made for:

- statutory organisations (including mainstream schools and hospitals), unless exclusively for a special needs unit
- fundraising events including appeals or events for national charities
- expeditions, exchanges or study tours
- playgroups and mother and toddler groups, unless for special needs groups
- medical research, animal welfare charities, conservation or environmental projects
- sports clubs, village halls, political or religious organisations (including the upkeep and repair of places of worship)
- advertising or sponsorship connected with charitable events or appeals.

Applications   In the first instance, visit the trust's website and follow the links to check eligibility and download the guidelines and application forms.

Highlands & Islands

Argyll and Bute Council Charitable Trusts

General
Not known

Beneficial area Argyll and Bute.

Finance Department, Council Headquarters, Argyll and Bute Council, Lochgilphead PA31 8RT

Tel. 01546 604471 **Fax** 01546 604411

Correspondent Bruce D West, Head of Strategic Finance

Scottish Charity No. SC025066

Information available Information was provided by the council.

General The council is responsible for a number of trusts, some of which are very small. Areas of interest include older people, people experiencing poverty and residents of the former boroughs of Argyll and Bute. It also provides funds for educational purposes, in particular grants and prizes for pupils and ex-pupils of schools in the area.

Applications In writing to the correspondent, who will then assess whether there is a trust that may be relevant. Some of the trusts do not accept unsolicited applications; many of those which do advertise in the local press when funds are available.

The Brownies Taing Pier Trust

Community groups
See below

Beneficial area Sandwick and Levenwick.

Tait & Peterson, Bank of Scotland Buildings, Lerwick, Shetland Islands ZE1 OEB

Tel. 01595 693010

Correspondent Eric S Peterson

Information available Limited information was provided by the trust.

General Grants are given to community projects in Sandwick and Levenwick. Projects which receive part of their funding from the local community are given preference. Several years ago grants totalled about £2,000 but the trust informed us that grants are not made every year and consequently does not commit to annual donations.

Applications Contact the correspondent at the above address for further information.

The Bute Charitable Trust

Education, medical and community projects
About £23,000 to organisations and individuals (2003/04)

Beneficial area UK, particularly Scotland and the Isle of Bute.

47–49 Borough High Street, London SE1 1NB

Tel. 020 7397 5660 **Fax** 020 7397 5669

Trustees *J C Bute; S Crichton-Stuart.*

Charity Commission no. 285226

Information available   Accounts were on file at the Charity Commission.

General   Grants are categorised into those given for 'education', including a number to individuals, and 'other donations'.

In 2003/04 the trust had an income of £14,000 and a total expenditure of £25,000. Grants were made totalling about £23,000. No information was available on beneficiaries during the year.

Previous beneficiaries include Rothesay Primary School, Rothesay Academy, Scottish Education Trust, King Edward VII Hospital Trust, Beach Watch – Bute, Battersea Summer Scheme, Crisis at Christmas, Help the Hospices, Terrence Higgins Trust and Jim Ross Coaching Clinic.

Applications   In writing to the correspondent.

The Davidson (Nairn) Charitable Trust

Social welfare

Not known

Beneficial area Nairn area.

Messrs R & R Urquhart, Incorporating MacGregor & Co Solicitors, Royal Bank of Scotland Buildings, 20 High Street, Nairn IV12 4AX

Tel. 01667 453278 **Fax** 01667 453499

e-mail partners.nairn@r-r-urquhart.com

Trustees   *Ian A Macgregor and others.*

Scottish Charity No. SC024273

Information available   Limited information was provided by the trust.

General   The trust gives grants in the Nairn area for social welfare causes. This includes making grants towards the provision of leisure and recreation facilities, relieving poverty, assisting elderly people, and educational concerns.

Exclusions   Only registered charities are supported or charities recognised in Scots law.

Applications   Write to the Agents for an application form.

Mrs A M Garnett's 1973 Charitable Trust

Medical, education, environment

About £20,000

Beneficial area Newtonmore area.

Chiene & Tait, Cairn House, 61 Dublin Street, Edinburgh EH3 6NL

Tel. 0131 558 5800 **Fax** 0131 558 5899

Correspondent   James G Morton

Trustees   *Eira Drysdale; J A Findlay; Alasdair J Findlay; John Drysdale.*

Scottish Charity No. SC003876

Information available   Accounts were on file at the Charity Commission.

General   The trust supports medical, educational and environmental charities in the Newtonmore area. In 2003/04 the trust had an income of £21,000 and a total expenditure of £22,000. Grants were made totalling around £20,000.

Previous beneficiaries include Game Conservancy Scottish Research Trust, HALO Trust, Patrons of National Galleries of Scotland, Sandpiper Trust, Diabetes UK Scotland, Countryside Restoration Trust, Macmillan Cancer Relief, Merlin, NSPCC, Roses Charitable Trust and SOS Farmers Appeal.

Exclusions   Grants are not given to individuals.

Applications   In writing to the correspondent.

Highland Council Charities

General

Not known

Beneficial area The Highland Council area.

The Highland Council, Glenurquhart Road, Inverness IV3 5NX

Tel. 01463 702000

Correspondent   Margaret Grigor, Finance Manager – Central Services

Scottish Charity No. SC025079

Information available Information was provided by the council.

General The council runs a number of common good and trust funds, which can award grants to support local community projects. These funds are administered through local offices as shown below:

Inverness Common Good Fund: Area Manager, Town House, Inverness IV1 1JJ (01463 724235)

Cromarty, Dingwall, Fortrose, Invergordon amd Tain Common Good Funds: Area Manager, Council Offices, High Street, Dingwall IV15 9QN (01349 868500)

Nairn Common Good Fund: Area Manager, The Court House, High Street, Nairn IV12 4AU (01667 458569)

Caithness Educational Trust Scheme, Area Education Manager, Rhind House, West Banks Avenue, Wick KW1 5LZ (01995 602812)

Iverness-shire Educational Trust Scheme, Area Education Manager, 13 Ardross Street, Inverness IV3 5NS (01463 663812).

No further information was available.

Applications Contact the appropriate division for further information.

The Jordan Charitable Foundation

General

£506,000 (2004)

Beneficial area Unrestricted, with strong local interests in Herefordshire and the Scottish Highlands.

Rawlinson and Hunter, Eagle House, 110 Jermyn Street, London SW1Y 6RH

Tel. 020 7451 9000 **Fax** 020 7451 9090

e-mail chris.hawley@rawlinson-hunter.com

Correspondent Chris Hawley, Secretary

Trustees *Sir Ronald Miller; Sir George Russell; Ralph Stockwell; Snowport Ltd; Parkdove Ltd.*

Charity Commission no. 1051507

Information available Full accounts on file at the Charity Commission.

General The trust does contribute to the core funding of some charities but this represents a fairly small proportion of its charitable spending.

The real aim of the trustees is to seek larger, more meaningful projects to support, including the refurbishment of buildings used for charitable purposes and the provision of essential medical or other equipment.

Funds are given towards welfare causes, including the welfare of animals and plantlife. Although the trust had an unrestricted beneficial area, virtually all of its grants are made in the UK, particularly Herefordshire and the Scottish Highlands. There were no overseas beneficiaries during 2004. Smaller recurrent grants are made to a broad range of UK charities.

In 2003/04 the trust had assets of £31 million and an income of £791,000. The costs of generating the funds and administration expenses were £198,000. Grants were made to 49 organisations totalling £506,000. Many recipients of grants had also been supported in previous years.

The beneficiary of the largest grant was The Royal Marsden Cancer Campaign, receiving £150,000. Other larger grants were distributed to Megan Baker House (£50,000), Women's Royal Voluntary Service (£48,000), Lifebuoy Charitable Trust (£35,000), Blue Cross (£25,000) and Eating Disorder Association (£20,000).

Among the other beneficiaries in the Scottish Highlands were National Trust for Scotland, Sutherland Schools Pipe Band – Golspie and Sutherland Young Carers Project (£5,000 each), Children's Hospice Association – Scotland and Highland Society for the Blind (£1,000 each) and Helmsdale Community Centre and Dunrobin Castle Piping Championship (£500 each).

Applications In writing to the correspondent.

Lewis Museum Trust

History, heritage

Not known

Beneficial area Stornoway and Isle of Lewis.

c/o 5 Mill Road, Stornoway, Isle of Lewis HS1 2TZ

Tel. 01851 703 812

e-mail deatfireflame@madasafish.com

Correspondent F G Thompson, Trustee

Scottish Charity No. SC019875

Information available Limited information was provided by the trust.

General   The trust gives grants to historical and heritage projects in Stornoway and Isle of Lewis. No further information was available.

Applications   Apply to the secretary at the address above by 31 December each year.

The William MacKenzie Trust

Older people

£7,000 to organisations (2003/04)

Beneficial area Former burgh of Stornoway.

26 Lewis Street, Stornoway, Isle of Lewis HS1 2JF

Tel. 01851 702335 **Fax** 01851 706132

e-mail jack@mannjudd.co.uk

Correspondent   Jack Kernahan, Trustee

Trustees   *Revd Stanley Bennie; Jack Kernahan; Donald MacDonald.*

Information available   Information was provided by the trust.

General   Grants of around £1,000 each are made to organisations which assist people in the former burgh of Stornoway who are elderly or infirm to remain in their own homes.

In 2003/04 the trust had assets of £803,000 and an income of £38,000. Grants to individuals totalled £17,000.

A total of £7,000 was given to other organisations to pass on to individuals. This included £2,500 each to Alzheimer's Group and Crossroads Care Group and £1,000 each to Provost's Coal Fund and Cul Taic.

Applications   In writing to the correspondent.

Lady McCorquodale's Charity Trust

Churches, cancer, retired nurses' organisations

£12,000 to organisations (2004/05)

Beneficial area Suffolk, Warwickshire and the Highlands and Islands of Scotland.

Pollen House, 10–12 Cork Street, London W1S 3LW

Tel. 020 7439 9061

Correspondent   Alan Winborn

Trustees   *The Cowdray Trust Limited.*

Charity Commission no. 268786

Information available   Full accounts were provided by the trust.

General   In 2004/05 the trust had assets of £518,000 and an income of £15,000. Grants were made totalling £16,000 of which over £12,000 was donated to organisations and £3,600 was distributed in payments to pensioners.

The main beneficiary was Charities Aid Foundation which received a grant of almost £12,000. Other grants were made to North Cerney Parochial Church Council (£500), Edith Cavell and Nation's Fund for Nurses (£200) and Macmillan Cancer Relief (£100).

Applications   In writing to the correspondent at any time.

James Paton's Charitable Trust

General

About £15,000

Beneficial area Inverness.

7 Muirfield Road, Inverness IV2 4AY

Tel. 01463 231025

Correspondent   R M Murray, Trustee

Trustees   *R M Murray; Hugh Hutchison.*

Scottish Charity No. SC000496

Information available   Information was provided by the trust.

General   The trust supports a wide variety of local charities in Inverness. It has about £15,000 to give in grants each year. Past beneficiaries have included Highland Regional Council's Social Work Department, Isobel Fraser Home of Rest and Highland Society for the Blind.

Exclusions   The trust does not normally fund national charities.

Applications   Applications are not encouraged as the trustees do their own research.

Ross and Cromarty Educational Trust

Education and training, children and young people

£10,000 (2005)

Beneficial area Isle of Lewis.

Comhairle nan Eilean, Education Department, Sandwick Road, Stornoway, Isle of Lewis HS1 2BW

Tel. 01851 709546 **Fax** 01851 709372

Correspondent The Director of Education

Information available Information was provided by the trust.

General The trust supports children and young people and education and training on the Isle of Lewis. Individuals are supported for educational purposes under the following categories:

- postgraduate scholarships
- special grants
- assistance in obtaining practical experience of trades
- travel grants
- educational excursions
- special equipment
- sports facilities
- support of clubs
- adult education
- promoting education in visual arts
- promoting education in music
- promoting education in drama.

Individual applicants must be ordinarily resident in the Isle of Lewis. Organisations must be Lewis based, although mainland organisations may apply for funding for Lewis-based branches. The trust stated that it has an annual income of around £10,000, the majority of which is given in grants. The usual maximum grant is £200.

Exclusions The trust only supports people living on the Isle of Lewis.

Applications In writing to the correspondent requesting an application form and further information.

Each application for a grant must be supported by cost estimates as all awards will be based on the cost of activities, projects or intended purposes.

Applications must be restricted to one trust section (category) at a time. Potential applicants should therefore determine their own priorities very carefully.

The Peter Samuel Charitable Trust

Health, welfare, conservation, Jewish care

£109,000 (2004)

Beneficial area South Berkshire, Highlands of Scotland and East Somerset.

The Estate Office, Castle Road, Farley Hill, Berkshire RG7 1UL

Tel. 0118 973 0047 **Fax** 0118 973 0385

Correspondent Miss Emma Chapman, Trust Administrator

Trustees *Hon. Viscount Bearsted; Hon. Michael Samuel.*

Charity Commission no. 269065

Information available Accounts were on file at the Charity Commission, without a recent grants list.

General The trustees' report states: 'The trust seeks to promote the family's interest in medical sciences, and the quality of life in local areas, heritage and forestry/land restoration'.

In 2004 the trust had assets of £2.9 million, which generated an income of £120,000. Grants were made to 15 organisations totalling £109,000.

By far the largest grants were £40,000 to Game Conservancy, £25,000 to Pippin and £20,000 to University College of London Development Fund.

Other beneficiaries included Worshipful Company of IT and Maidenhead Synagogue (£5,000 each), Barkingside Jewish Youth Centre (£3,000), Norwood and Jewish Care (£2,500 each), Community Security Trust (£2,000), Hemihelp, London String Quartet and New Bridge (£1,000 each), Jewish Memorial Council (£350), Lord Mayor of London Charity (£200) and Child Bereavement Trust (£100).

Exclusions No grants to purely local charities outside Berkshire or to individuals.

Applications In writing to the correspondent. Trustees meet twice-yearly.

Shetland Amenity Trust

Conservation, heritage

£61,000 to individuals and organisations
(2003/04)

Beneficial area Shetland.

Garthspool, Lerwick, Shetland ZE1 0NY

Tel. 01595 694688 **Fax** 01595 693956

e-mail shetamenity.trust@zetnet.co.uk

website www.shetland-heritage.co.uk/amenitytrust

Correspondent The Trustees

Trustees *Andrew Blackadder; Lawrence Robertson; Cecil Eunson; Florence Grains; Brian Gregson; Martin Heubeck; Roger Riddington; Frank Robertson; Douglas Sinclair; John Scott; James Henry.*

Scottish Charity No. SC017505

Information available Accounts were provided by the trust.

General The trust's stated objectives are:

- the protection, improvement and enhancement of buildings and artefacts of architectural, historical, educational or other interest in Shetland with a view to securing public access to such buildings and the permanent display for the benefit of the public of such artifacts for the purposes of research, study or recreation
- the provision, development and improvement of facilities for the enjoyment by the public of the Shetland countryside and its flora and fauna, the conservation and enhancement for the benefit of the public of its natural beauty and amenity and the securing of public access to the Shetland countryside for the purposes of research, study or recreation
- such other purpose or purposes charitable in law as the trustees shall from time to time determine.

In 2003/04 the trust had assets of £3.4 million and an income of £4.5 million which included £3.1 million in grants and donations received, mostly from Shetland Islands Council Charitable Trust.

Grants were given to 26 projects totalling £61,000. Beneficiaries included SAT Property Acquisition (£13,000), Glasgow University (£5,500), British Trust Conservation Volunteers (£4,000) and Viking Stories Project (£3,500).

The trust operates a grant aid scheme which provides financial assistance for the preservation of architectural heritage, environmental improvement initiatives and archaeological projects. During the year, £45,000 of the trust's grant total was awarded to 16 projects, including:

SAT Old Scatness Broch Phase 3 – £10,000
SAT Old Scatness Broch Phase 3 Consolidation (3 years) – £10,000
Whalsay History Group – £7,500
BTCV Scotland – £7,000
Peter Johnson Partnership – £1,500
Royal Commission on Ancient and Historical Monuments – £1,000
Shetland Organic Producers' Group – £500
Fetlar Museum Trust – £500
Scalloway Waterfront Trust – £350
Foula Heritage – £300
Shetland Heritage Association – £200

Applications In writing to the correspondent.

Shetland Arts Trust

Arts

About £50,000 (2004/05)

Beneficial area Shetland.

Pitt Lane, Lerwick, Shetland ZE1 0DW

Tel. 01595 694001 **Fax** 01595 692941

e-mail admin@shetland-arts-trust.co.uk

Correspondent Jacqueline Clark

Trustees *Anne Dickie; J Hutton; W H Manson; F A Robertson; Dorota Rychlik; B Stove; Celia Smith; Jane Thomas; Mr Skimmer; Mr E Knight; Mrs T Redmond; Mrs F Grains.*

Scottish Charity No. SC003098

Information available Information was provided by the trust.

General The trust promotes visual, performing and creative art in Shetland. It also assists in arranging a widespread service of performances, exhibitions and lectures about any artistic-related pursuits. It coordinates the efforts of government agencies, local authorities, societies, trade unions and local people. It operates an arts development grant scheme, the guidelines for which are as follows:

Who can apply?
Individuals who have practiced in their particular art form for two years or more. Individuals must

submit a portfolio/examples of their work with their application and have a bank account. References may be requested.

Groups who are planning an arts based project/event. Groups must submit a constitution with their application and have a bank account. Groups must submit examples of their work and previous publicity material with their application. Office bearers should be 18 years old or over.

Groups/individuals undertaking a commercial venture may apply for a Guarantee Against Loss. Further information on this aspect of the scheme is available through your grant contact.

How do you apply?

By completing the scheme's application form and submitting a project report. Each applicant is allocated a grant contact who will provide assistance and advice.

The majority of applications are considered by Arts Trust officials. On occasions the advice of our grants panel, sub-committees or board of trustees may be sought.

When can you apply?

Applications are considered throughout the year. However, our budget is limited and we would advise that you apply in the initial project planning stage of your project.

What do SAT look for?

- Originality within an arts project.
- Benefits to the wider Shetland community and the project participants.
- Developmental potential.
- Quality.
- Increased access to and awareness of the arts.
- Advancement of artistic skills.
- Financial assistance for equipment purchase will not be provided.
- Financial assistance for framing costs will not be provided unless it is part of a larger development project.
- Educational bursaries/grants are not currently provided.
- Funding will not be awarded retrospectively.

What happens if you are successful?

Funding will not exceed 50% of the total project cost. The grant amount will not exceed £750 (£1,000 if travelling outside Shetland). The grant amount for individuals will not normally exceed £500.

Grants under £500 will be paid in full prior to the project start date. For grants of £500 or over a 10% retention will be withheld. 90% of your grant will be payable prior to the project start date, the 10%

retention once all conditions of grant aid have been complied with.

The trust reserves the right to consider an Interest Free Loan or a Guarantee Against Loss as a more appropriate method of support on certain projects. Please ask your grant contact for further information.

What is matched funding?

Funding will not normally exceed 50% of the total project costs. The remaining 50% project shortfall must be covered from other sources, e.g. box office takings, Shetland Enterprise, Scottish Arts Council etc.

The trust stores information on funding agencies and general arts information. Please ask your grant contact for further information.

You will be required to vouch for the total cost of your project.

What is retrospective funding?

Retrospective funding is when an applicant submits a bid for funding for a project which has already been paid for in part or in full.

You are required to inform the trust of the project start and finish dates. If the money has been spent prior to these dates your project may be deemed to be retrospective.

Any bid which is submitted too near to the project start date runs the risk of being classified as retrospective. The trust advises all applicants to submit bids at least four weeks in advance of the project start date.

Is there anything else you need to know?

- Each application will be considered on its merit.
- The Development Grant Scheme is a discretionary one.
- Shetland Arts Trust reserves the right to reject an application.
- Any award will depend on the availability of funds.
- It can take between four and seven weeks to process any application.
- The trust encourages applicants to investigate other funding options.
- The trust operates an appeals procedure.
- Only one application can be submitted in any financial year (1 April to 31 March).
- Shetland Arts Trust funding must be acknowledged on all publicity material.

In 2004/05 the trust gave grants totalling about £50,000. No details of the beneficiaries were available.

Applications On a form available from the correspondent, to be returned with recent accounts and publicity material.

The Shetland Charitable Trust

Social welfare; art and recreation; environment and amenity

£16 million (2003/04)

Beneficial area Shetland only.

22–24 North Road, Lerwick, Shetland ZE1 0NQ

Tel. 01595 744991 **Fax** 01595 690206

e-mail mail.charitable.trust@sic.shetland.gov.uk

Correspondent Jeff Goddard, Financial Controller

Trustees *24 trustees, being the elected Shetland councillors (acting as individuals), the Lord Lieutenant and the Headmaster of Anderson High School. The chair is Bill Manson.*

Scottish Charity No. SC027025

Information available Annual report and accounts were provided by the trust (for the reasonable charge of £2).

General The original trust was established in 1976 with 'disturbance receipts' from the operators of the Sullom Voe oil terminal. As a clause in the trust deed prevented it from accumulating income beyond 21 years from its inception, in 1997 most of its assets were transferred to a newly established Shetland Islands Council Charitable Trust, which is identical to the old trust except for the omission of the prohibition on accumulating income. This has now been renamed Sheltland Charitable Trust.

The trust was run by the Shetland Islands Council until 2002. The trust is currently administered by its own separate staff.

The trust aims to provide public benefit to and improve the quality of life for the inhabitants of Shetland; ensure that people in need receive a high standard of service and care; protect and enhance Shetland's environment, heritage, culture and traditions; provide facilities that will be of long-term benefit to the inhabitants of Shetland; build on the energy and initiatives of local groups, maximise voluntary effort and input and assist them to achieve their objectives; support a balanced range of services and facilities to contribute to the overall fabric of the community; support facilities and services and

jobs located in rural areas and maintain the value of the funds in the long term to ensure that future generations have access to similar resources in the post oil era.

In 2003/04 the trust had assets of £211 million with an income of £32 million and grants totalling £16 million.

The funds are used to create and sustain a wide range of facilities for the islands, largely by funding further trusts as follows (with their 2003/04 grant totals):

Shetland Welfare Trust – day care and running costs (£2.8 million)
Shetland Recreational Trust (£2.5 million)
Isleburgh Trust (£1.1 million)
Shetland Amenity Trust (£1 million)
Shetland Amenity Trust – new museum and archives (£1 million)
Christmas Grants to Pensioners / Disabled Households (£938,000)
Shetlands Arts Trust (£516,000)
Independance at Home Scheme Grants (£278,000)
Voluntary Bodies (£212,000)
Island Games 2005 Capital Projects (£518,000)
Specialist Aids & Social Assistance (£319,000)
Shetland Recreational Trust – Replacement Running Track (£844,000)
Walter and Joan Gray Eventide Home – running costs (£160,000)
Shetland Alcohol Trust (£152,000)
Shetland Citizens Advice Bureau (£130,000)
Shetland Council of Social Service – VRC (£454,000)
Other grants totalled £3.1 million.

Exclusions Funds can only be used to benefit the inhabitants of Shetland.

Applications Applications are only accepted from Shetland-based charities. The trustees meet every two months.

Voluntary Action Orkney

Disadvantaged people, especially children and young people

£7,000 available (2006)

Beneficial area Orkney Islands.

Anchor Buildings, 6 Bridge Street, Kirkwall, Orkney KW15 1HR

Tel. 01856 872897 **Fax** 01856 873167

e-mail enquiries@vaorkney.org.uk

website www.orkneycommunities.co.uk/vao/

Correspondent Gail Anderson, Administration/Training Officer

Scottish Charity No. SC010691

Information available Information was provided by the trust.

General Voluntary Action Orkney receives a sum of money each year from Talisman Energy UK. The trust confirmed that around £7,000 would be available to voluntary groups for grants in 2006. Priority is given to groups concerned with people who are disadvantaged by:

- poor health
- age
- disability
- poverty
- geography.

Children and young people's groups are especially supported. The maximum grant is £500. It gives grants for one-off costs such as equipment, repairs, surveys and travel.

Exclusions The total cost of the project should not exceed £5,000. Running costs are not supported. Grants are not paid retrospectively.

Applications In writing to the correspondent. The trust advertises for applications in January, the closing date is 25 February. Applications should include the following documents:

- letter of confirmation of charitable status (if applicable)
- constitution
- most recent annual accounts and report (all applicants must submit these).

To claim a grant, proof of expenditure, either a receipted invoice or an invoice to be paid is required.

The Westminster Foundation

Church, conservation, youth, education, medical, arts, social welfare

£2.4 million (2004)

Beneficial area UK, and local interests in central London (SW1 and W1 and immediate environs), the north west of England, especially rural Lancashire and the Chester area, and the Sutherland area of Scotland.

70 Grosvenor Street, London W1K 3JP

Tel. 020 7408 0988 **Fax** 020 7312 6244

Correspondent Colin Redman, Secretary

Trustees *The Duke of Westminster, Chair; J H M Newsum; R M Moyse.*

Charity Commission no. 267618

Information available Accounts were on file at the Charity Commission, without a full report or explanation of grants made.

General The foundation makes almost 200 grants a year, mainly for welfare and educational causes, but with substantial support for conservation and rather less for medicine and the arts. Grants appear to be all for UK causes and perhaps half by number, though less by value, are in the areas of special interest given above.

Though grants can be every large, all but a handful are usually for amounts of not more than £60,000 and most are between £5,000 and just a few hundred pounds. About half of the beneficiaries were also supported in previous years.

The foundation has previously noted that: 'It is usual that the trustees have knowledge of, or connection with, those charities which are successful applicants. The trustees tend to support caring causes and not research.'

This is assumed to be a largely personal trust, created by the present duke. He is well known in the charity world for his active personal involvement in many organisations, and no doubt a significant number of the regular beneficiaries are organisations with which he has developed a personal connection that goes beyond grantmaking.

In 2004 it had assets of £28.5 million and a total income of £2.7 million, mainly due to it receiving donations totalling £2.2 million. There were 222 grants made totalling £2.4 million. They were broken down as follows:

Church	£1,039,000
Social welfare	£537,500
Education	£311,000
Conservation	£200,500
Arts	£161,000
Medical	£112,000
Youth	£79,000

Grants in 2004

Church (14 grants)
Accounting for almost half of the grant total during the year was the £1 million grant to the Deans and Canons of Windsor. Other grants included those to St George's House Trust and Chester Cathedral Development Trust (£10,000 each), Aldford Parochial Church Council (£7,000), Eccleston and Pulford Parochial Church Council (£4,000) and Over Wyresdale Parochial Church Council and St Mary's Without the Walls (£1,000 each).

Social welfare (65 grants)
Beneficiaries included Centrepoint and CRISIS (£40,000 each), Business in the Community (£30,000), Cardinal Hume Centre and Passage 2000 (£20,000 each), Royal Agricultural Society for the Commonwealth (£17,000), Television for the Environment (£14,000), Lionheart and Esther Benjamin Trust (£10,000 each), Fundacion Victims del Terrorisme Catastrophies (£7,000), Chester Aid to the Homeless and Joint Commonwealth Societies Council (£5,000 each), City of Westminster Charitable Trust and Lord Mayor's Christmas Parcel Appeal (£2,500 each), Chester CVS, Home Farm Trust Ltd and Parents Against Drug Abuse (£1,000 each) and City of Westminster Family Placement Unit and Ullapool Tourism & Business Association (£500 each) and London Homeless Division (£200).

Education (14 grants)
Three larger grants were made to University of Liverpool (£100,000), University of Cambridge (£70,000) and Royal United Services Institute for Defence (£55,000). Other beneficiaries included Training for Life Limited (£24,000), Investment Property Forum Education Trust (£12,000), Foundation of Nursing Studies (£8,000), Eccleston School (£5,000) and Watergate School PSFA (£1,000).

Conservation (16 grants)
The main beneficiaries in this category were Game Conservancy Trust (£54,000), Soil Association (£50,000) and Atlantic Salmon Trust (£30,000). Other grants included those to Green Alliance Trust (£14,000), County History Trust (£10,000), West Sutherland Fisheries Trust (£5,000), Woodland Trust (£2,000) and Royal Geographical Society (£500).

Arts (18 grants)
The main beneficiary in this category was the Tank Museum – Bovington, which received £100,000. Other beneficiaries included Battle of Britain Monument, English Sinfonia and Liverpool Carters' Horse Monument Appeal Fund (£10,000 each), New Eden Court Appeal – Inverness (£5,000), Chester Summer Festival (£2,000), Chester Mystery Festival (£1,000) and Friends of Lancaster City Museum (£500).

Medical (29 grants)
Beneficiaries included Dyslexia Institute (£23,500), Mecenat Chirurgie Cardiaque (£21,000), Fund for Epilepsy and Fine Cell Work (£8,000 each), British Kidney Patient Association (£6,000), Vision Aid and Claire House Children's Hospice (£5,000 each), St Lazarus Charitable Trust (£3,000), King Edward VII's Hospital for Officers (£2,000), Alder Hey Children's Hospital, Deafness Support Network and Guide Dogs for the Blind (£1,000 each). Small grants included those to Hearing Dogs for Deaf People, Hope House, Highland Society for Blind People and St John Ambulance.

Youth (18 grants)
Beneficiaries included Chester Youth Club (£24,000), Kidscape (£12,000), Youth Sport Trust (£11,000), Farms for City Children (£5,000), Duke of Edinburgh Awards (£4,500), Pimlico Family Workshop Toy Library (£2,500), Galgate Youth Centre (£1,500) and Kinlochbervie Pre-School Centre Association (£500).

Exclusions Only registered charities will be considered; charitable status applied for, or pending, is not sufficient. No grants to individuals, 'holiday' charities, student expeditions, or research projects.

Applications In writing to the secretary, enclosing an up-to-date set of accounts, together with a brief history of the project to date, and the current need.

Index

W

Y

Z